MENTAL!

MENTAL!

THE TOUGHEST, BLOODIEST AND HARDEST CHALLENGES IN THE WORLD

HELEN SUMMER

JOHN BLAKE

Published by John Blake Publishing Ltd,
3 Bramber Court, 2 Bramber Road,
London W14 9PB, England

www.johnblakepublishing.co.uk

www.facebook.com/Johnblakepub 🅵

twitter.com/johnblakepub 🅑

First published in paperback in 2014

ISBN: 978-1-78219-923-6

British Library Cataloguing-in-Publication Data:

A catalogue record for this book is available from the British Library.

Design by www.envydesign.co.uk

Printed in Great Britain by CPI Group (UK) Ltd

1 3 5 7 9 10 8 6 4 2

Papers used by John Blake Publishing are natural, recyclable products made
from wood grown in sustainable forests. The manufacturing processes conform
to the environmental regulations of the country of origin.

Every attempt has been made to contact the relevant copyright-holders,
but some were unobtainable. We would be grateful if the appropriate
people could contact us.

All care has been taken to provide accurate and current information,
however, due to the regular updating of events and their websites, the author
takes no responsibility for any amendments or alterations that may have
taken place since the time of writing.

CONTENTS

ACKNOWLEDGEMENTS

No book is ever written by the author alone, and this book is no exception. I owe a huge debt of gratitude to the following support crews:

First, to all those who participate in the events contained in this book, who allowed me to take extracts from their blogs or provided me with accounts of their experiences and in so doing brought the book to life. They are: James Adams, Tim Adams, Paul Ali, Mimi Anderson, Robbie Britton, Dan Cartwright, Mark Cockbain, Paolo De Luca, James Elson, Sharon Glenister, Chris Heaton, Anton Inckle, Sandra McDougall, Paul Navesey, Rob Pinnington, Ann Richardson, Joel Richardson, Sam Robson, Adam Seldon, Liz Tunna, Elina Ussher, Richard Ussher, Marcus Wadsworth, and John Wellington, with a further special word of thanks to Paolo De Luca who also assisted me with the cycling and swimming overviews.

Second, to those who provided me with leads to events and participants: Jack Archer, Andy Chandler, Matt Dunn, Angela Elder, Helen Gowin, Malcolm Hargraves, Ali Humphrey, Lynn Pawsey and Allan Rumble.

Third, to my special support crew at John Blake Publishing: Liz Mallett for coming up with the original idea; Anna Marx for all her support throughout and for her and her team's immeasurable editing skills; Sarah Cattle for all the Twitter leads she had to find during her week's work experience and who, as a result, has probably been put off working in the publishing industry for life (sorry, Sarah!); the design team at Envy Ltd who came up with a cover that is utterly brilliant (I only hope the inside lives up to the outside), and last, but by absolutely no means least, the man himself – the lovely, incomparable John Blake, for giving me the opportunity to write a second book, and for all the wonderful lunches and laughs at that special place!

Thanks also to my favourite employers and colleagues at Bookends in Christchurch, who not only display *Running Crazy* face out at all times (even when I'm not there to check – don't you?) and put up with my general incompetence with amazing good grace on a daily basis, but who allowed me the time out to write *Mental!* – no matter how short-staffed that sometimes made them.

I would further like to give special thanks to my very dear friends who, as always, have been with me every step of the way, listening, encouraging, believing in me, and understanding when I haven't always been able to come out to play (we will make up for lost time, I promise); my dad for his patience and forbearance in not being able to see as much of his daughter as he might wish; and, finally, and as always, to my son, Jack Matthew Archer, who continues to shower me with sunshine and joy, and to his partner, Steph Stafford, who does the same for him and for whom, as a mother, I am so thankful.

And one last special mention for Nina, Lyn and Linda – may improved good health rain down upon you all for many years to come.

Final thanks, and apologies, to anyone I may have forgotten.

I dedicate this book to my son, Jack Matthew Archer, just because…

INTRODUCTION

There is an ultra-run in this book called the Piece of String Fun Run. It is a race that takes place in the UK at the end of November, just as the weather can't make up its mind whether to hang on to autumn for a bit longer and endow us with glorious clear blue skies, still-warm sunshine and crunchy, multi-coloured leaves to run through; or whether to rain down upon us with fierce intent – or maybe even snow – flooding rivers and roads, freezing puddles and blackening ice so that just walking, never mind running, becomes an extreme sport.

But enough of the weather – back to the Piece of String Fun Run, the race that does exactly what it says in the title. It doesn't know how long it is, at least the runners don't, it's kept a secret from them even while they are running it – all they know is that it starts on a Friday, will be longer than a marathon, and will, hopefully, finish before they have to return to work on Monday…and apparently it's fun…I'm not going to tell you anything more than that, you can read the whole story of the race inside this book; the only reason I'm telling you about it here is that the runners probably feel like I did when writing this book – when was it going to end?

This may seem a daft question because, obviously, I had a deadline, so it had to be finished by then, but normally with writing you know when you have reached the end – the story or the facts or the information you wish to impart are all in there, written as well as you are able, or the story has reached its natural, or otherwise, conclusion: in other words, the ending of a book is finite.

However, that is not the case with *Mental!* – which started out with the rather more wordy working title of *The Toughest, Bloodiest and Hardest Challenges in the World*, and was renamed *Mental!* because the more I researched events, the more often I was heard to utter out loud and with gusto, 'That's mental!' But, perhaps more pertinent, was the fact that it was quickly apparent that taking part in any of the events in this book (and those not in it – more of which in a minute) is as much, if not more, about mental fortitude as it is about physical strength and fitness.

Which takes me back to the connection between the Piece of String Fun Run and the writing of this book. Just as the Piece of String has no known end, neither does this book – there are so many extreme sporting events out there that it would be impossible to incorporate them all into one volume. Certainly, at one time I considered changing the name of the book a second time to *War and Peace* – not because it's about fighting, (other than the mind trying to force the body to keep going at the same time as the body is trying to force the mind to submit to the pain and give up), but because if I had written about every single challenging event out there, three things would happen: first, I would never finish the book because new events are starting up every five minutes and current ones are ending; second, the book, if it did get finished, would be encyclopaedic and would have to be published in numerous large volumes; and third, nobody would ever have the time to read it.

So, with some reluctance, I decided it was necessary to rein in the book by writing only about events that complement one another in some way and are reasonably accessible to most people. For example swimming, cycling and running events that can be tackled singly or together in one form or another, such as triathlon or Ironman. Running also brought in muddy challenges, such as Tough Guy and Tough Mudder, to name but two, and also adventure racing, which touched on extras like rock climbing and kayaking, plus a little bit of rowing and canoeing. Undoubtedly, however, the book leans towards running events – simply because there are more extreme challenges in running than in any other discipline.

Then, of course, I was faced with the decision of what was tough enough to go in the book? It didn't take a genius to work out that this wasn't so much a decision as an invitation to be slaughtered by readers who, naturally, being human beings made up of millions of individual cells, would have differing opinions on what is tough and what is not. So the entries in this book have made it because they are, by and large, events that those who partake in such things have told me should be included – but even then I've had to exclude some purely on the grounds of this not being the 'War and Peace of Extreme Challenges'. I apologise unreservedly to those events, event organisers, participants, spectators and anyone else who has a view on it, for all those events that are not included.

For all events I have included a website address, and of those sites about 90 per cent of them will provide links to other events. So, one way or another, if this book gives you a taste for challenge and adventure and you fancy having a go at something similar, just get online and you will find something that suits you.

I have also, where possible, included first-hand accounts generously given to me by people who have actually taken part in the events. These accounts bring this book to life, and will make you feel as though you have shared the struggle with those who really did run 3,200 miles across America, swim the English Channel or cycle the Dolomites.

Oh, and I almost forgot to mention – there is another rather special category of challenge in this book made up of events that may not qualify as the 'toughest' of challenges, but certainly represent the 'quirkiest'! What is a book without any humour?

FOREWORD

BY RICHARD USSHER

Having been involved in endurance sports for almost 20 years I've had my fair share of mental battles within races and events. Endurance events are unquestionably as much to do with the battle in one's mind as the actual physical nature of the events. While physically brutal, it is the ability to move that pain and suffering to one side and push on 100 per cent, often in the face of seemingly insurmountable challenges, in search of a finish line, that for most provides only a temporary respite before the next challenge engulfs one's world.

Extreme endurance events are no longer solely the domain of elite athletes, with participants from all walks of life striving for the next challenge to conquer. With the graduation from marathon to ultras, triathlon to Ironman, adventure racing and all sorts of ultra-distance tests, it would seem that the appetite to discover just where our boundaries are set and to prove to oneself that these can be continually reformed time and time again, is only just being whetted.

FOREWORD

Maybe it is the replacement for those expeditions to the farthest corners of the earth hundreds of years ago, our natural curiosity to see where our limits lie, or just the desire to test if we can remain unbroken in the face of the seemingly impossible? Whatever it is, there is nothing so empowering or uplifting as reaching rock bottom, the point where continuing feels utterly futile, and battling through to reach the finish, even if for no other reason than to prove it didn't break you.

Like an addiction, promises made the last time dissipate within seconds of the finish and plans already begin to seed for the next challenge.

There are so many adventures out there waiting to be added to people's bucket lists – this book will definitely help feed those ideas of where that next box to tick might be and provide a huge amount of inspiration along the way.

Richard Ussher

Former professional multi-sport athlete, five-times winner New Zealand's Coast to Coast Multisport World Championship, former New Zealand triathlon Ironman-distance record holder, two-times Adventure Racing World Champion, Olympic skier 1998.

ULTRA-RUNNING
AN OVERVIEW

An ultramarathon race is one that is more than 42.2km/26. miles in distance. The most usual distances are 80km/50 miles, 161km/100 miles, 50km/31 miles, and 100km/62 miles. There is no maximum distance, with the longest crossing entire continents, such as the Trans America ultra from Los Angeles to New York, a total of 5,150km/3,200 miles.

Ultra races may be categorised as either 'non-stop' races or 'stage' races.

A non-stop race does exactly what it says – the clock starts when the runner starts and doesn't stop until the runner reaches the finish. No time allowance is made for stoppages, whatever their purpose. Consequently, runners in these races make their own decisions as to when, where and for how long to rest.

A stage race is pretty self-explanatory too – it is run in stages. Generally, racers run a stage each day, then sleep and do another stage the following day. Occasionally, racers will run a stage and will then be required to stop for a requisite period of time only, not necessarily overnight, before continuing. While the non-stop race may on first glance appear to be the hardest of the two, it is not always the case, as much depends on the distances to be covered at each stage. For example, a stage race where you are running an average of 45 miles per day for 70 consecutive days, such as in the Los Angeles to New York race, will have the effect of gradually wearing you down over a long period of time and is mentally especially hard. Each day you must wake up, still exhausted from the previous cumulative days' runs, and go out and do it all again, knowing that you must do so again the next day, the following one and for the foreseeable future, until you reach the finish. Arguably, this is as hard as running 483km/300 miles over the course of, say, 72 hours or three days, albeit with little or no sleep but with the knowledge that it will be over in a relatively short space of time.

Either way, there can be no argument that running ultra-marathons is hard.

Another specific to ultra-running is what is known as the 'X' factor, that's to say extreme heat, extreme cold or extreme altitude, with races taking place in extreme locations such as Death Valley, the Arctic or India.

Wherever the races take place, they are likely to feature severe weather conditions, elevation changes and a variety of difficult terrain, from Alpine tracks to forest trails, from frozen lakes to snowy mountains, from rocky boulders to sand dunes.

Ultramarathons may be supported or unsupported.

A supported race means that runners will be allowed to engage the services of a 'support crew', who may be made up of people he or she knows or a group of people supplied by the race.

Dependent upon the length and type of race undertaken, a support crew may be responsible for anything from carrying a runner's spare kit and camping equipment to checking their medical condition along the way. They will also be responsible for carrying and preparing food and drink for the runner, ensuring the contestant receives the right mix of nutritional drinks and gels, as well as providing psychological support and encouragement.

They may also be required, if the race allows, to 'buddy run'. Buddy running helps keep the racer motivated and may also be used where terrain is dangerous or difficult to run along safely, particularly in the dark.

Depending on the length and type of race, support crews will use a support vehicle to take them from one part of a course to another, where they will meet up with their runner, feed, water and nurture him, tend his blisters and any other wounds, and, if necessary, push him back up on to his feet to get him running again!

Unsupported races mean a runner must race with complete autonomy. In other words, he must carry all his own kit, including camping/sleeping equipment, food, water and anything else he requires or that the race organisers consider mandatory, such as safety equipment like a whistle, emergency flares, maps, waterproof jacket and trousers, etc., and must not seek or accept any outside help whatsoever for the duration of the race.

In both supported and unsupported races, runners will check in during the race at a number of different 'mandatory checkpoints'. Dependent upon the type of race, the checkpoints may be manned, with showers and overnight facilities, as well as cooking facilities, or they may be a simple hut or tent where a runner must register with an official or sign a book to prove he has been there.

These mandatory checkpoints serve as a safety measure, allowing organisers to keep a tally on how all the runners are progressing, or if any are missing. If an official or medic, who are also often positioned at these mandatory checkpoints, considers a runner to be unfit to carry on, they will have the authority to withdraw that person from the race or to keep the runner there until they consider he is fit to continue.

As well as mandatory checkpoints, many races will also provide aid stations where additional food and drinks may be obtained or rest taken.

Runners may also be withdrawn from a race if they fail to meet any of the cut-off times. Cut-off times are put in place at the start of a race and applied to all runners equally. Put simply, a cut-off time will be an amount of time allocated to reach a certain point or points in a race. Some cut-off times err on the side of generous, others are notoriously tough and can sometimes be the hardest part of running an ultra – the distance may be doable but having to run it in a certain time at a certain pace all the way through in order to meet cut-off times has proved many an ultra runner's undoing.

All of the above races may take place as point-to-point (starting at one place, finishing at another) races, or single loop or multi-lap loops (starting and finishing in the same place). The races may take place on any type of terrain anywhere in the world, in any weather and under any conditions – provided runners are prepared to pit themselves against whatever the race offers, the race will prevail!

Another type of ultra-racing comes in the form of non-stop running for a specified period of time – 6 hours, 12 hours, 24 hours, 48 hours – rather than over a specified distance. The winner is the person who runs the furthest in the time set. These types of ultra races are usually run around a 400-metre running track or a circuit of a specified length, such as a mile or two, usually on road.

For further information on ultra-running and races, please visit: www.100kmassociation.org.uk or www.100marathonclub.org.uk

KEEP YOUR COOL...

YUKON ARCTIC ULTRA
CANADA

Run, bike, ski – 692, 483, 161km (430, 300, 100 miles)
– non-stop – 40°F/-40°C

Adventure runner Robert Pollhammer has two loves in his life – adventure and sport. So in some ways it's not too surprising that he runs a company called the Great Outdoors, which specialises in organising multi and extreme sporting events.

The Yukon Arctic Ultra is one of Robert's designer events and takes extreme adventure running to the max, with an annual 161km/100-mile and 483km/300-mile race along the supremely snowy and notoriously tough dog sled trail, the Yukon Quest. There is also a biannual 430-miler, just in case 100 or 300 miles of frozen rivers, lakes, snow-ridden hills and forests isn't challenging enough. Competitors can choose to run/trek, cross-country ski or mountain bike the trail and may enter as individuals or in teams of two or more.

Whatever the desired mode of transport or elected distance, all participants start together next to the Yukon River in Whitehorse, Yukon Territory, Alaska, at 1030 on a winter-white day at the end of January in temperatures of around -40°C/-40°F, and, all being well, will finish at various locations and within varying stipulated times, according to distance. In the case of the 430-miler, this is eight days. All cut-off times are strictly enforced and, due to the extreme nature of the weather at this time of year, the trail may from necessity change and distances vary accordingly.

The adverse weather conditions, specifically fresh snow and wind, can make finding the trail difficult at times, despite being well marked with Yukon Quest markers (wooden sticks with fluorescent tops), and the use of a GPS (Global Positioning System) is recommended.

Also recommended are waterproof/windproof jacket and trousers, gaiters, over-boots, waterproof/thermal socks and underwear, a wicking fleecy layer (that draws moisture away from the body), head-cover, ear protectors, thermal/shell gloves, sunglasses and goggles, snowshoes, trekking poles, sled and cover.

Sled? Yes – this is an unsupported event, so all equipment must be carried by the competitors themselves, hence the sled (although you can use just a backpack if you can find one big enough).

En route, there is a maximum of 10 checkpoints (on the longest course), where a meal and hot water can be obtained, but the chances of coming upon a shopping mall or hotel are pretty much a big fat zero.

Given the autonomous nature of this event, and the fact that it occurs in the harsh Canadian wilderness in night-time temperatures that can drop as low as -50°C/-58°F, presenting a serious risk of frostbite and a potential loss of fingers, toes and ears, and with other life-threatening situations a very real possibility, the race organisers strongly recommend attending their instructor-led survival-skills course, which is held the day before the race.

Taking into account all of the above, it would be hard to argue with Mr Pollhammer's assertions that the Yukon Arctic Ultra is the world's coldest and toughest human-powered winter ultra. Certainly the following quote given by him on the race website makes for interesting reading: 'People will think that you are absolutely crazy if you decide to do this. The way I look at it, people who have never faced such a challenge are a lot crazier. Those of you who have done similar races previously know what I am talking about. The feeling of finishing such a race won't be that new to you any more. However, for you it will be a new and exciting challenge and an event you won't want to miss.'

Who would do this?

Highly experienced and successful ultra runner, 41-year-old Mark Cockbain, director of Cockbain Events, took part in this race in 2006. This extract was taken with kind permission from the company's website: www.markcockbain.com.

It's 10.30am, Sat, 11 Feb, 2006, and I'm on the starting line of this gruelling race, at downtown Whitehorse, along with 38 other international competitors. We all have a fully loaded sled and a nervous smile.

The starting gun is fired and we set off across a makeshift starting line, heading north along the frozen river edge of a skidoo trail set into snow.

I soon generate enough heat to wear only a few layers and the sled moves smoothly, although I feel its weight on my hips, despite long tyre-pulling training sessions.

I decide to run the race in small sections, walking mostly, adding and removing clothes as required. It's tough-going pulling the sled through soft snow, sinking and sliding up the trail wearing my huge Neoprene over-boots to give me a bigger footprint and grip and protect me from any dangerous overflow.

I reach the 26-mile checkpoint at Sir North Ranch and take the mandatory four-hour stop which includes a kit inspection, a test of my sleeping system and my ability to light my gas stove.

Mark completes the Yukon Ultra

At 9.20pm I head north still following the frozen river. It's much colder during the night and a 40-mile stretch lies ahead. It's frustrating travelling at 3 miles per hour but only possible to run on the flat icy sections; the dense undulating woodland has such steep inclines that I require trekking poles which I jam into the ice to pull me up.

Around 4am I put on my big down jacket and mitts and get into my bivvy bag for an hour's rest.

I am now running with three others; we get lost, ending up on what looks like quite thin ice.

Trudging around in the dark getting ever colder, we eventually relocate the main trail and continue through some dangerous overflow areas wearing our over-boots for protection.

Day two through energy-sapping, hilly wooded areas; I eat as much as possible to keep my strength up. The scenery is amazing, pine forests with mountainous backgrounds.

Checkpoint two, *Dog Grave Lake* – we re-fill our water

canisters, then head further north and higher uphill towards Braeburn, the 100-mile point, a 14 – 15 hour section of relentless pulling through the evening and night.

Temperatures drop and wind speed increases, with higher altitude making it even colder. The chill goes straight through your body and our pace slows. It is at least -20°C/-4°F.

We reach checkpoint three at Braeburn in just under 48 hours. We are given stew and one of the largest cinnamon buns in the world!

More steep hills follow, and we need trekking poles to pull the sleds upwards, until we start to access a chain of vast frozen lakes. These are easier to cross but more exposed and temperatures drop fast.

We move on till nightfall. The temperature plummets, my hands and face are freezing. I try warming my hands with two pairs of gloves but still feel frost nip in my fingers. The end of my nose is also freezing and I have to keep twitching it to break the ice. My trail shoes freeze on me, the laces are solid and ice forms over the top of the shoes and cuts into the material itself. I'm shocked by how cold it has become in such a short space of time. It is now -30°C.

We light a fire and sleep but wake to find our shoes and water frozen solid. We're all suffering from blisters and sore hips, but moods lift with the light.

All morning we cross frozen lakes miles long until we reach checkpoint four at Ken Lake where we are treated to semi-warm stew inside a makeshift tent.

Night falls and we continue climbing hills in the dark thick woods. I start hallucinating with the various shapes of heavy clumps of snow on trees.

It's extremely cold, Hugh's moustache is frozen solid and my nose is crunching with ice! But later, the sun rises giving the most amazing 'Arctic red' glow across the frozen valley.

We are now crossing huge, jagged, frozen slabs of ice. It's hard pulling sleds over these frozen obstacles and difficult to keep balanced and move safely without twisting an ankle or falling.

We reach checkpoint five and find another runner inside coughing up blood as he's been breathing the ice-cold air in too deeply and has hurt his lungs.

We eat some soup, take a few hours rest on the floor, then leave with some others. It's below -30°C and we're wearing everything we have.

We've completed just over 200 miles and been going for nearly five days with only a few hours' sleep; adrenaline and coffee are the only things keeping me awake, but I'm confident I'll make it. It's just a case of mentally hanging on.

Mile 270 checkpoint – we all look a total mess. My face and eyes are swollen with cold, my lips chapped and my nose blistered. My shoes are totally torn to pieces and my blisters are terrible. I have a pulled hamstring and shin splints.

At around 7pm, we hobble away. It's a long painful night and the most monotonous section so far. Exhausted, we barely speak to each other, just trudge onwards, heads down, concentrating on putting one foot in front of the other. Long into the cold night we pull our sleds up the frozen river. My sled is like a dead weight, jarring my hips with every step. It seems never ending.

In the early hours we reach the farm checkpoint and bed down in a frozen barn; later though, we're invited into a warm kitchen and given coffee and pancakes. The father even shows us his grizzly bear photo album and stuffed claw collection!

We head out for the last 30 miles with shattered legs and badly blistered feet, but it's the last section and spirits are high.

Night, and the temperature falls, our bodies start to shut down, we are now so tired we hallucinate at almost everything we see, but eventually the orange glow of streetlights at the Pelly Crossing finish hone into view. Boosted, we attempt to run a little but soon settle back into a desperate hobble, our legs and feet totally useless.

Using every last drop of strength and stubbornness we eventually shuffle across the finish line. We're presented with finishers' medals and collapse exhausted in a heap on the floor.

It has taken me 6 days and 12 hours to cover 320 miles, finishing in sixth place out of 38 starters and 16 finishers.

This is certainly one of the hardest races I've ever completed. Not only because of the distance and lack of sleep, but because of the extreme cold and slow pace due to the sled and terrain. I would certainly think twice about doing another 'cold' race ever again!

Mental Miscellany

- The first Yukon Ultra took place in 2003.
- In 2013, there were a total of 81 starters doing a variety of distances.
- In 2013, less than half of all starters finished any of the races, apart from the mountain bikers who only had one participant in each event.
- In 2013, times for the winners of the 430 miles were: foot: 186 hours 50 minutes; mountain bike: 180 hours; skis: 225 hours 10 minutes.
- In 2013 times for the winners of the 300 miles were: foot: 146 hours 22 minutes; mountain bike – no bikers took part; skis: none finished.
- In 2013 times for the winners of the 100 miles were: foot: 24 hours 35 minutes; mountain bike: 42 hours 10 minutes; skis: no skiers took part.
- One year a runner slept beside the trail and another athlete camped next to him. When the first runner woke up he looked at where the other racer was still sleeping, and based upon the direction the sleeping runner was facing, made the decision to run in the opposite direction, believing that to be the way forward. He was wrong – four hours later, he ended up back at the checkpoint he'd come from.

For further information, please visit: www.arcticultra.de

BAIKAL ICE RUNNING MARATHON
SIBERIA
A marathon on ice – 20°C/-44°F

Imagine this if you will – Russia, Siberia, mid-winter, Lake Baikal – the oldest and deepest fresh-water lake in the world (it may not have the huge surface area of the North American Great Lakes, but its depth is such that it holds more water than all of them put together), the surface of which is frozen so solid that lorries can be driven over it – and runners can run over it, for 42.2km/26.2 miles.

Yes, the ice will move – you will hear it – and yes, as you run you will encounter great fissures and cracks along the way, not to mention huge slabs of ice forced up from the surface creating hummocks of ice rubble, the only raised areas of an otherwise totally flat race surface. And yes again, you will need to be dressed from head to foot, including your face, in warm/thermal clothing as protection against the 20 different general and locally formed winds, which are not only notoriously difficult to predict but variable and omnidirectional and whose chill factor can lower the temperature from -12°C/10°F to -20°C/-4°F in as many seconds.

Photo by Mariya Shalneva

And sure, with Lake Baikal claiming more sunshine hours than southern Italy, you will also need polarised UV-protective sunglasses and factor-50 sunscreen to protect your eyes and any minute areas of skin that may be exposed to that sunlight, which, on a clear day, reflects off the ice and snow in air so pure that the effect of solar beams on skin and eyes is tripled.

And, oh yes, once you've 'packed up your body', as the race organisers so aptly describe getting dressed appropriately against the elements, you will then need to don ice spikes, as the entire race will be run on the frozen surface of the lake, from the western shore at Irkutsk Oblast to the eastern shore at the Buddhist Republic of Buryatia.

But, if you are willing to accept all the above and enter the Baikal Ice Running Marathon, then you will find yourself taking part in what is widely regarded as one of the most impressive foot races in the world.

Oh, just one other thing, you will also need to develop a taste for vodka.

Vodka?

Yes, vodka.

For once you are on the start line you will be offered the opportunity to partake in the precautionary ritual of 'vodka sprinkling' – a custom developed to pacify the spirits of the lake, which basically involves imbibing a shot of vodka immediately prior to setting off on your run and sprinkling some in/on the lake. Alternatively, you may opt for milk. Either way, the organisers advise you to partake, saying anyone who doesn't runs badly.

Potentially, that shot of vodka (and any further shots you may choose to imbibe at the 5km/3-mile spaced checkpoints along the way, which also offer hot drinks and food as well as vodka) may help soften the fact that although from the start line you can virtually see the finish line on the far side of the lake, what lies between you and it is a long, cold, lonely, barren, feature-less white landscape that offers no sense of perspective or distance.

Although the course is predominantly flat, it is blisteringly hard and uneven, covered in a light layer of snow with areas of ice so highly polished that it is almost translucent. And there is no escaping the strong winds and bitingly cold temperatures that both chill and create resistance to progress as they howl wildly and unhampered across the open surface of the lake.

Despite all this, the race attracts around 100 runners each year and is, at least according to its organisers, Russia's most exotic marathon.

Who would do this?

Chris Heaton, a 55-year-old adventure runner and accountant, who in 2013 ran 30 marathons in 30 days in hilly Cumbria to raise funds for the Brathay Trust (www.brathay.org.uk), took part in this race in 2012 to raise money for a cancer charity.

It all looks and is flat – by and large you run in vehicle tracks, but it really saps your energy because you sink in a bit and don't quite get the traction for the effort, like walking on compact snow. You make decent progress but feel more tired than usual and of course some bits were deeper snow, other bits just plain ice and a few bits uneven, broken ice. The weather when I did it was magnificent, cold of course, but sunny and clear. After a while you actually felt too hot, but if you slowed down or took any clothes off you quickly got very cold again.

Running was fine until about 25k when I hit a bad patch, as did others, but I got going again around 30k. It was actually quite harsh on knees, hips and feet. Unusually, my feet

An unforgiving landscape; photo by Mariya Shalneva

were trashed by the end and required a little home surgery later on. The surface and unevenness constantly put you at awkward angles and make your feet move around too much I think.

Definitely one of the most unusual races I've ever run in – when you're out there in the middle of the lake, wherever you look it is just ice to the horizon.

Mental Miscellany

- The race was founded by friends, Alexei Nikiforov from Russia, and Andreas Kiefer from Germany, in 2004.
- The inaugural race in 2005 saw 15 runners and was won by a 57-year-old professor in 3 hours, 8 minutes, 43 seconds.
- The fastest crossing is purported to be 2 hours, 53 minutes by a Russian, but this does not appear to have been adopted as an official record.
- The race 'Ice Captain' and a team of volunteers plot a safe course across the lake only on the day prior to the race, due to the constant movement of the ice, which could otherwise render any earlier plotting too dangerous.

MENTAL!

- The race logo is: 'Clean Waters Conservation Run' – for the preservation of clean water.
- The marathon is part of a larger winter games festival that includes a swimming race in the frozen lake, golf, fishing, volleyball and football.
- Lake Baikal is the same length as England and contains one-fifth of the world's fresh water supply.

For further information please visit: www.baikalexpress.de

ARROWHEAD 135
MINNESOTA, USA
Run 217km/135 miles – -50°C/-58°F

To state that the Arrowhead 135 is a cold race would be like saying the sea is salty. Taking place in an area known locally as 'America's friendly icebox', and starting out from International Falls, nicknamed 'Frostbite Falls', the names should tell you all you need to know about the climatic conditions of this race, which can be run, cycled or skied, and which, incidentally, is held in January at what race organisers cheerfully say is 'hopefully the coldest time of the year'.

Such hope is undoubtedly easily fulfilled in a race that is described as: 'a human-powered ultramarathon taking place in the coldest part of winter in the coldest city in the lower 48 states', with average temperatures falling somewhere between -30°C/22°F and -40°C/-40°F, often accompanied by snow. As such there is an average finish rate of just 50 per cent, lower for novice ultra runners.

Following the rugged Arrowhead State Snowmobile Trail situated in northern Minnesota's stunningly scenic Superior National Forest, the race follows the trail's wide, well-groomed and well-marked route, crossing roads and ski trails, and is fairly flat on the northern part between International Falls and the Ash

17

River. Along this section of the course, should you be interested and have enough wit about you, it is possible to spot mice, wolves, deer, lynx, fox and snowshoe hares.

After the first 11km/7 miles, there are trailside shelters approximately every 19km/12 miles, with the longest distance between any two shelters being 37km/23 miles. Additionally, there are three race checkpoints spaced around 56km/35 miles.

Once you hit the southern section, however, the trail becomes heavily timbered and rugged with rolling hills and large areas of exposed rock and enormous boulders, as well as numerous lakes and streams, all of which rather wonderfully attract snowy owls, ospreys and bald-headed eagles, but which, perhaps not so wonderfully, make running, especially in the dark, far more onerous. However, at about mile 69 (111km), there is a little respite as racers may opt to take a shortcut across Elephant Lake to the next checkpoint, carefully following the snowmobile trail markers.

But it is the frigid temperatures and inhospitable weather conditions that really mark this race out as tough, factors which are not helped by competitors having to be self-supporting with no outside help except other racers or race officials. As the organisers say, 'Arrowhead is about you, the wilderness, your inner dogged spirit and self-sufficiency.'

As such, racers must carry all their own gear on the course and must finish with a stipulated amount of food and fuel. Mandatory gear includes sleeping bag, insulated sleeping pad, bivvy sack or tent, fire starter, insulated water container, headlamp or flashlight, and whistle. Should any racer fail a mandatory gear check, which may be carried out at any point during the race, they will be instantly disqualified. The rules also state that iPods are not allowed, followed by the arguably helpful suggestion to instead, 'Listen to nature and your own hallucinations'.

The final cut-off is 60 hours from the 0700 hours Monday morning start, or 1900 hours on the Wednesday, at the Fortune Bay Casino.

While there are special awards for the winner (one being a guaranteed entry to the Iditarod Trail Invitational Race) and a unique trophy awarded to all finishers, the race organisers say that the main award is the satisfaction of finishing one of the hardest ultra events in North America.

There is also one further award known as the 'Ernest Shackleton Endurance Award', which is given in recognition of the racer/official finisher who remains on the course, making forward progress for the longest period of time. In deference to Ernest Shackleton and his hard-fought-for achievements, this special award is presented in the spirit of perseverance, fortitude, steadfastness and bravery.

The event aims only to break even financially, but if there are any proceeds, these are donated to the Special Operations Warrior Foundation and the Minnesota Safe Families charities.

Who would do this?

In the first race in 2005, just 10 people took part, but by 2013, there were, fittingly enough, 135 competitors in total, being a mix of runners, cyclists and skiers, from a number of states and countries.

On the race website, one runner reported that the temperature at the start of the 2013 race was unexpectedly warm and the snow slushy, with the first 32km/20 miles of flat trail passing fairly quickly, as the snow had been packed down by the bikers having already cycled over it.

However, it then started to snow pretty heavily and got dark, causing people to drop out, till he was only seeing other people every couple of hours. The early hours of the morning were especially rough on his own with the wet snow sapping his energy and forcing him to stop constantly to empty snow from his sled.

By the time darkness fell again, the runner was finding it hard to stay motivated, with boredom a major factor, and, having been alone for 25–30 hours, he said he was running out of subjects to take his mind off the weary state of his legs.

By midnight, he reports the onset of delirium, stopping to close his eyes and waking after a couple of minutes, trying to push on but stumbling off one side of the trail.

As a freezing dawn arrived the snow became firmer and he was able to pick up some speed, although he had no idea by now what mile he was on and kept hearing voices, which turned out to be just the whistling wind.

A few hours later, he reached the hilly part of the course, which consisted of 35–40 significant hills close together. The hills were so steep he needed to dig in with his poles to pull his legs up.

And that is where this particular runner's race ended. He didn't make the next checkpoint before the cut-off time and was out of the race.

He was not alone. Just 49 racers from a starting field of 135 from all three disciplines actually finished the 2013 race. However, the organisers described the 2013 event as, 'the best and most competitive Arrowhead yet'.

Mental Miscellany

- The first Arrowhead 135 was held in 2005 with 10 starters across all three disciplines.
- In 2013, there were 135 starters across the three disciplines.
- The first to cross the line in 2013 was a cyclist, in just over 14 hours, followed by a skier in around 39 hours, and finally the first runner crossed in 45 hours 40 minutes.
- 2013 saw the warmest starting temperature in the race's nine-year history at -3°C/25°F.
- In the middle of the 2013 race, an unpredicted 8–10 inches of heavy, wet snow, sleet and ice pellets fell on the competitors – the heaviest snowfall of the season and the event's most significant precipitation ever – and was probably partly responsible for the second lowest finish rate in the race's history, of just 35 per cent.
- Only 7 of the 42 runners who started the 2013 race finished, with no women making it past the 112km/70-mile checkpoint.

For further information, please visit: www.arrowheadultra.com

THE SPINE RACE
UK

431km/268 miles – 11,759m/38,579ft ascent –
Pennine Way

A new race was added to the ultra-racing calendar in 2012 – the Spine Race is a 431km/268-mile run along the whole of the Pennine Way, encompassing some of England's most beautiful, wild and challenging terrain, including the Peak District, the Cheviots, the Yorkshire Dales and the Northumberland National Park, before finishing on the Scottish borders.

Held in January to give competitors a taste of the worst of a British winter consisting of deep snow, ice, chilling rain and savage winds, and temperatures averaging around or below freezing, the organisers claim this to be Britain's most brutal race, as well as its longest, coldest, most demanding mountain marathon.

Competitors have seven days in which to complete the race, with each day bringing 15 hours of darkness, soul-searching solitude and a vastness of landscape that can rival pretty much any other wilderness worldwide.

The gruelling, non-stop race starts at Edale in the Peak District and follows the Pennine Way all the way to Kirk Yetholm, on the edge of Scotland, and is considered so tough

21

that it serves as a four-point qualifier for the notorious Ultra-Trail du Mont-Blanc race.

As such, the creator and joint race director, Scott Gilmour, takes safety very seriously and insists that competitors have previous appropriate experience of ultra-running and mountain racing; they must carry all of the compulsory equipment listed in the race rules and, they are warned, kit may be inspected on the course or at checkpoints. Failure to meet the requirements results in a time penalty being incurred or even disqualification from the event.

Additionally, with the potential for hypothermia, there are appropriately skilled professionals on hand at all times who are able to deal with emergency situations and the course is monitored 24/7 during the race, with support vehicles on standby. Runners may also use their own support crews.

The race itself starts at 0800 and has a maximum field of 75 runners, all of whom must carry their own equipment, although there are five manned checkpoints along the way where athletes may rest, refuel and top up their drink bottles and other equipment from a drop-bag.

It is mandatory for runners to visit every checkpoint so they can be checked for signs of exposure, hypothermia and cold-weather injuries by the medical team who will, if they deem it necessary, hold a runner for a minimum of four hours, or withdraw them from the race to prevent further injury.

The longest stretch between checkpoints is around 97km/60 miles, which occurs on day two. In 2012, it took competitors an average of between 22 and 30 hours to cover the distance, and most withdrew from the race at this stage.

Who would do this?

Anyone looking for the ultimate in ultra-running mountain races in the UK, who enjoys running in the dark, and can cope with sleep deprivation and fatigue, as well as mind-numbing, bone-chilling snow, sleet, rain, hail and wind, periods of total isolation, empty vistas and mental despair.

Certainly, in only the second race to be held in 2013, the

competitors had no idea they were about to be pushed to their absolute limits when they set off along the narrow tracks of the Pennine Way on their steady ascent to Kinder Scout in seemingly average wintry conditions.

At that point the going was good, the usually boggy ground made firm by a covering of ice, which allowed them to run more easily, but the mental stress soon began taking its toll with the realisation that it can take 20 hours to reach checkpoint one along this trail.

As darkness set in, navigation became more difficult and moving more arduous, increasing both physical and mental tiredness.

Leaving the checkpoint, they then set off on the longest stretch of the entire race – the 96.5km/60-mile trek that includes the awesome Pen-y-Ghent and is considered the make-or-break section of the race.

And that's when the weather decided to make itself noticed by dumping around 30 cm (almost 12 inches) of snow in about 12 hours on the highest sections of the course, with winds decreasing visibility and making navigation more difficult. Unsurprisingly, beaten by the weather, falls and the severe physical and mental demands being made upon them, several runners withdrew at this stage.

On the upside, the disaster brought out the qualities that make human beings what we truly are – looking to one another for support and help, banding together to face the challenge as one, and groups of runners began to form.

Which was just as well, for by the time they reached the Yorkshire Dales the snow was waist deep and concerns about hypothermia were becoming more real with every minute that passed.

The further north they progressed, the further the distances between landmarks became, with the stark moors offering no shelter or protection from the worst of the weather.

The lead runner, a Spaniard called Eugeni, who was out alone in the dark, was met by one of the race's support crew and had a tracker placed on him for safety.

Ultimately, just 14 of the 29 starters finished the race. All, apart from Eugeni and three others, finished together in groups.

To quote from the website: 'It was a dramatic end to an incredible race and a fitting reminder to us that nature should always be respected, and safety always comes before racing.'

Mental Miscellany

- The first Spine Race was held in 2012 and had just three finishers.
- In 2013, the winners recorded times of 5 days, 4 hours, 52 minutes (men) and 7 days, 4 hours, 59 minutes (women).
- All checkpoints are indoors and offer medical support, hot food and water, beds and showers, providing a haven from the hostile weather.
- The Spine Challenger is a shorter race starting at the same time as the Spine Race, and is a 174km/108-mile, non-stop, 60-hour winter mountain marathon that follows the Pennine Way from Edale to Hawes.

For further information, please visit: www.thespinerace.com

FEELING THE HEAT...

BADWATER 135
CALIFORNIA, USA

*217km/135 miles – non-stop through
Death Valley – 54°C/130°F*

If you think that training for a race like the Badwater 135 is simply a matter of upping the number of miles you run each week, think again. For this is a race that will test not only your endurance, but also your ability to cope with extreme heat for long periods, with temperatures reaching over 49°C/120°F even in the shade.

Accordingly, participants have been known to prepare for the race by trying to replicate the extreme race conditions by running in saunas, cycling in greenhouses, and even jogging on treadmills with clothes dryer vents blowing hot air over them! They will also be running around 161km/100 miles a week and refusing to sit down at every opportunity so they can get used to being on their feet for prolonged periods.

Held deliberately during the hottest month of the year in July, when weather conditions are at their most extreme with temperatures soaring as high as 54°C/130°F, it is said that entering

25

the area is like stepping into a giant oven; what little breeze there is will be hot and your skin will burn from the relentless heat of a perpetual sun.

It is in these exceptionally intense conditions that you will attempt to traverse three mountain ranges totalling a massive 3,962m/12,998ft of vertical ascent.

Hardly surprising, then, that very few people actually ever make the finish line.

The race, which is one of the many in this book to describe itself as 'the world's toughest foot race', starts at 85m/282ft below sea level, the lowest elevation in the western hemisphere, in the Badwater Basin in California's Death Valley, and finishes at Horseshoe Meadow, the trailhead to Mount Whitney, at an elevation of 3.048m/10,000ft.

With an imposed maximum number of 100 participants, the runners set off in three more-or-less even waves, the first at 6am, the second at 8am and the third at 10am. They then have 48 hours from their start times to complete the gruelling event.

During the race the runners will have to contend with the sight of miles of visible flat, open roadway lying ahead, simmering in the heat and offering no shady relief from the searing sun, while passing signs that read 'Caution! Extreme heat danger'. Consequently, most runners take the precaution of wearing long-sleeved shirts and sun hats.

With dehydration being a very real danger, most runners will have a support crew who will monitor their fluid intake and check their weight throughout the race to judge how much water they have lost while racing.

To help the runners keep cool, the organisers provide a Moeben hemp wrap (like a bandana), which is soaked in iced water and filled with ice. This is then worn around the head and shoulders and replenished as necessary.

The support crew vehicles are equipped with huge fridges which are stocked with food and drink and bags of ice, with one fridge full of ice and water. Only one ice scoop is used, solely for putting ice into bottles, to ensure that no bacteria can accidentally contaminate the runner's drinking water.

James Elson on an unforgiving stretch

The vehicles also carry a two-way radio, a chair and a brolly, the latter being used to hide the runner when changing clothes or urinating – there are no bushes in the desert!

All racers who officially complete the event within 48 hours will receive a finisher's T-shirt and commemorative Badwater Ultra marathon buckle.

Who would do this?

James Elson is a 31-year-old ultra runner and Ironman. He has been running ultras since early 2006 and organises 50- and 100-mile trail races in the UK through Centurion Running. James ran the Badwater 135 in 2010, aged 28. This extract was taken with kind permission from centurionrunning.com/blog

Death Valley was something else. This was it for me, the pinnacle, the hardest race on Earth, how could anything compare with 130 degrees and 135 miles of road, uphill?

Well, my luggage was lost on the way to the race, I was

forced to buy all my supplies for the event in Walmart the day before and suffered horrendous chaffing and nausea. My crew poured gallons of water over my head and by mile 42 I'd already lost most of the skin on the insides of my legs/ undercarriage. I had to walk the final 65 miles like John Wayne in order to finish in 39 hours. I would say that the heat, the elevation changes and the final 13 miles being up the side of a mountain are what make this so spectacularly hard. I think it's the hardest race finish I've ever endured.

When I got back, I was out of it for three months. That race took more out of me than any event I'd done before or since.

And then there's Mark Cockbain, a highly experienced, 41-year-old ultra runner and director of Cockbain Events. In 2003, 2005 and 2009, Mark ran the Badwater 135. However, in 2007 Mark decided to tackle it twice. Consecutively. Back to back. A total distance of just under 300 miles. This extract was taken with kind permission from: www.markcockbain.com

It's near midnight on 24 July 2007, and I'm back in Death Valley, approaching the end of my third Badwater Ultramarathon, with just 13 miles left to go, including a final push up Mount Whitney to the finish line. I've just managed to recover from severe dehydration yet again as I shuffle out of the baking heat of Owens Valley with the help of my chief crew and pacer, Liam.

However, this year is different. I'm attempting a 'double crossing', which means I will run the 135 miles back to the start at Badwater at -282ft, after summiting the 14,497ft peak of Mount Whitney.

As I cross the finish line in 46 hours, 12 minutes and receive a coveted sub 48-hour belt buckle, I wonder just how I will push myself on, as I'm already exhausted and my feet are badly blistered.

My crew [Liam, Cheri and Julia] bundle me into the [support] van for food and rest while they pack clothing and equipment ready for the big climb ahead.

I change into my trail shoes with thicker socks to give relief to my aching feet, put on some warmer clothing and a camelback for my water supply.

The trail is beautiful, but the sun is up and it's getting quite hot, slowing my progress.

Hours later storm clouds roll across the pinnacles of the mountain, the skies darken and thunder roars as it starts to rain heavily. This could be a huge setback as if I can't summit the mountain and sign the visitor's book inside the summit hut, my race is over.

I take temporary cover under some cliffs, and meet some descending climbers who describe terrible conditions of snow, hail and flooding on the top. With no escape from the elements up on the mountain crest, my double attempt looks in serious doubt, as it could be a fatal mistake to continue with the threat of lightning being a strong possibility.

Eventually the rain stops and I climb a little higher to evaluate conditions. I discuss options with my crew. Liam decides he doesn't want to risk it as further heavy rain could cause hypothermia and he feels responsible for Cheri, who is new to all of this.

I respect their decision as I certainly don't want anyone to get hurt, but am determined to get to the summit to continue with my double attempt. So I ask Julia, an experienced climber, her honest opinion: she's not happy with the situation but is prepared to push on a little further.

Just as we set off, I see a cougar, apparently a very rare sighting, which I take as a good luck omen.

Another runner and crew is heading down the mountain; they have been forced to turn back just a mile from the summit due to freezing conditions, hail and rain, I explain my predicament and they lend me extra warm clothing and food.

It's not ideal trying to climb to the summit in the dark, the crest veers up and down with sharp rocks underfoot and a sheer drop, and as we reach 13,000 feet it's very cold and I have a dull altitude sickness headache.

I'm really tired now, with aching feet and legs and it's hard to concentrate on the terrain, but a fall here would be fatal.

However, in the early hours of the morning we approach the huge shark fin silhouette of the summit peak and through a freezing wind we reach the summit hut at 4am, clambering inside to shelter from the elements, and signing the visitor book which is outside in a steel box.

We eat some freeze-dried cheesecake mix and then I nod off for a few minutes. We are now halfway at 150 miles; it has taken almost three days to get this far and I'm cold and tired.

We decide to get back down the mountain as soon as possible and it's still dark as we leave the hut to descend the steep, winding trail. Each step is agony on my blistered feet over rocky ground, my ankles twist and turn making me yell out in frustration, swearing and cursing at the mountain.

Eventually, the sun rises and my spirits lift, as I marvel at the magnificent view across Owens Valley in the distance.

As we descend down through the Whitney Park zone, my altitude headache disappears and I feel the strength of the early morning sun, and strip back down to my running gear.

After a while, I feel dizzy with the heat as we follow the winding river trail. We stop to fill up our camelbacks with river water using a purifier and I take off my shoes and socks and dip my feet in the cool mountain water. It feels fantastic as the swelling goes down and I manage to pop a few annoying blisters.

It's mid-afternoon as we approach the end of the trail; it's taken us just over 24 hours to summit and return to the Whitney portals. I'm tired, dehydrated and hungry.

I eat and sleep for an hour, then wake to start the 13-mile stretch of mountain road to Lone Pine. I run at a decent pace once my stiff legs loosen up.

After a good night of running I slow down as dawn breaks and start the long climb up towards the Darwin turnoff, just avoiding stepping on a dozy looking rattlesnake!

By the time I set off towards Panamint Springs, the sun is beating down on me and my hands are swollen with heat. It is slow going and I feel like I'm being boiled alive, but I keep drinking regularly and Julia drenches my hat and back to create a false sweat to cool me. I've been on my feet for four days now and I'm becoming much slower as I battle the heat and pain in my feet.

Several hours later, I start the long descent of sharp switchbacks towards the valley floor, easing myself carefully around blind corners to prevent collision with an occasional oncoming vehicle.

My face is bloated and flushed as I start to overheat, so I keep drinking and taking electrolytes, trying to move forward with minimum exertion.

Eventually the road flattens out and I meet my crew where I take a rest in the shade and bathe my feet. But I'm still overheating so we move inside a small information booth with a ceiling fan that helps cool me down.

I drink another large iced Pepsi and then a Gatorade, then wet my hat and start trudging across the valley floor towards the 10-mile long hill ahead.

It's hard work on the backs of my legs and my feet still ache as I push up the hill, I'm dizzy and slow and stare at the mounds of rocks either side of the road, which have started to look like piles of skulls as my mind plays tricks on me.

It's the hottest part of the day and I feel irritated and confused, classic signs of heat exhaustion and another all-time low. I just want the whole thing over.

But at last I finish the last big climb, take a short rest and down a cup of noodles, pleased the sun is setting and a slight breeze cools my skin.

It's time to make a push for Stovepipe Wells, a long downhill section, which usually I would welcome but not with the way my legs and feet are feeling. But once I settle into the pain, my legs start moving more freely and I run at a decent pace.

Although it's dark it's still very hot with a slight headwind that feels like a hairdryer in my face sucking the moisture from me.

After a few hours I hit a brick wall. I've misjudged my

pace in the heat and I'm empty and confused and start hallucinating about the rocks and bushes either side of the road. I feel terrible, but I keep drinking and trying to hold myself together.

Then to my relief the lights of Stovepipe appear and I stumble into a hotel room and onto a nice soft bed, which feels great.

My crew remove my shoes. I just want to sleep but know I must eat first to put back some energy. I'm confused; my mind is racing. I force down some noodles then try to sleep, but the room appears full of people examining me and I'm having the wildest dreams. I'm rabid with heat exhaustion.

I wake after a few hours feeling very confused and still dehydrated to a dangerous level. I decide not to leave the room until I can urinate, as the last 42 miles is the hottest section below sea level.

My crew worry about me overheating, so Cheri gives me her long white leggings which I cut into shape, and a long-sleeve top to wear over a layer of total block suncream.

I'm back on my feet again following the winding road out of Stovepipe past the giant sand dunes and through an area known as the Devil's Cornfield.

I take it nice and easy as the full power of the sun beats down on me and am glad to have Cheri pacing me, amusing me with stories and chat.

I regularly jump into the van to cool my feet with the deck chair now set up inside providing the only shade, but there's no escape from the heat as I sit dripping sweat with my feet submerged in the bucket.

There's less than a marathon to go now, and I'm confident I can make it.

I see the green oasis of Furnace Creek and am relieved the sun is setting for the last time on my journey.

At approximately mile 275, I wander into Furnace Creek, totally exhausted. It's hard to believe we stayed here five days earlier before the start of the race; the runners and their support vehicles have long gone.

I'm now into the last 17 miles and all I can do is walk. Liam walks alongside me as we turn right at the junction signposted Badwater to take the long road back to my original starting point. The support van drives alongside, blasting out music.

I am moving on empty and in a bit of a daze with a strange bittersweet feeling of reaching the finish. On one hand I don't want to take another painful step, but on the other I will be sad this life-changing adventure will be over.

With the combination of sleep deprivation and exhaustion, I point out shapes of dancing women in the clouds to Liam as the moon lights up the sky.

Then the crew announce I'm inside the last mile.

I walk in silence and am overcome with relief and emotion as I think about all the highs and lows of this amazing journey. I shake Liam's hand to thank him for helping me achieve my dream.

I cross the imaginary finish line at the point where the race had started and it feels like the world has been lifted from my shoulders. I hug Liam, Cheri and Julia; I could not have done this without all of their hard work and dedication.

I've made it! What seemed an impossible dream has become a reality. It's taken me 5 days, 19 hours and 44 minutes; I'm only the 20th person in the world to complete this crazy ordeal, and the 5th Brit!

We all then lay on our backs and stare up at the beautiful desert stars as Liam passes around whisky and cigars to celebrate a true moment of magic.

Mental Miscellany

- Al Arnold was the first person to run from Death Valley to Mount Whitney in 1977.
- The first Badwater race took place in 1987.
- The organisers of the inaugural 1987 race, Richard Benyo and Tom Crawford, became the first runners to complete a double Badwater in 1989.

- Rhonda Provost became the first woman to complete a double Badwater in 1995.
- Britain's Chris Moon was the first amputee to complete the race in 1999. He has since completed the race a further four times.
- Badwater also organises cycling events such as the 'Fall Death Valley Bike Challenge' – a ride of 322km/200 miles within 24 hours – and a chance to view the Valley in moonlight.

For further information, please visit: www.badwater.com

SPARTATHLON
GREECE

*250km/153 miles – 1,200m/3,937ft ascent –
Athens to Sparta – 36 hours*

As might be expected of a race that takes place in Greece, the Spartathlon comes steeped in history and culture.

The race follows the footsteps of the mighty Pheidippides, the Greek soldier who was sent to Sparta from Athens to seek help in the Battle of Marathon in 490 BC and who, according to historians, duly arrived in Sparta, over 150 miles away, just one day after his departure from Athens, despite travelling solely on foot!

That claim roused the curiosity of Colonel John Foden to such an extent that in 1982 he organised for himself and five officers of the British Royal Air Force, all long-distance runners, to tackle the identical route that Pheidippides would have followed to see whether it really was possible to cover such a distance in that time. They proved it was possible, completing their run in less than 40 hours.

So inspired was Colonel Foden that he envisioned a race bringing runners from around the world to run the trail of Pheidippides, and the following year a multinational team led by Michael Callaghan organised the first international Spartathlon, the name deriving from the Greek words for 'sparta' and 'feat'.

The race has since been held every September, being the month that Pheidippides is reported to have carried out his epic run.

As for the route itself, this traverses rough tracks and boggy pathways across vineyards and olive groves, while also climbing steep hillsides, including, at the 161km/100-mile point, a 1,200-metre, night-time ascent and descent of Mount Parthenio (the mountain where Pheidippides is said to have met the God, Pan). It is still very much the same as it must have been in Pheidippides' day, a gruelling test of stamina and mental strength, with no actual pathway over the mountain (although the ascent is marked by battery-driven flashing lights) and biting winds that lower the temperature to around 4°C/39°F.

But it is the final stages that really test the runners, as exhaustion leads to hallucinations and a lost sense of time and reality, their minds capable only of focusing on keeping going to the finish line at the Statue of Leonidas in Sparta.

With only around a third of all starters making it to Sparta within the 36-hour time limit, it is little wonder that those who do make it struggle to express what finishing such a punishing race means.

Who would do this?

Thirty-one-year-old race director with Centurion Running, James Elson, took part in Spartathlon in 2012 and 2013. In 2012, he was forced to drop out of the race at mile 99; in 2013, he returned with just one aim in mind – to finish. This extract was taken with kind permission from: www.centurionrunning.com/blog.

I woke up at 5am on race morning and smiled, thankful that the pressure of waiting for the massive effort to begin was over. I wore a plain white cotton tee that would absorb the water continually being poured over my head to stay cool, shorts with deep pockets to carry food and gels, and a buff over my head to pack with ice.

We ran out of the Acropolis at 7am and I dropped into a

comfy pace as we ran through the Athens streets with blaring horns and police blockades which shut the city rush hour down to allow us to pass.

After about 10km, we were on the hard shoulder of the motorway heading west towards Corinth, and rolled through the checkpoints efficiently while the heat was manageable, taking on food and water consistently.

The heat got up at around 11am and I made heavy use of the ice at the checkpoints along the coast road. The difference it makes is astounding; from the heat forcing your pace down everything seems to suddenly free up and allow you to move well again.

We rolled into the 50-mile checkpoint in 7 hours, 47 minutes. I felt great.

After Corinth the course evolved into olive groves and smaller villages.

I reached mile 76 in 13 hours, 5 minutes and flicked on my headlamp for the first time. I was way ahead of where I'd been in 2012, my time better by about 90 minutes. My legs felt great and I was starting to believe this was going to be my day. I can't explain why, but I felt incredibly calm.

At Nemea I raced down a can of baked beans, two cups of soup and a handful of other bits, my stomach still co-operating well.

I reached mile 91 [146km] which displays the read-out showing 99.3km [62 miles] to go. Any other day, knowing you had 62 miles to run would be a stomach churning prospect, not least after already having covered 91 miles, but somehow at Sparta, this is a vision.

The hike up the switchbacks to the base of the mountain are long but not too steep and it was with a big smile on my face that I looked up at the mountain, flashing lights rising high into the sky, realising I was about to pass into unknown territory, pushing through the place my race had ended last year. I felt good and with 18 hours, 50 minutes on the watch we'd covered 100 miles and passed on to the third and final part of the race, the final 53 miles.

The mountain was steep and rugged but easy enough to negotiate. Hiking hard, I was sweating under my windproof, but every time I stopped my temperature plummeted. On the summit it was pretty blowy, so I started the descent immediately. The downhill was way worse than the climb with the track covered in substantial scree. Twice I nearly went backwards but I managed to run the majority of the drop into the next village at mile 104.

After the CP [checkpoint] I dropped back on to the road, alternating between a purposeful hike and a steady 10-minute-mile running pace. Then the worst happened. My trusty Petzl headlamp blinked three times at me, signalling the impending death of the batteries. It was pitch black on the road. As my torch died I ran hard to catch a runner in front with a blinking red LED on her back. I told her [Brenda] my predicament and she kindly offered to let me draft her light by running alongside her. A few minutes later, however, I had to stop to tend to business and with no light I didn't realise but I stepped right into the big pile of my own crap. Things weren't looking up.

Again I ran slightly harder than was comfortable to catch Brenda and we made our way through a few more checkpoints. Half-an-hour further I reached a friend who kindly swapped her lamp for mine while she found me some batteries. Independent again I felt rejuvenated and was finally able to clean my stinking shoes and push on.

By now it was 5am and the temperature was through the floor. I was getting cold quickly and knew I needed a solution. I took a bin bag from the next CP [checkpoint] and wrapped myself in it. That quickly failed to be enough and I ended up picking up further bin bags at the next three aid stations. I had one between each layer of clothing and one on top of the lot wrapped tight around me like a blanket and up over my head. I looked like a tramp.

Eventually I knew I was going to get myself in serious trouble, so I began searching among the trash and multiple dead dogs (seriously) at the sides of the road for any items of clothing I could add to my growing collection of tramp style. I am embarrassed to say that had I seen any houses with clothes or sheets on a line outside, I would have found it hard to resist grabbing something. When the sun came up it seemed to take an age to bring any heat whatsoever, but all of a sudden I went from shivering wreck to overheating and quickly stripped off all of the bin bags, extra layers and headlamp.

At the 124-mile mark, I was expecting the 'second mountain' – a long drag up to the top, perhaps only 4 or 5 miles but at a steady climbing grade, there were some tight bends where enthused Greek drivers waving frantically out of the window at us with no hand on the wheel could easily swipe down a runner. Crossing the road to avoid this seemed a monumental waste of dwindling energy. As I crested the climb with a marathon to go, it seemed like the end was nigh. 127 miles down.

Time was pretty irrelevant at this point, I had plenty in the bank under which to meet the 36-hour cut-off. I just needed to ensure I didn't overheat. Back to the old routine of ice over the head, soaking the shirt and moving ever forward. This last 50 were not fun in any way, shape or form. But somehow, knowing we were in the midst of the fight to finish Spartathlon, was enough not just to stay motivated but to keep moving well.

With 12 miles to go I found the gradual downhill leg-battering grade was without doubt the worst end to a race I'd ever endured. Despite all that, I still had a smile on my face and felt relatively good for how late in the race it was. I jogged intermittently and hiked a lot of it as I made sure I was always working between 4 and 5 mph, reducing the time left on my feet from 6 hours to 5, 4, 3, 2...

Arriving at six miles to go, I toughed out five of those miles and found myself passing under the blue banner welcoming Spartathletes to Sparta. My mind started to fill with the thoughts of running up that final street to the statue, the same memory I'd let build over the course of a year to keep me moving every time running hard started to hurt a little bit, and the thought I'd kept at bay for the whole race as I focused only on the next checkpoint ahead at any one time.

Finally I made checkpoint 74, 1 mile to go, 152 done. I'd been moving consistently forward, with the exception of that 10 minutes reheating, for a little over 33 hours. A police bike joined me and escorted me through the streets of Sparta. I was running well at this point, then I turned a street after 10 minutes or so and saw quite a long climb ahead. I asked him how close we were and he said 1.5km! I swore and dropped back into a hike without caring too much that he was forced to ride so slowly he almost fell off. When I saw the final turn and the national flags streaming in the wind along the boulevard past the waiting crowds, I did begin running again and this time held it [the run] to the statue. High-fiving friends and being handed the Union Jack were exactly what I'd imagined for the past 12 months. Reaching the steps to the statue, I took a second to walk slowly up to it and kissed the foot of Leonidas in the tradition of Spartathlon finishers from the last 31 years, started of course by Pheidippedis, whose footsteps we retraced 2,500 years later.

My finish time 33 hours, 45 minutes, 2 hours, 15 under the eventual cut-off; 59 runners beat me to the statue, 90 more would finish before 36 hours passed and over 200 more would be beaten by the race.

How hard was it? It took almost all of what I had, mentally and physically,

Having conquered the gruelling race

to get there. It isn't just race day, it's the dedication of 100s of hours over the course of 12 months to running the miles you need in order to condition your body to the hammering that 153 miles on the road puts it through. The sacrifices you need to make are huge. Without the support of your friends and loved ones, it simply isn't possible to do what's necessary to finish. I still puked one less time at Sparta than I did the previous weekend at a 5km park run-though. That feels wrong.

Mental Miscellany

- The first Spartathlon took place in 1983 with 45 runners, including women, from 11 countries.
- In 2013, there were 350 runners from all over the world; 146 finished.
- The inaugural race was won by a Greek who went on to win it four times, producing one of the best ever times in 1984 of 20 hours, 25 minutes.
- Only those meeting strict qualifying requirements may enter Spartathlon.
- Participants have included a Japanese blind man with a guide.
- The oldest man ever to finish Spartathlon was a 75-year-old German.
- All finishers must kiss the foot of the statue of Leonidas.
- There are medical support groups and physios for 36 hours at checkpoint stations, and medical cars run between with medics and physios.
- Local hospitals along the route are on standby during the whole of the race.

For further information, please visit: www.spartathlon.gr

ULTRABALATON
HUNGARY

212km/132 miles – 40°C/104°F –
Lake Balaton – within 32 hours

It's 0600 in Hungary and the start of another beautiful sunny day in May. The temperature is still comfortable enough to take a relaxing stroll beside the lovely calm and gentle waters of Lake Balaton, which derives its name from the Slavic word *blato*, meaning 'mud' or 'swamp', and which is the largest freshwater lake in central Europe, as well as being one of the most shallow with an average depth of just 3.2m/10.5ft, although it does venture further downwards to 12.2m/40ft at its deepest point. As a result, the lake is ideal for children and swimming, with an average temperature of 26°C/80°F, while older visitors may take advantage of the health-giving qualities of its water and mud, which purport to offer excellent remedies for nervous complaints, anaemia and nervous fatigue.

However, despite the serene setting and comfortable climate, this particular day is not a day for strolling, swimming or partaking in spa-styled treatments; today is a day for running 212km/131 miles non-stop around the entire lake within a time limit of 32 hours. For today is the day of the Ultrabalaton.

Runners will set off from Tihany, a hilly promontory that juts out into the lake, the only real hill in the whole of the course, racing gleefully down the hill at the start, clambering up it rather more sedately near the finish 210km/130 miles later, should they get that far within the strictly enforced time limit; for once the temperature begins to climb – it can reach as high as 40°C/104°F, and many will falter and fail.

Some 50km/31 miles after crossing the start line, they will reach the lake, whose shores they will then follow for the rest of the race, passing along its flat, southernmost shores where the sunshine reflecting off the mirrored lake produces the perfect climate for successful wine-growing, and along the opposite mountainous northern shores, which offer beautiful scenic views that attract tourists from all over the world.

Fortunately there are plenty of water stations along the way providing fuel and fluid, and runners can also take advantage of the plastic, shallow 'baby baths' filled with cooling water to dunk their heads in should they feel so inclined, although this is not recommended during the night-time when head torches are worn.

Although the race is not high in absolute terms, after 210km and 30-odd hours of running, that one hill near the finish is a killer, and many resort to using the handrail on the side of the road to assist them.

Who would do this?

Ultra runner and self-employed management consultant, Robert Pinnington (51), who lives in Germany, has attempted this race twice, once in 2011 and again in 2012. He completed it successfully in 2011, but the heat got the better of him in 2012 and he got timed out at 80km.

The course is flattish, but you just have to keep going in the heat. Then the end is a climb and saps the will to finish.

2011 was my first attempt at that sort of distance and I remember chatting to a couple of Polish guys during the first day who'd done the Marathon des Sables; they thought the Ultrabalaton was far tougher.

We ran together for a while and then they disappeared into the distance at around 8pm. In the middle of the night one of them popped up next to me again because his quads were shot, so we ran together for a while but he dropped out at the next rest stop and I promised to finish it for him.

I was very tired at around 2am and stopped at a rest point where a young girl asked me if I was okay. I told her I was okay but tired. She offered to get me some food, a banana or a biscuit or something, and I told her that if I saw another banana, I would scream and if I ate another biscuit, I'd throw up. She didn't really know what to say to that. So then I told her that what I really wanted was a big fat juicy cheeseburger. She apologised and told me that McDonald's was closed. So I asked her to pass me a bottle of cola, which she did. I drank about a litre of it. Then I noticed some cigarettes and asked whose they were. She said they were hers, so I asked her if I could have one, and she agreed. Then she asked me if I was giving up on the race now, and I told her that I wasn't, I just wanted a fag.

I lit up the cigarette and walked off into the night smoking, much to the amazement of the crew at the rest stop. It kept me awake though!

I also remember going past a lakeshore disco that lit up the night sky for miles around and a rather drunk lad ran alongside me and quizzed me on what I and the other runners were doing. His reaction was a picture.

I got over the tiredness and was within the time limit at 164km [102 miles], by at least an hour, but at around 7am, my left achilles seized up and it was a death march from then on.

When I reached the final hill to the finish, my achilles was so swollen, the foot was frozen in place and an old dear with a zimmer frame was moving faster than me and offered to help!

I finished in 31:30, and would have liked to have improved on that in 2012, but it was really a lot hotter at over 40°C, and I pulled out at 80km.

Mental Miscellany

- The first Ultrabalaton took place in 2007 and was won in 18 hours, 15 minutes (men); 28 hours, 32 minutes (women).
- In 2013, the race was won in 20 hours, 34 minutes (men); 22 hours, 47 minutes (women); 115 started the race, 75 finished.
- The race can be run as an individual or in teams.

For further information, please visit: www.ultrabalaton.hu

JUNGLE ULTRA
PERU

230km/143 miles – through the Amazon rainforest

Billed on its website as the 'toughest, wettest, hottest and most beautiful ultra race in the world', the Jungle Ultra runs 230km/143 miles from the Andes to the Amazon rainforest and is organised by Beyond the Ultimate, a company who hold four races on four continents to form the 'Ultimate Ultra Race Series'. The four races offer a vast range of terrain from the Amazon jungle to the Rocky Mountains, the Namib Desert to the Arctic Circle, and each contain a Red Jersey Stage (a race within a race), which tests competitors over relatively short distances across the toughest section of each race.

In the case of the Jungle Ultra, which is held every May, this takes place during stage four of the five-stage race, testing quads and calves to the max during a climb of 1,000m/3,281ft through thick jungle trails with a timed run to the top, battling with nature and humidity on the way.

The race itself starts in a cloud forest at Cuzco, one of the highest cities in the world at 3,200m/10,499ft, with stunning views of the Amazon before descending into the thick of the jungle, where temperatures of up to 38°C/100°F and 100 per cent humidity are the norm.

Each day, competitors will run anything from 30km/19 miles to 92km/57 miles along rough jungle tracks and mountain trails, facing numerous ascents and descents, and more than 70 river crossings which they need to wade, zip-wire or raft through. On their journey they may come face-to-face with black caimans and jaguars or any of the other 13 species of primate that inhabit the jungle, as well as numerous mammals, reptiles and an estimated 30 million species of insects and snakes that carpet the jungle floor or dangle from tree-top canopies!

It may therefore be reassuring to know that the race organisers state that safety is their prime concern, and have therefore designed the course in loops with each section ending in an area accessible by road, which is manned by a medic, with the ratio of medics to runners being 1:10. There is also plenty of other race support with multi-lingual staff, medical support, 4x4 support vehicles, and helicopters, as well as an evacuation arrangement in place, though whether this is considered reassuring or alarming is a matter of personal opinion!

With this being a self-sufficient race, runners will also have to carry their own hammock, sleeping bag, food and supplies for the entire race, refilling water containers at various checkpoints and base camps along the way.

Who would do this?

Anyone adventurous and fit who is into virgin forests, diverse wildlife, forest basins, flowing rivers and vast open grassland, not to mention insects, snakes and primates, and with a penchant for running long distances in extreme heat and humidity – and sleeping in a hammock of a night.

According to the results of the 2013 race, competitors came from as far afield as the UK, Denmark, the USA, South Africa, Canada, Argentina and Italy, and consisted of lawyers, coaches, journalists and public speakers, among other professions.

Mental Miscellany

- In 2012 the winners finished in a cumulative total time of 21 hours, 22 minutes (men) and 32 hours, 45 minutes (women).
- In 2012 there were 24 starters – three did not finish.
- The race takes place through the Manu National Park.
- During stage 1, runners will climb and descend 2,743m/9,000ft.
- Runners will wake up above the clouds!

For further information, please visit: www.beyondtheultimate. co.uk

FIRST IT'S COLD, THEN IT'S HOT...

WESTERN STATES 100
CANADA

161km/100-mile trail race – Sierra Nevada Mountains –
-6°C/21°F to 43°C/109°F

One of the most unusual histories of any ultra race must be the one behind the Western States 100, which no doubt accounts for the website's claim that this is the oldest and most prestigious 100-mile race in the world.

Way back on a scorching day in July, 1955, a man named Wendell T Robie and five other horsemen rode 100 miles along the rugged Western States Trail from Squaw Valley to Auburn to prove that it was possible for horses to cover that distance in one day.

Following successful completion of the mission, Mr Robie set up a foundation and organised an annual Western States Trail Ride known as The Tevis Cup – '100-Miles One-Day Trail Ride'.

Then, in 1974, a man named Gordy Ainsleigh joined the horses to see if he could complete the course on foot. He did so in 23 hours, 42 minutes.

The following two years saw two other men take up the personal challenge, the first withdrawing just two miles from the finish, the second succeeding in 24 hours, 30 minutes.

A year on, in 1977, the first official race was held. It was called the 'Western States Endurance Run', and took place in conjunction with the Tevis Cup Ride. Indeed, the 14 runners who took part were monitored at the three vet stops – by a doctor, not a vet!

There were just three finishers – the winner in 22 hours, 57 minutes, with the second- and third-placed runners finishing in a dead heat in 28 hours, 36 minutes. Consequently, the silver-buckle award for anyone completing the run in less than 24 hours was born, with a bronze buckle award going to anyone finishing within 30 hours.

In 1978 the foot race took place independent of the horse race, a month earlier in June. This time there were 21 aid stations with 6 medical checks and 63 runners, including the first woman, who finished in 29 hours, 34 minutes.

By 1979, the field had increased to 143 runners from 21 states and three overseas countries. Today, the field is more likely to reach its limit of around 400 runners, who will come from a myriad of states and countries.

The race itself starts at 0500 from the base of the Squaw Valley Ski Resort, and continues through the night before finishing 100 miles later at the Placer High School running track in Auburn, and imposes a 30-hour time limit.

The terrain is extremely rocky, rugged, and at times, remote, passing through deep canyons, high mountains, ice-cold water, and dirt trails, and includes a cumulative total climb of 5,500m/18,000ft and a potential temperature variation of between -6°C/20°F and 43.3°C/110°F.

Due to the toughness of the event, entrants must meet the following qualifying standards: they must either have completed 50 miles in sub-11 hours, 100km in sub-15 hours, or 100 miles in sub-30 hours. They must also produce proof that they have carried out 8 hours of voluntary work on trails or at an ultra event in the 12 months prior to the race.

Unsurprisingly, the website warns that the race may present

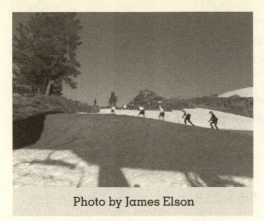

Photo by James Elson

extremely serious or fatal medical risks, such as extreme physical and mental stress/exhaustion, renal failure, heatstroke and low blood sodium. As a result, prior to the race all athletes must undergo a medical examination, which will include weight, blood pressure and pulse checks. Readings from these tests will then be used as a baseline throughout the event.

The race also warns of snow hazards, rattlesnakes, bears, mountain lions and Poison Oak, and recommends flashlights for night running and the use of guide ropes or personal assistance when crossing rivers.

Although support crews and pacers are allowed, the pacer must not carry any provisions for their runner or assist in any way.

Who would do this?

James Elson (31), experienced ultra runner and race director of Centurion Running, took part in this race in 2011. This extract was taken with kind permission from: www.centurionrunning.com/blog.

The race manual gives 'trashed quads' as one of the main reasons for not finishing Western States 100. I had never really had trashed quads before, but let me tell you it hurts bad.

At the medical check they took our blood pressure, pulse and weight, but the weight thing is annoying as they checked us regularly throughout the race and if our weight differed by more than 3 per cent up or down of registration weight, we might be asked to wait at an aid station to drink/eat/pee until our weight normalised before we could go on. If our weight differed by 7 per cent or more, we would be pulled from the course on medical grounds – dehydration or hyponatraemia [low sodium levels].

I was one of the few without designated crew or pacers, but I didn't worry given the number of aid stations.

I got up at 3am to drive to Squaw Valley; it was freezing.

The first few miles climb up gravel paths under ski lifts to the escarpment and over the top of the mountain. There is no downhill or flat and the ski slope was still covered in thick snow.

I slid a lot but the views across Lake Tahoe were incredible.

By 20 miles, my quads were already sore and I still had 20,000ft of downhill to contend with. The lack of training due to injury was mainly responsible.

The single track winding through trees around the edge of a lake and crossing small streams to Duncan Canyon was stunning.

There followed a long downhill descent on trail and road, then a steep climb in the now building heat back up to Mosquito Ridge at mile 31. I knew then I'd gone out too hard because people were passing me on the downhills where I was in pain, but I made up for it on the climbs with strong climbing legs.

By mile 35 my quads felt like they were being jarred out of my legs.

The next 20 miles descend deep down into a canyon and back up the other side – three times. It was in the heat of the day and there was no air down there. Luckily it was only 90°F degrees instead of the usual 110°F.

My quads were so battered I was forced to walk most of the descent with every step causing more pain.

The climb up Devils Thumb is intense, 1,500 feet in a mile or so with 36 switchbacks. It's the kind of climb where you look up and the runners ahead look like they're perched on a cliff directly above you.

By the time I got to the top at mile 43 I felt totally spaced out and my weight was down to the limit. I forced some food down and kept moving so my legs wouldn't seize up.

I wanted to reach mile 62 before dark and give myself a boost psychologically. Apart from my quads, everything else was pretty okay, no chaffing or blisters.

I tried everything to ease my quads, snatching sticks out of the bushes to push down my legs and try and run the lactic acid out, stretching. Nothing worked. When your quads are shot to pieces there is nothing you can do to recover them.

A medic sweeper who was out running sections of the course kindly found me a pacer whose runner had dropped out. He knew every nook and cranny. Having someone pace you when it's getting dark and you've been on your feet for 16 hours already, telling you exactly how long the next climb is or how far to the next run-able section, is invaluable, and his help at the aid stations was out of this world. I let him know what I needed and he did it, allowing me to stretch, puke or just stand at the food table eating everything I could.

I say puke because over the next 10–15 miles I started to get pretty nauseous. By the time we reached the aid station at mile 70, I suffered a total evacuation of everything I had in my system. Retching really hard made me pull my stomach muscles, but once it was all out I felt tons better and we proceeded on through the dark to the American River crossing.

At Rucky Chucky, mile 78, we donned life jackets and climbed into a raft for a quick journey to the other side. It would have been spectacular had I not been freezing cold and in pain, but it was still an experience I'll never forget.

On the other side, I found all the skin had come away from the bottom of my feet, so I placed clean socks over the flaps of skin and pressed down into my shoes to get it to all stay put.

The light started to come up just as we hit Browns Bar at mile 90. I'd gone a little quiet because of the pain in my legs but my pacer kept pushing me to eat salt and drink a little as my hands were pretty swollen and my weight still up a few pounds at the previous weigh in.

The last 10 miles is almost all straight up or down, nothing severe, but rough going. I was having real trouble negotiating the descents now at any speed and felt pretty sick with the pain but didn't want to puke again, so just gutted it out best I could, but we were really crawling along.

We descended down to No Hands Bridge at mile 96.5; it was a death march, but it was the last downhill and I started to lighten up a little.

Then we made the climb up to Robie Point at mile 98.9 on to the last mile to the track at Auburn at a gentle stroll.

I couldn't have cared less about the overall time at that point. We ambled in, trying to loosen up my quads so we could run round the track at the end.

The reception was fantastic, people cheering all the way round to the finish. It felt good to cross the line, total time – 28 hours, 25 minutes.

I was elated that I'd got it done, mentally it was my strongest ever performance. Not once did I even come close to contemplating taking extended time at an aid station, let alone sleeping, stopping or dropping out.

Western States lived up to everything it pertains to be; the Trail holds this race up there at the top, it's awesome.

As I crossed the line a medic took my pulse and told me it was high. I'd just covered 100 miles and run to the finish. No shit my pulse was high.

Mental Miscellany

- Course records as at 2012 are 14 hours, 46 minutes, 44 seconds (men); 16 hours, 47 minutes, 19 seconds (women).
- The minimum age is 18.
- The race now provides 25 aid stations and 10 major medical checkpoints.
- The Western States 100 is one of four events comprising the Grand Slam of Ultra-running (the others are: Vermont 100, Wasatch Front 100 and Leadville Trail 100).

For further information, please visit: www.wser.org

IN THE DESERT YOU CAN'T REMEMBER YOUR NAME...

TRANS 333
WORLDWIDE

*Longest annual non-stop desert
foot race in the world*

Perhaps unsurprisingly, the Trans 333 is 333km/207 miles long, and is usually held in a different desert location each year.

As such it is the longest annual non-stop desert foot race in the world and is only open to the world's most experienced ultra runners.

The race itself is so hardcore that its checkpoints offer only minimal assistance and water top-ups, and runners must navigate the course using a wrist GPS, to which they will have programmed in a list of coordinates given to them by the race organisers.

Runners are required to supply their own freeze-dried food, energy bars, gels, torch and batteries, sleeping bag, survival gear and mandatory emergency satellite phone; bag drops (the facility to arrange for bags containing further supplies to be dropped off and accessed from checkpoints en route) are allowed.

Whichever desert, there will always be the same challenges

and difficulties to contend with, such as scorching sun and strong winds, pitch-black nights, sand dunes, rocks and mountains, heat-swollen fingers, face, legs and toes that make it almost impossible to get shoes back on, blisters sorely aggravated by the sharpest of stones, dust, hallucinations and mirages, and last, but by no means least, sheer exhaustion from wading through endless miles of energy-sapping, foot-sinking, deep, soft sand.

As one runner put it, 'The race strips life back to essentials, nature, run, sleep, eat and drink, and camaraderie', and race organiser, Alain Gestin, says that he believes the minimal assistance throughout the race means the runners succeed by triumphing over themselves.

Who would do this?

Forty-one-year-old electronics engineer and director of Cockbain Events, Mark Cockbain, took part in the 2006 race in Niger, Africa. This extract was taken with kind permission from: www.markcockbain.com

There were just 20 runners and the race started deep in the Ténéré Desert.

I was carrying 2 litres of water in my backpack, and another 1 litre in bottles strapped to my front, as well as all the mandatory equipment in a backpack.

The race started at 8am at 'The Tree of Ténére', a metal post that used to be the only tree for miles around. It was in the middle of nowhere, but apparently it was the only mapped landmark for miles.

We set off running straight ahead into a strong headwind, with the soft sand underfoot taking a lot of effort to move through. It felt like I was going nowhere fast, and it was hard to keep up a decent pace.

There was nothing as far as the eye could see apart from the other runners and the occasional mound of bleached white camel carcasses.

A few hours after leaving checkpoint two, I could see

nothing around me at all; it was just flat dusty white sand right up to the horizon. I had never been to a place where there were no landmarks at all, not even a rock.

I was making good progress through the hottest part of the day, with the burning sun deceivingly masked by the strong wind.

Eventually, the sun started to set on a long day of running, and I took out my head torch.

At the next checkpoint I re-filled my water, and left into the pitch-black night while eating one of my freeze-dried meals, to try and restore some energy.

There was no moon yet, and I could only see the beam of my head torch, as I constantly monitored my GPS for directions.

It felt eerie running into the night, alone in the middle of such a vast expanse of land, and it was becoming much cooler, with a sharp wind. There wasn't a sound, but it felt like I was being watched. I quickly scanned around with my head torch beam, and was shocked to see two bright green eyes shining back at me! I ran a lot faster, looked around again, and once more I saw the eyes. It was following me!

I had nothing I could use as a weapon, and there were no rocks or sticks, so I decided to hold my emergency whistle in the hope that the noise would scare it off if it got any closer.

I continued running fast, regularly spinning round with my torch, looking for the eyes, but after several miles, and to my relief I realised it was gone.

The sand was getting deep again, and I was sliding around making slow progress as I trudged on towards checkpoint four at around 50 miles. It was approaching midnight and my feet were already swollen and blistered from the soft sand.

The moon was rising, and soon visibility was much clearer. The terrain was becoming rocky now; tiredness was catching up with me and I began to trip up over rocks, so I decided that I would try to sleep for an hour at the next checkpoint, just before sunrise.

I was paranoid I wouldn't wake up, and after nodding off a few times I saw that it was getting light and decided to get myself together. I inspected my feet and found plenty of blisters to burst, and again put on a fresh pair of socks. My shoulders were sore with the weight of the backpack, and my nose and ears were full of sand dust.

I hobbled out of the tent. My feet were very sore, and it would take a while before my leg muscles loosened up. A huge black mountain dominated the horizon, and there were now large mounds of rocks and hills, and the GPS was taking me on a direct line over them. There was no wind today, and it was feeling hot already as the sun peaked over the hills.

It felt great to get some shelter from the sun as I reached the checkpoint. My fingers and face were swollen with the heat, and feet felt as though they were on fire.

The next section was a long, dusty winding track, which was easy to run and seemed to be slightly downhill, before heading up again across a vast open range and through a herd of camels, which noticeably had their front legs roped to prevent them wandering too far.

I was getting a reading of 42°C on my thermometer, and I was feeling a bit dizzy. I was glad when the midday sun had passed its hottest point again, and it was starting to drop in the sky, just as I arrived at checkpoint 7, at around 90 miles.

It wasn't long before it was pitch black again, but this time it wasn't flat at all, and I kept arriving at huge mounds of white rocks that I could only cross directly, because I couldn't see around them as I followed the GPS.

After several hours of climbing over mound after mound, I was starting to think that my GPS coordinates must be wrong, and I checked them against the master list. They were right, but because it was so dark I couldn't see an easier route, so it was slow going.

It was late evening when I saw the lights of checkpoint 8, but I was now over halfway and I aimed to try and get to checkpoint 10 without sleeping. This turned out to be harder than I thought, and after a few hours of leaving the checkpoint I was struggling to stay awake.

It was around 2am, and I was starting to hallucinate. This

wasn't a problem, as I had experienced it many times before, but I was now starting to walk a lot more, and making very slow progress. The occasional small bushes looked like crouching men, and I swear that I saw several sleeping ducks, which I now realise were definitely rocks!

I then entered a small grass-hut village; I kept as quiet as possible, as everyone seemed to be sleeping. This section seemed to go on forever, and when I eventually got to checkpoint 9, at around 4am, I knew I needed sleep before I could go on.

I lay down and shut my eyes for an hour. I woke with a start. My legs were very stiff now, and it took a while before I could run. I was back on flat open desert, and it was good for running, but my feet and legs were so sore that I was very slow.

The sun was baking hot again, and I could see the heat rising from the ground ahead. In the distance I saw what looked like a brown tidal wave heading towards me, with white tips at either end. As I got closer, I could see that it was a huge herd of camels being 'driven' at each end by men on white camels. The men waved at me!

This was the hottest day so far, and I took time to cool off, and rehydrate at checkpoint 10.

I looked for an easier path to follow to avoid the painful rocks, cowering to keep my face down and out of the sun blasting directly at me. After a long, painful afternoon, I reached the shade of the next checkpoint and collapsed exhausted inside the tent.

When I left I was aching, but pushed on through another grass hut village, then I was back on to deep soft sand as night fell, and tried to follow some jeep tracks to keep from going through the scrubland on either side. The deep sand was making this the slowest section so far, as I reached the 160-mile point. It was pitch black again, and I just wanted to sleep. I was hallucinating again, and I tried to fight it. I needed to sit in the sand and just rest for a few minutes.

Checkpoint 12 was my lowest point in the race, as I could hardly put my shoes on because of my swollen feet, and once I stood up, it was taking me longer and longer until I could ignore the pain. Shuffling off into the night, I knew that if I could make it to the next checkpoint before dawn, then I had almost beaten the race.

I kept a steady pace, taking the occasional break to get my breath back again, and after a long night came into the checkpoint, again resting before setting off on the last 26 miles towards Agadez.

There were now a few signs of life, like some goats, the odd grass hut and the occasional camel rider and I was on a major track that was nice and flat approaching the last checkpoint. I gathered up my last water supplies to take on my final leg into town.

After a few hours I was delighted to just make out the box-like sandy buildings of Agadez on the horizon, but it was also the hottest part of the day again and I was desperately low on water. I could see the town a lot more clearly, but was walking slowly trying not to overheat. Then, luckily, a cameraman turned up in a jeep, and passed me some spare water, which I gulped down.

On the outskirts of town, children were playing in the dirt. This was a desperately poor country, but at least they looked happy. I gave out whatever energy bars and gels I had left to the children, along with my empty water bottles. It was heart-breaking to see such gratefulness at the smallest of gifts.

As I turned the last corner, I got my first glimpse of the finish line, and ran over the line, in second place! It had taken me 81 hours and 34 minutes.

Mental Miscellany

- The first Trans 333 race was held in 1999.
- The 14th edition, in 2013, was held in Morocco.
- Typically, around one-third of participants fail to finish.
- Runners will wear shoes at least one size larger than normal to allow for swelling of feet in the heat.

For further information, please see: www.extreme-runner.fr

4 DESERTS RACE SERIES
CHINA, CHILE, JORDAN, ANTARCTICA
250km/155 miles x 4 – Gobi, Atacama, Sahara, The Last

Founded in 2002 in Hong Kong, the 4 Deserts Race Series consists of four separate trail races across four different deserts. These can be run individually at any time, or all four can be tackled within a year.

The inaugural race of the series was held in 2003 in China across the Gobi Desert and is known as the Gobi March. This was followed in 2004 with the Atacama Crossing in Chile, the Sahara Race in Egypt in 2005 and, finally, and somewhat aptly, The Last Desert in Antarctica in 2006.

Anyone attempting all four in a calendar year will need a current passport and understanding employers, so they can be in Jordan in February, China in June, Chile in October and Antarctica in November.

All four races follow an identical structure in that they are all 250km/155 miles long, run across a desert over a seven-day period, and are self-supporting – a tent and water being the only 'luxuries' provided by the race organisers, although there are checkpoints with experienced hikers, ultra runners and wilderness-specialist medics on hand. There are one or two notable variables, however, and these are the weather and climatic conditions, geographical features and the terrain that the runners will face at the various destinations – not all deserts are formed from sand, though all will undoubtedly satisfy their dictionary definition of being uninhabited and desolate.

The organisers claim that the series of four races is widely recognised as the most prestigious outdoor foot race series in the world. However, apparently not satisfied with such accolades, they decided to introduce a fifth race in 2008, known as the 'Roving Race'.

The Roving Race, which is sponsored by affiliate company, Racing the Planet – an online store selling outdoor gear and associated products – follows the exact same format as the other four races, but takes place in a different location each year, with the first edition having been held in Vietnam. Since then, participants have raced in Namibia in 2009, Australia in 2010, Nepal in 2011, Jordan in 2012 and Iceland in 2013, with Madagascar planned for 2014.

According to the company's website, the objectives of the 4 Deserts Race Series are not only to challenge individuals to go beyond their athletic limitations, but also to, '…contribute to improving the lives of ethnic minorities and tribes in areas we explore and encourage competitors to raise funds for their charities'.

Mental Miscellany

- Anyone completing all four deserts in one calendar year can claim membership to the prestigious Grand Slam Club – there are 28 members as of 2013.
- Anyone completing all four deserts at various times can claim membership to the 4 Deserts Club – there are 125 members as of 2013.
- As of 2013, more than 7,000 competitors from 100 countries had participated in the 4 Deserts Race Series and Roving Races.
- In 2012, a 22-year-old American, completed all 5 races within one calendar year, becoming only the second person ever to do this.

- The 4 Deserts Race Series itself claims to have raised over US$750,000 (around £460,000) for various charities, with millions more being raised by competitors.

For further information, please visit: www.4deserts.com

ATACAMA CROSSING
CHILE

250km/155 miles across Earth's driest desert – 40°C/104°F – altitude 3,500m/11,480ft

Take the driest place on Earth, a place that is known to be 50 times more arid than Death Valley, California, with a daytime temperature of up to 40°C/104°F, a night-time temperature of 5°C/40°F, and a landscape so lunar-like that it is used by NASA for testing planetary rover vehicles, and then gather together a group of paying volunteers and get them to run for 250km/155 miles (a distance that would take them horizontally across the whole of their host country) at 2.3km/1.4 miles above sea level – and you've got yourself the Atacama Crossing – one of the series of four desert races that forms the 4 Deserts Race Series.

The Atacama Desert lies in Chile and consists of salt lakes, sand and felsic lava and has an average rainfall of just 15mm a year; it is believed that some areas have never received any rain, making this the oldest continuously arid region on Earth. So, really, what better place to take part in a self-supporting, seven-day ultramarathon that requires competitors to carry all their equipment in a rucksack on their backs and ascend and descend up to 3,500m/11,480ft?

Certainly, the potential maximum field of 200 who will stand

64

on the start line at Arcoiris Valley, 3,000m /9,800ft above sea level, at 8am on an October day, must believe this to be the case, for here they will gather, rucksacks, reflective sunglasses and musket-caps-with-removable-neck-flaps firmly in place, skin awash with sunscreen, lip balm and insect repellent, anxious to get going over the sand dunes, salt flats, gravel, loose rock, hard earth, waist-high grass and river crossings that will greet and test them to their absolute limits over the course of the next seven days.

Most days they will run, walk or hobble between approximately 35km/21 miles and 42km/26 miles, except for day five, the day of the notorious 'Long March', a feature included in all four of the series races, during which they will cover around 73km/45 miles. On the final day, they will face a mere 10km/6 miles to the finish line.

Who would do this?

Mark Cockbain, 41, electronics engineer, ultra runner, and director of Cockbain Events, ran the Atacama Crossing in 2009. This extract was taken with kind permission from: www.markcockbain.com.

Atacama was a unique and beautiful place, with hot desert surrounded by snow-capped volcanoes on all sides! It was arranged for us to climb up one of these volcanoes as a form of pre-race altitude training.

This first camp (Rio Grande) was the highest (3,263m), and it was in a spectacular valley location, with red coloured mountains on all sides. We were assigned our tents, in groups of seven to nine per tent.

Stage 1 (Distance: 35km; Starting altitude: 3,263m, +245m, -973m) – After a restless cold windy night we woke to make final preparations to our kit, before lining up at the start line at the foot of the rocky gorge, with pink flags indicating an early climb upwards across the steep valley walls.

As soon as I started pushing up the first gravel slope I felt

Mark takes on Atacama in 2009

like I could hardly breathe. A combination of altitude and exertion was leaving me light-headed and I thought my heart was going to burst from my ribcage. I had to keep taking huge breaths as I slipped and slid up the hill. Everyone was struggling with the altitude, and it was a relief to eventually reach the top.

The view was spectacular, desert and rocks as far as the eye could see, and once down the other side, the course flattened off into a long, winding trail. The temperature was rising, and I tried to stay cool by getting into an even pace and trying to relax my breathing.

After checkpoint three, though, the route slowly went up through a rocky plain and it was now very hot. I was sweating lots and just couldn't breathe. I entered a long, winding gorge that seemed to go on upwards forever, and the temperature seemed to be magnified. I finished in 4 hours, 27 minutes.

Stage 2 (Distance: 42km; Starting altitude: 2,627m, +243m, -535m) – This stage was described as difficult, and would follow the River Grande and take us to the 'Dead Valley'! I had pushed hard yesterday and today I was lacking energy.

Before long we headed down into a canyon and actually into the river. It was a gorge with steep sides, and at some points we were up to our knees in the water. I didn't mind this as it cooled off my hot feet and helped my sore legs.

Once out of the gorge, we were back into the baking sun and heading up a long incline up a ridge overlooking the spectacular Dead Valley. This looked like an enormous version of a ploughed field, but with huge red rocks, like something out of the Jurassic period.

From the summit, the path took us over the edge, and down the biggest sand dune; it was like running down the side of a mountain! From here, it was pretty flat, but the heat was draining us as again we ran down a long dried riverbed that seemed to trap the heat. We were struggling and using a lot of water and we were pleased to reach the final checkpoint and begin the last leg of the day, but it was horrible crusty sandy terrain that seemed to go on forever.

Stage 3 (Distance: 40km; Starting altitude: 2,335m, +260m, -150m) – Crusty 'un-runable' mounds of dried grass and salt. The terrain was really cutting into our shoes and twisting our ankles, making it hard going. It was a pretty featureless section, which seemed to go on forever because of the slow progress we were making, and I was getting through my water quickly as it seemed hot down in the valley.

The last section was a hard, rolling, rocky and sand dune section that was energy zapping. After over six hours of running we were all just hanging on. Then to our relief we saw the white tents in the distance. However, there was still a deep valley to navigate first, before a long heart-pounding climb to the stage finish line. We arrived exhausted.

The camp was exposed to the elements here up on a ridge, and the high winds gave the tents a beating during the night, making it difficult to sleep.

Stage 4 – The infamous salt flats (Distance: 42.8k; Starting altitude: 2,453m +155m, -294m) – Sharp rocky canyon entrance and steep crevasses until we reached a long sandy descent into a lush green river valley. Once again, we were knee-deep in water and pounding our way downstream through jungle-style plantation.

From here on things got hotter, as we were exposed to the sun across an endless desert plain. Eventually, the heat wore us down and our water was almost gone, so we used a walk/run strategy to conserve energy.

We reached the next checkpoint quite dehydrated, and were advised to take the maximum amount of water into the salt-flat section.

After half an hour, I could see why: this was a horrendous section. The salt flats were like huge hard, crusty ploughed fields that tore away at our shoes and twisted our ankles. Every so often you would break through the hard, crusty surface and enter knee-deep into salt mud. Several times my foot went so deep into the mud that I almost lost my trainer. We were only doing about 2 miles per hour now, but we were using so much energy as the sun beat down on us.

Eventually this turned into a more solid trail and we could begin to run again. There was just 8km to go into the next camp, but I was drained and my pace slowed.

This new camp was situated on the edge of a stunning light-blue lagoon dotted with a few groups of pink flamingos, which seemed a fitting reward for the day's running. Later that evening, just as the sun was setting, I took off my socks and shoes and waded out into the cool water. It felt great.

Stage 5 – The long day (Distance: 73.6km; Starting altitude: 2,412m +342m, -263m) – Effectively the race would be over after today's long section, just leaving a final 10km 'jog' into San Pedro. I ate double portions for breakfast to try and give me extra energy for this long day. I was tired now, and my feet were bruised.

It was a struggle to get my legs moving again. Straight away we encountered more salt flats, but at least these were easier to run through, then the trail turned into hard grassy mounds that I managed to cut myself on before we were out into the heat of the day along dusty tracks.

Hours passed by as we headed into what looked like snow-covered plains. These were bright-white salt flats, littered with rocks that magnified the sun and startled us.

Far in the distance we could see what looked like a mountain, with runners climbing up it, but as we got closer, we could see that it was the biggest dune ever. We reached the base and began our climb. It was so steep and the sand was packed hard. We didn't look up, but kept stopping to catch our breath. The view from the top was spectacular across the white flats with the volcanic background.

We dropped down the other side through some amazing rock formations. More long dry riverbeds followed and I was beginning to run low on energy. The sun was setting already.

This last 10 miles was mainly on a track that took us past a worrying sign that read: 'Beware. Land mines'! As it got dark I turned on my head torch and ran up a long steep road to the entrance of Lunar Valley. Exhausted, I ran carefully through the strange rock formations of the valley, following a series of green glow sticks for directions. In some sections I was squeezing through crevasses and ducking under huge overhangs. It was like some strange maze, with some quite dangerous dry waterfall descents.

The twists and turns seemed to go on forever until I hit a track that took me on the last mile into the base camp in around 11 hours.

The final day and I just wanted to get to the end. I went as fast as I could and finished in seventh place overall in a total accumulative time of 36 hours, 19 minutes. I was met by a magnificent reception in San Pedro town square with bands playing, locals and runners cheering – and my huge Atacama Crossing medal ... one that I had dreamed of for quite a while.

Mental Miscellany

- The race has checkpoints every 10km/6 miles.
- The race starts at above 3,000m/9,842ft above sea level, descending to the finish at 2,400m/7,874ft above sea level.
- Records as at 2013 stand at 23 hours, 46 minutes (men) and 29 hours, 49 minutes (women).
- Campfires are an integral part of the race, tended by staff that keep a constant kettle of water boiling and rekindle the flames every morning before competitors wake.
- The Atacama Desert is estimated to be 15 million years old and has the oldest mummies on Earth dating back 7,000 years.

For further information, please visit: www.4deserts.com

SAHARA RACE
JORDAN
*250km/155 miles across the world's
hottest desert – 6 days*

It is probably fairly safe to suggest that running across the Sahara Desert would not conjure up romantic images for most people. However, according to the race website, for a group of Chinese runners who took part in the 2012 Sahara Race in Egypt it was the special romantic meaning arising from novels they had read about the Sahara that was one of the main inspirations behind their decision to run 250km/155 miles across the hottest desert in the world.

Of course the novels were really only responsible for the choice of location; the inspiration for the running came from reading the stories of other runners who had gone before them and it was those stories that prompted them to enter a race that would see them facing six consecutive days of running an average of 40km/25 miles a day, except for on the fifth day when they would cover a gruelling 990km/56 miles, in energy-sapping temperatures of up to 50°C/122°F, battling the softest sands and steepest dunes, while carrying all their equipment in a rucksack on their back. Reading is a dangerous sport.

However, it was not just those Chinese runners who were

so inspired to take part in a race which makes up one of the 4 Deserts Race Series, for alongside them on the start line were more than 150 runners from 38 different countries, among them were professional poker players, students, chefs, catering managers, documentary-makers, journalists, filmmakers, medics, consultants, and a man with type 1 diabetes who had already climbed Everest and finished four Ironman triathlons. Aside from the shared inspiration, all were there for their own good reasons – some to find out why others were there (film- and documentary-makers), some for self-discovery, some for the competition, some to complete all four desert races, and others were there to escape their frantic lives and take time out for inner contemplation.

But no matter what their reasons, their backgrounds or nationalities, all would share the same suffering, experiences and ultimate triumph over the six days of running.

The race itself starts out at Wadi Rum (the largest wadi, or desert valley, in Jordan, made famous by Lawrence of Arabia and his *Seven Pillars of Wisdom*), at 0700 on a warm February day, and the competitors will cross four different desert areas – Wadi Rum, Kharaza, Humaima and Wadi Araba.

Throughout the race, they will have to deal not only with the varying hard and soft, resisting, sands of the flat desert, but also the mountainous dunes that rise as high as 180m/590ft, cross salt lakes, negotiate rocky dirt tracks, and navigate canyons, riverbeds, valleys and villages.

If they're not too tired to notice, they will have an opportunity to enjoy some of the wondrous sights along the way, as the course passes through some unique rock and natural arch formations, before finishing at the renowned World Heritage Site of Petra, famous for its rock-cut architecture and water conduit system.

During the race, runners will pass through a total of 30 checkpoints, which are spaced at approximately 10km/6 miles, where they will be logged on arrival and informed of any changes in the course conditions, such as thunderstorms, sandstorms, fog or terrain changes etc. They can also restock their water supplies, take a short rest in the shade and seek advice and any necessary treatment from a doctor.

Overnight checkpoints will provide a Bedouin tent where competitors can sleep, and there will also be a campfire or stove for boiling water for drinks and preparing freeze-dried meals.

Who would do this?

Aside from romantic Chinese readers, as already mentioned above, competitors come from all over the world and from all walks of life to partake in this race. For most of them it is ultimately about the personal challenge, the self-discovery and the shared experience and camaraderie.

It may also be about the opportunity to discover new lands, new people and new meaning that races and events such as this offer those who take part.

Mental Miscellany

- In 2012, 174 entered the race, 168 started the race, 18 withdrew during the race and 150 finished the race.
- In the 2012 race there were 124 men and 26 women.
- In 2012, the youngest competitor was 19, the oldest 64.
- The management team for this race consists of three women and one man.
- The Sahara Desert is the third largest desert in the world after the Antarctic and the Arctic.

For further information, please visit: www.4deserts.com

GOBI MARCH
CHINA

250km/155-miles across the Gobi Desert – 7 days

From the four desert races that make up the 4 Deserts Race Series, the one with the most curious background must be the Gobi March, which takes place annually in June.

As with the other three desert races, the Gobi March consists of a seven-day, self-supporting, 250km/155-mile race, this time across the largest desert region in Asia (the fifth-largest in the world), as well as the windiest non-polar desert on Earth.

As such, competitors face a widely varying climate according to topography, ranging from lush plains and barren deserts to snow-capped mountains; a mixed terrain of green pastures, dusty tracks, narrow ridge paths, rocky riverbeds and crossings; as well as a veritable yo-yo of temperatures from 15°–30°C/59–86°F in the daytime, right down to freezing at night.

On the plus side, assuming they're not too tired to notice, they get to see the mysterious rock valley containing the largest group of strange rock formations in Western China, a Mongolian settlement, cable bridges, a view of Tian Shan peaks, the famous Sayram Lake, and a memorial to the founding father of Mongolia, Genghis Khan.

But it is the backstory to the origins of the Gobi March (China) that gives it its own peculiarly unique appeal.

Back in the early part of the 20th century, three Christian

missionaries, Mildred Cable, and sisters Francesca and Eva French, who had been carrying out routine missionary work in China for over 20 years, got itchy feet and took off for the Gobi Desert – and beyond. Those who knew them were shocked and dared to suggest that there were 'no fools like old fools'.

Undeterred, the trio sallied forth by ox cart to the City of the Prodigals, so named for its reputation for attracting criminals, where they set up camp for the winter and spent the rest of the year travelling the extensive trade routes of the Gobi Desert preaching Christianity. They also fed orphans, visited the poor, tended the sick and educated girls. By way of a thank you, bandits assaulted them and they found themselves getting caught up in local wars. Even the weather had it in for them, throwing the occasional brutish blizzard their way. It was with due cause, therefore, that Mildred Cable was one day heard to remark, 'Only a fool crosses the great Gobi without misgivings.'

Despite that comment, as Mildred pursued her course across the desert, she began to see parables for a life that embraced the message she wanted to deliver: 'In this trackless waste, where every restriction is removed and where you are beckoned and lured in all directions ... one narrow way is the only road for you. In the great and terrible wilderness, push on with eyes blinded to the deluding mirage, your ears deaf to the call of the seducer, and your mind un-diverted from the goal.'

And so it was with that message in mind, and in deference to the trio's resolve, that the very first of the 4 Deserts races, the Gobi March (China) was held in 2003.

And just as Mildred Cable had crossed the length of the desert more than five times, becoming 'part of its life', so does each participant of the Gobi March become a part of the history and legacy of that same land.

Furthermore, a special award, the Cable-French Trophy, is presented to the competitor who best epitomises the remarkable characteristics of the three maverick missionaries.

Who would do this?

As with all the 4 Deserts races, competitors come from all over the world – in 2013, countries represented included the Ukraine, Vietnam, Japan, Korea, South Africa, the USA, Canada, Australia, China, Singapore, Hong Kong, Argentina, Turkey, Switzerland, Spain and Great Britain – and from all walks of life, including in 2013, marketing and management consultants, lawyers, events organisers, bankers, engineers, detectives, behaviour analysts, and many, many more!

Just as all the 2013 competitors came from varying countries and had varying careers, so they all had varying reasons for wanting to take part in such an event, ranging from those who wanted simply to challenge themselves or to check their training programmes were effective (!), to those who were attempting to complete all four desert races, and those who were raising money for charity. For others it was as much about experiencing the personality of the Gobi Desert itself, from its beautiful butterfly valleys and Buddha-faced rock carvings to its rather more unusual inhabitants, such as yaks, camels and antelopes, as it was about the race.

Mental Miscellany

- In the first Gobi March in 2003, there were 40 competitors; in 2013 there were 150.
- In the 2013 race, 118 men and 32 women took part.
- In 2013, the youngest competitor was aged 20; the oldest was 63.
- The men's course record is 23 hours, 12 minutes; the women's is 27 hours, 53 minutes (both in 2012).
- Most runners finish in between 24 and 70 hours.
- The majestic Altai Mountains provide a stunning backdrop for the race.

For further information, please visit: www.4deserts.com

THE LAST DESERT RACE
ANTARCTICA

250km/155 miles – in the largest, coldest, windiest,
driest desert in the world

For some people, running is about solitude; they slough off the cheering crowds of London, the incessant beat of rock 'n' roll marathons and seek instead somewhere more tranquil, more natural, more silent to run. Such as Antarctica.

In point of fact, it was only as recently as 2006 that the first ever 100-mile race was held on Esperanza (base), Antarctica, where the only spectators were the penguins. That race was the precursor to a 6-day, 6-stage, 250km/155-mile race that now takes place biannually in November on and around the Antarctic Peninsula and forms the fourth race in the highly acclaimed 4 Deserts Race Series. It is known as The Last Desert race.

Unlike the other races in the series, runners can only compete in The Last Desert race by invitation, and having successfully completed at least two of the other three desert races. Also unlike the other three races, rather than sleeping in tents, competitors will sleep on board an expedition ship, which will take them from Argentina across the Drake Passage to the start of the race, and will then serve as their base for the duration of the event.

Over the course of the six days, competitors will race across several of the 10 islands that make up Antarctica, and may even bathe in the thermal waters on Deception Island and camp on the shores of Antarctica should they so wish.

Whichever islands the race inhabits, though, there is one thing that will remain unchanging throughout, and that is the extreme and harsh conditions the runners will face. For not only is Antarctica the driest continent on Earth, being a polar region with little precipitation and no lakes or rivers, the extreme cold freezing the water vapour out of the air, but it is also the largest and windiest desert in the world. Not to mention the coldest, with temperatures in its interior dipping as low as -70°C/-94°F in the winter months, although it is much warmer on the coast with temperatures ranging from -32°C/-25°F in the winter to a positively balmy 5°C/41°F in the summer!

There is also snow, lots of it, from a few centimetres to over a metre and it is this and the resulting reflection of sunlight that may cause competitors to suffer severe sunburn to face and lips, and snow blindness should they take off their sunglasses.

Despite the relentlessly uncompromising conditions, The Last Desert race makes no exceptions and the competitors will face the exact same race conditions as set for the other three desert races, that is to say they will run 250km/155 miles over six days. During this time they will have to be self-supporting and carry a minimum amount of safety equipment. They will also have to conquer not only the discomfort the unique arctic conditions will undoubtedly bring, but also the rocks, hills, glaciers, volcanoes, snow and sand that make up the terrain on the islands.

On the plus side, they will be treated to a visit to an exceptionally beautiful and rarely seen part of the world, with wildlife and landscape experts on board the ship who will share their knowledge freely with the runners, making this undoubtedly the trip of a lifetime, even if running a very long way in exceptionally harsh conditions is a prerequisite.

Who would do this?

In 2012, 35 men and 14 women from various countries around the world took part in The Last Desert race, including one married couple. They came from countries as diverse as Beirut, Australia, Canada, USA, Brazil, Hong Kong, Turkey, Switzerland, Spain, the UK and Wales, among others.

Just as diverse were their professions, which ranged from sports scientists to accountants, from bankers to exercise physiologists, from IT managers and consultants to researchers. There was even one who worked as a wrought-iron artist.

Ages too ranged across the board, from the youngest at 22 to the oldest at 63.

As for their reasons for taking part in the event, these ran from 'personal development' and 'wanting to see what is possible' to 'completing all four of the desert races' and 'living life with no regrets'. Most simple of all, perhaps, was the desire to 'see the penguins'! Many were doing it for charity.

Some of those who took part kept blogs which give vivid descriptions of their experience, including the wildlife they saw, such as humpbacks, penguins and orcas; the incredible 'thunder-crash' of a glacier dropping off the snow into the water; and the blue of the ice beneath the sea. They also mention the seasickness – apparently it was a pretty rough crossing in 2012. Oh yes, and they occasionally mention the running too.

Mental Miscellany

- The Last Desert race is the only multi-stage race on the continent of Antarctica.
- The inaugural Last Desert race took place in 2006 with 15 competitors – almost 50 per cent were from the USA.
- Generally, 75 per cent of competitors in the race are men; 25 per cent are women.

For further information, please visit: www.4deserts.com

MARATHON DES SABLES
MOROCCO

*250km/155 miles – 6 days – across the hottest
desert in the world*

Founded in 1986 by Frenchman Patrick Bauer, following his own epic 200-mile walk across the Sahara Desert in 1984 – carrying all his needs on his back and with nothing to think about other than how he could create a similar experience for others – the Marathon des Sables – or MdS or 'Marathon of the Sands' – is probably the best-known ultramarathon in the world.

Of course Patrick made one or two slight adjustments to his own personal challenge, such as turning the whole thing into a multi-stage running race rather than a solo walk, and lowering the total distance to be covered to somewhere between 150 and 156 miles over the course of six days, but fundamentally the same challenges, such as coping with temperatures of over 50°C/100°F, strained lungs, a parched mouth, dripping sweat that evaporates in the baking heat, not to mention the occasional sandstorm, would still need to be overcome. The self-sufficiency, too, remained intact, with competitors having to carry everything they might need on their backs (apart from a tent, which is provided for them to sleep in at night).

That first race back in 1986 attracted 186 competitors; today around 1,000 runners will stand on the start line. They will travel on foot for up to six days through extreme heat beneath a meltingly hot Moroccan sun, running across salt pans, up desert mountains and sand dunes, and through ruined towns, covering a distance that is the equivalent of around five-and-a-half marathons in six days.

They will need to be wearing trainers that are at least one size larger than their usual shoe size to allow for feet swelling in the heat, over the top of which they will affix gaiters to protect their shins from the stinging sand; they will need layers of sunscreen, the strongest sunglasses and head protection against the sun's fierce rays; they will have to carry food, spare clothes, medical kit and a sleeping bag, not to mention a whistle, a metal-bladed knife, tropical disinfectant, anti-venom pump, a signalling mirror and an aluminium survival sheet. They must also constantly be on the lookout for dangerous snakes and insects (hence the tropical disinfectant and anti-venom pump), although these are reported as rare and mostly harmless.

At night they will be given a place to sleep in a bivouac village comprised of open-sided tents with approximately eight competitors per tent who will often become lifelong friends or, on occasion, sworn enemies!

Every day they will rise early and set off to run varying distances: most days this will be around 40km/25 miles, but the fourth day will be longer and even tougher, usually around 80km/50 miles across the barren desert wilderness when most competitors will finish in the dark. On the positive side, there will be a rest day following the longest run.

Each year the route will change and distances will therefore vary slightly, with the exact course being kept a closely-guarded secret by the race director until the day before the event starts, when all competitors will be given a book detailing each day's route.

As might be expected of a race this size, safety and good organisation is paramount and the course is well marked, with critical points marshalled every 500m and luminous markers for night sections. Headlamps must be switched on after 7pm and all competitors must supply a medical certificate and a resting

ECG report before being allowed to enter the race. In the case of sandstorms, which can lower visibility to zero, competitors must literally stop in their tracks and await instructions.

The race director, Patrick Bauer, is as passionate about individuals fulfilling their dreams and developing their potential as he is about the charitable foundation he set up in Morocco to support the education of women and children and to encourage sports development for the disadvantaged, to which a percentage of the entry fee is donated.

Who would do this?

British double-gold-medal winning Olympic rower and adventurer, James Cracknell, took part in this race in 2009, with a broken bone in his foot!

Prior to taking on the challenge though, in spite of his already supreme level of fitness, and unlike most other competitors entering the race, James had the unique opportunity of working with scientists who helped him to condition his body to perfection for the challenge of running 250km/155 miles in the searing heat of the Moroccan desert.

In the short video that accompanies the race that was filmed for the Discovery Channel, James says of the race that it is 'brutal' and comments on how his mind would be telling his legs to work, but they just wouldn't cooperate.

In his view, those competitors most likely to finish were the ones with a positive mental attitude, who didn't look too far ahead, dreading the thought of another desert marathon the following day, and who considered themselves simply lucky to be there running across the Sahara Desert.

James himself managed to finish the race in a highly credible 12th place, the highest ever managed by a Brit.

Mental Miscellany

- Places for the 2014 Marathon des Sables were sold out within 11 minutes of the opening of registration.

- The oldest person to finish the Marathon des Sables was 78, the youngest 16.
- There are 2 helicopters, 7 aircraft, 100 all-terrain vehicles and 4 camels available for emergencies throughout the race.
- 120,000 litres of mineral water will be imbibed during the race.
- The race has been won 10 times by the same local Moroccan, his brother having won it three times.
- The Saharan runners cover the distance in a cumulative time of around 19–20 hours; the fastest Brit to date took 25 hours, 13 minutes.

For further information, please visit: www.marathondessables. co.uk

UP WHERE THE AIR IS CLEAR...

THE HIGH
LA ULTRA
INDIA

222km/138 miles – 5,395m/17,700ft – the highest ultramarathon in the world

Wandering happily along the Leh–Manali Highway in the Himalayas one particularly hot summer afternoon, Dr Rajat Chauhan, ultra runner, took to considering whether it would be possible for man to run along what is the highest motorable road in the world – or whether running non-stop for 222km/138 miles through two of the world's highest mountain passes with an average altitude of 4,500m/14,764ft rising to 5,395m/17,700ft, and with 66 per cent less oxygen content than at sea level, might actually kill him.

Of course Dr Rajat Chauhan wasn't considering carrying out the experiment on himself; oh no, Dr Rajat Chauhan had a much better idea – he would set up a race, imaginatively naming it 'The High' or 'La Ultra' – and then wait to see whether anyone would be brave/foolhardy (or a word of your own choice) enough to enter and take up the challenge of a race that claims to '... push human endurance to the limit and redefine what the human body and mind are capable of'.

It turned out three people were prepared to put themselves on the start line that searingly hot and head-meltingly humid day in July 2010 – two Americans (one male, one female) and an Englishman. The two Americans ended up in hospital, one suffering from dehydration, the other from severe chest pains (both recovered); the Englishman successfully completed the race.

The race itself starts a few miles outside the beautifully verdant Khardung Village, at approximately 4,267m/14,000ft, along a reasonable stretch of road surrounded by snow-capped mountains.

However, as the road climbs up towards Khardung La at 5,395m/17,700ft, underfoot conditions worsen into a rocky track, but provided you have enough air in your lungs, you can allow yourself to be mollified by admiring the towering mountains and stunning rock formations that now surround you.

Fortunately, the rocky track turns back into a smoother surface as it descends back down to Leh at 3,500m/11,483ft, and you pass through an achingly beautiful yet utterly hateful canyon, whose walls trap the heat, turning the temperature up to above 40°C/104°F.

For every down, there must be an up, and so you begin your second highest climb up to Tanglang La mountain pass at an altitude of 5,359m/17,582ft – and plunge back into the bone-numbing chill of snow-covered mountains.

Assuming you're still alive at this point, you then start your final descent to More Plains – a beautiful desert valley lying at 4,572m/15,000ft – and the finish line.

Overall, the race offers a cumulative vertical ascent of 3,106m/10,193ft, with the two highest points hitting you at 41 and 160km/26 and 100 miles, a descent of 2,704m/8,873ft, and a mind-menacing temperature variable of below freezing to plus 40°C/104°F.

It also offers the opportunity to suffer from altitude sickness

The dramatic scenery of The High

and HAPE (high altitude pulmonary oedema), which can be life threatening.

However, Dr Rajat Chauhan is a kindly, caring man and therefore he tempers these risks with three cut-off times along the way, and a final cut-off time of 60 hours. Just in case you're still a little nervous about giving this one a go, the website reassures you that these cut-off times are there for your safety and will be followed very strictly.

In the further interests of safety, you will also be relieved to know that you can hire a race crew consisting of local people – just in case you don't happen to know three people who would like to trot alongside and support you over the two-and-a-half-day race that claims to be the toughest high-altitude ultramarathon out there.

Who would do this?

Mark Cockbain is a highly experienced, 41-year-old, ultra runner and director of Cockbain Events. Mark ran his first marathon in 1997 and moved up to ultramarathons three years later. In 2010, Mark became the first person in the world to complete The

High. This extract was taken with kind permission from: www.
markcockbain.com.

*For me, this sounded like a fantastic and unique challenge
and I decided to find out if I could complete such a race at
altitude.*

*I only had five days to acclimatise and was soon introduced
to my crew before starting my altitude training. My training
in Leh consisted of travelling higher each day, eventually
to the maximum 18,000ft [5,486m]. Initially this was a real
struggle, walking uphill was a heart-pounding action that
left me breathless. Over the next few days, I increased my
pace and my confidence grew. My biggest concern was how I
would cope with the altitude while fatigued.*

*Just three of us lined up at the start. As soon as I started
to run my chest was much tighter than normal, and I had to
control my breathing. I set my sights on summiting Khardung
La as quickly as possible. My body felt under such strain, and
it was a bit like breathing through a straw. My heart was
pumping overtime.*

*As I turned a corner, a fresh avalanche had totally covered
the route. I was lucky that I had just missed it, as it would
have surely knocked me off the ridge. I just clambered
over the huge pile of snow and continued on my way to the
summit.*

*I felt quite sick as I attempted to jog down the other side of
the pass and running still left me fighting for breath until I was
below 15,000 feet. A magnificent golden eagle soared above
me on what had become a very hot afternoon, and I could feel
the sun biting at my legs as I ran down towards Leh.*

*It was dark at around 8pm, but the highway was very busy,
so I wore reflective gear on all sides with a head torch and
flashing lights. I found it easier to run on the softer sand at
the roadside. A full moon lit my way and it was eerily quiet
in the middle of the night.*

*At around 80 miles I started to get low on energy. My body
had been working overtime because of the altitude, and*

I had not consumed enough calories, which caused me to 'blow up', and I had to stop for a while to eat and recover.

I set off again slowly into the night, only to be surrounded by numerous barking dogs. It was quite unnerving, but the Himalayan dogs seemed quite harmless, so I marched on and ignored them.

The second day was extremely hot, around 40°C, so I covered up with long sleeves and a desert-style hat. At 15,000 feet I could again feel the unnatural demand on my system. Rajat [the race director] joined me as I began my steep ascent. It was around 30k to the summit. The mountain switchbacks got progressively steeper and I could only manage to walk as I was breathing fast again. It was great to have Rajat pace me up the mountain and I think we were just both hoping that I could at least be the one person to finish this race! Up and up, it felt like my head was slowly being squashed as I was over 16,000 feet, and I was aware of how cold it was becoming as the sun disappeared behind the snowy mountains.

I knew I was slowing down, but I was determined to beat the second mountain. Hours passed and the summit never came, and I started to deteriorate, becoming very cold and dizzy with a nasty headache. It felt like I was a little drunk and confused. I put on several more layers of clothing, including two jackets, as the temperature dropped below zero. I was getting a little annoyed that I could not see the summit. My feet were blistered and stepping on sharp rocks caused me extra misery.

I felt very anxious at this point. On reaching the summit I felt dizzy and sick and knew I needed to get down fast. I was losing a lot of body heat. It had been a long night and the altitude had drained me. I was quite spaced out, and I remember shivering a lot. The air was still too thin. I knew I would only feel better if I got lower.

I had only around 18km to go and I ran the best I could through the valley. I kept asking my crew how much distance was left, and they counted it down for me.

The end never seemed to come...but eventually I could see

Mark Cockbain: the first finisher

the white finish banner ahead. I smiled and knew that I was going to finish what had been the greatest ultra-running adventure I've had.

I crossed the line and celebrated with my crew. They had been fantastic.

I was the first and only finisher, in 48 hours and 50 minutes, and I was so proud to have been part of such an extremely tough, exceptional race. I had managed to achieve what many had said could never be done.

I will truly never forget how kind and welcoming everyone was and the sights and sounds of India. This was not just a race, but a true adventure and an experience of a lifetime.

Mental Miscellany

- The first time The High took place in 2010, there were 3 starters and 1 finisher; in 2012 there were 11 starters and 9 finishers.
- The winner in 2010 completed the race in 48 hours, 50 minutes; the winner in 2012 completed the race in 36 hours, 36 minutes.
- The Leh–Manali Highway is maintained by the Indian Army and is only open for three summer months a year, hence the race taking place at the hottest time of year.
- The race route usually takes 5 days for a walker to complete, with sleep breaks included; the race itself allows 2.5 days (60 hours) maximum.
- Acclimatisation prior to the race takes place at around 15,000ft.

For further information, please visit: www.thehigh.in

LEADVILLE 100
COLORADO, USA

161km/100 miles – 4,800m/15,600ft of ascent/descent

The Leadville 100, or 'the race across the sky' as it has popularly become known, was conceived back in the eighties by marathon runner Kenneth Chlouber, who saw it as a way to make Leadville famous and bring visitors during an economic downturn.

According to the website, this is a race 'where legends are created and limits are tested'. The latter in particular is probably no idle boast with 161km/100 miles of extreme Colorado Rockies' terrain to negotiate and elevations of between 2,804m/9,200ft to 3,850m/12,600ft. As the website goes on to say, 'You will give the mountain respect, and earn respect from all'.

Starting at 0400 hours during the month of August when average temperatures reach a comfortable high of between 18°C/64°F and 21°C/69°F and lows of 3°C/37°F to 6°C/42°F, but with humidity striking at a rather less comfortable 85 per cent on most days, the race takes in the very heart of the Rocky Mountains, with ascents and descents of 4,800m/15,600ft and a 30-hour time limit. Accordingly, on average, less than 50 per cent of those starting out will finish.

Passing along attractive forest trails and mountain dirt roads, the course is predominantly a 50-mile out and back dog-leg, which starts at around 3,100m/10,200ft and at the heart of which lies the climb to the highest point at Hope Pass at 3,850m/12,620ft, followed, not unnaturally, by the descent.

There are 11 aid stations along the route, each with their own cut-off time, and all runners are subject to a pre-race medical check. Runners are allowed to use pacers after the first 50 miles, although the organisers may consider making an exception under special circumstances if requested.

Who would do this?

Thirty-one-year old race director and ultra runner, James Elson, took part in the Leadville 100 race in 2011. This extract was taken with kind permission from: www.centurionrunning.com/blog.

The first 13 miles were downhill and flat but on a low grade, making time disappear. As I left Mayqueen and made my way up Sugarloaf Mountain, a lot of people ran past giving me the 'Jeez dude you're walking NOW, there is NO WAY you will finish if you are walking here!' kind of look. Well, I'm finally becoming a bit more experienced at 100-mile races (this was my 8th) and I trusted my judgement.

Sure enough in the 4-mile climb I ate back the crowd that came past me lower down who were forced into a walk by the later stages. The descent down Power Line the other side is a steep and rocky/rutted trail but I flew down it.

I cruised down into the Fish Hatchery aid station at mile 23.5 in good shape and had some more gels and a bag of cheese cubes – pure gold. I was still eating and drinking well out on to the 4-mile stretch of road to Half Pipe aid station and cruised all the way into Twin Lakes at mile 39.5 after a long grinding climb and an awesome quick 3-mile descent.

I came down the iconic little bit of rocky trail into Twin Lakes outbound, had a quick pit stop to eat a bagel, some bananas, coke and crammed my pockets full of gels, crisps and sandwiches for the climb up Hope Pass. I also grabbed my poles. I wasn't sure that I'd need them, but in the end they were a big help in the section before I ditched them again at mile 60.

On route to Hope Pass there are three water crossings and one significant river pass, which soaked sore feet and left debris in shoes. I pushed on and began the ascent of Hope, which runs from 9,000 to 12,600ft in the space of 4 miles or so.

I was disappointed to find that on this stretch everyone was forced to power hike, and I lost ground. I couldn't work out what was going wrong but I think the altitude was finally starting to bite.

The climb up Hope begins in the woods before breaking out into mountain meadows at the top. I knew I was nearing the aid station 'Hopeless' just shy of the summit when I saw a runaway llama used for fast packing the aid equipment up to the summit being chased by a volunteer!

I came into the aid station, grabbed some food and moved straight on up the grinding last 600 feet to the top of the pass. Up here were just scree slopes and falling grass. The altitude really came into play up here though, and it was even harder to breathe than down at the Lakes.

The descent into Winfield was totally unexpected and brutal. The pitch of the slope that side of Hope is something people don't warn you about. It drops hard and fast and is pretty technical in places. At the bottom we were spat out on to the road for a 2-mile dusty run into Winfield aid station at mile 50, which I reached in around 11 hours.

I headed out onto the road and began the run back down to where we came off the mountain. Leadville's sting in the tail is the fact that it is an out and back, and the climb back up the near side of Hope was twice as severe as the front side, made worse by the fact that it had begun to rain and I was getting cold. The climb broke me twice on the way back up the mountain.

My one issue was that I was without a pacer and ideally wanted one for the long night ahead. As soon as I began climbing the short rocky ascent out of Twin Lakes, a huge bearded runner in a chequered shirt stormed up behind me with a pacer bib on. I asked him where his runner was and he mentioned he didn't have one, so was just headed off on his own accord. I asked him if he'd perhaps want to stick with me and to my utter delight he responded yes.

Things only started to unravel once we hit Half Pipe. I quite quickly felt nauseous, and just as we pulled into the mile-long stretch of people parked up watching runners, I started hurling. I puked most of the stretch while continuing to walk, silencing a lot of the clapping and cheering, but once I'd finished I said sorry to everyone and got a huge cheer, which was pretty nice.

I was now on to the final climb; Power Line is a brute of a hill, it is steep, rutted, uneven and worst of all has four false summits pushing you on higher every time you think you've finished the climbing. At the top I felt ropey and it was with a grimace that I shuffled down the other side.

I pushed on around Turquoise Lake which seemed to be never ending in the dark.

When I finally came back out on to the road, I hit a steep descent where inexplicably the organisers had a photographer out at 5am in the pitch black shooting us coming through, and then began the slow climb from the 95-mile marker up to the finish, ascending all the way on dirt roads.

I crossed the line in 26 hours, 29 minutes to a small crowd and a very loud speaker.

Mental Miscellany

- In the inaugural race in 1983 there were 45 entrants; in 2013 there were 1,219.
- In 2013 the race was won in 16 hours, 30 minutes (men) and 20 hours, 25 minutes (women).
- Course records as at 2012 stand at 15 hours, 42 minutes (men) and 18 hours, 06 minutes (women).
- The oldest person ever to take part in the Leadville 100 was aged 70.

- The minimum age for taking part in the Leadville 100 is 18.
- There is now a Leadville series of races held over three months, which includes running and mountain-bike races of varying distances.

For further information, please visit: www.leadvilleraceseries. com

ULTRA-TRAIL DU MONT-BLANC
FRANCE, ITALY, SWITZERLAND
166km/103 miles – 9,400m/31,000ft elevation gain

Regarded by many as the toughest foot race in Europe, the Ultra-Trail du Mont Blanc (also known simply as the UTMB) is a non-stop mountain race covering approximately 166km/103 miles, which basically follows the Tour du Mont-Blanc hiking path and is pretty much a complete tour of the Mont-Blanc Massif, passing through three countries – France, Italy and Switzerland.

Held annually in August, the race starts in the late afternoon from Chamonix, France, at 1,035m/3,396ft, before climbing first to 1,653m/5,423ft at Col de Voza, then on to the Croix du Bonhomme at 2,479m/8,133ft before descending to Les Chapieux at 1,549m/5,082ft and the first checkpoint.

The course then continues upwards to the Col de la Seigne at 2,516 m/8,255ft to enter Italy, following the ridge of the Mont-Favre and descending to Courmayeur at 1,190m/3,904ft, and the second checkpoint.

From there, it climbs again to the Refuge Bertone, and again to Arnuva, and yet again to reach its highest point at Grand Col Ferret at 2,537m/8,323ft, which marks the border with Switzerland.

The route then descends to La Fouly and Praz de Fort at

1,151m/3,776ft, before climbing back up slightly again to the third checkpoint at Champex d'en Bas at 1,391m/4,564ft.

Passing through Bovine and Les Tseppes on its way down to Vallorcine at 1,260m/4,134ft, the route then returns to France, crossing Argentière, and winding back down to the finish at Chamonix.

Occasionally, due to bad weather and resultant safety aspects, the route may be varied slightly, but most runners will complete the race in a time somewhere between 30 and 45 hours (the final cut-off time is 46 hours with 10 other strict cut-off times along the way), although the front runners will do it in around 20 hours. Hikers following the normal route usually take between seven and nine days!

As the organisers stress the principle of the race is self-sufficiency and autonomy (not to be confused with 'autotomy' – the casting off of a body part), they insist that all competitors must carry safety equipment, such as waterproof jackets, warm clothing, food, water, whistle, survival blanket and headlamp, although there are checkpoints every 10–15km along the route, where runners may obtain hot meals, massages and beds, and drop-bags are also allowed at two of the checkpoints.

Apart from the obvious difficulties of such a tough mountainous course, with its high passes and altitude, narrow ridges and steep downhill tracks, runners will also face extreme weather conditions, with freezing winds, sleet and snow.

It is with those difficulties in mind that the organisers offer courses in physical preparation, nutrition, equipment and materials, as well as in mental training, technique and pace-management.

It is also the reason that, despite the generous maximum number of 2,300 possible entrants allowed into the race, the selection process is based on a runner's capability and experience, rather than on a first-come, first-served basis.

Who would do this?

Forty-one-year-old electronics engineer, Mark Cockbain, ultra runner and director of Cockbain Events, competed in the UTMB in 2008 and described the course as 'soul destroying'. This extract was taken with kind permission from: www.markcockbain.com

I started the race in the town square in Chamonix at 6.30pm along with around 2,000 other runners. After only running a few miles I came to the first heart-pounding climb of 1,799m at La Charme. Most runners used hiking poles to help push them upwards over the uneven rocky terrain, but I had not brought any with me.

I was quickly out of breath and gasping for oxygen as we snaked up the steep mountainside and I pushed down on my legs with my hands to help power me upwards.

The sun was setting as I reached the top, and the view of the Mont Blanc mountain range was spectacular, with the silhouettes of runners dotting the orange horizon.

A long, steep, uneven, leg-pounding descent into the village of St Gervais followed. Crowds of supporters cheered us as we grabbed water and snacks.

It was now pitch black as I headed out of the village and up the next gut-wrenching climb to Les Contamines, which was a long slow hike. I was beginning to wish that I had never entered the race! Sweat was pouring out of me as I took step after step up the mountainside following the line of bright head torches in the distance.

Coming down the other side of the mountain in the dark was terrible, and a powerful head torch was essential as I concentrated on the rocky terrain below. I couldn't wait to reach the bottom to ease the pressure from my burning quads.

I could now see that each stage was to begin with a huge mountain climb and I found that at altitude it was much colder and I needed my windproof jacket to keep warm.

After a long night of running, the sun was starting to rise as I arrived at Lac Combal at 65km. I was feeling quite tired, and it was a good chance for me to wake myself up with some strong coffee and freeze-dried breakfast.

The sun was already strong on my back as I started yet another long climb to Arete Mont Favre at 2,435m. I was soaked with sweat, but after I had reached the summit another runner told me we were almost at the first major checkpoint at Courmayeur (50 miles), but it was a very steep descent down to the checkpoint and my knees were in agony.

Here we were given our drop-bags and a hot pasta meal. I changed into a dry T-shirt and let my feet cool off before changing into fresh socks as my feet were already blistering.

I left the CP [checkpoint] about half an hour later and headed out of Courmayeur and was again faced with a huge climb on the mountain trail. It was tough going in the heat of the day and my progress was slowing as I stopped regularly to catch my breath and try to cool down. My feet were burning with the friction of uphill climbing, and at one point I stopped by a beautiful mountain stream, took off my socks and shoes and just sat with my feet in the cool water … it felt great!

After a long hot day, I was pleased when the sun set and the temperature cooled. I'd reached La Fouly, in Switzerland now and knew I had plenty of time to make it to the next major CP at Champex Lac.

However, this stage seemed to go on forever through pitch black woods and small villages and after several hours it was a relief to finally reach the checkpoint at around 11pm.

This was to be my second night without sleep, so I knocked back several cups of coffee before I left the checkpoint to keep me awake.

At 3am I was cold and tired, and staying awake was a problem, but I needed to stay alert coming down the steep mountainside, as one false move could be fatal.

After what seemed like an endless night I reached Vallorcine at 149km (about 90 miles) at around 7am and knew I would finish within the time limit, so I took plenty of time to rest and eat some breakfast before heading off on the final 18km back to Chamonix.

I left the checkpoint running fast, determined to get as much distance behind me as possible, but of course it wasn't long before I came to another mountain to climb. I just wanted to get this race finished now; I had really hated every step, apart from the magnificent views.

I pulled myself up the mountain, desperate to reach the top. I marvelled as I saw a little brown mountain goat skipping over the boulders ahead of me with such ease, and wished I could do the same.

I eventually reached the summit cairn and sat down for my final breather before the last five miles into Chamonix. Each downward step was agony on my feet and knees as I slipped and stumbled on the steep rocky path, but each step was a step closer to the finish. Beyond the pine trees in the distance I could see Chamonix.

Down and down I ran until the track eventually turned into a road on the outskirts of Chamonix, and I was directed towards the town centre along streets lined with cheering supporters.

It was a relief to be back in Chamonix town square where I had started from, and all that was left for me to do now was to run a lap of honour around the town hall, before crossing the finish line in 41 hours and 28 mins…Never again!

Mental Miscellany

- The first UTMB race was held in 2003.
- The men's race in 2003 was won in 20 hours, 5 minutes and 58 seconds; the women's race was won in 29 hours, 38 minutes and 23 seconds.
- In 2013, the men's race was won in 20 hours, 34 minutes and 57 seconds; the women's race was won in 22 hours, 37 minutes and 26 seconds.
- To enter this race, qualifying points are required from other similar races.
- The Mont-Blanc range has 7 valleys, 71 glaciers and 400 summits.

For further information, please visit: www.ultratrailmb.com

HARDROCK 100
COLORADO, USA
161km/100 miles – 10,360m/33,992ft of ascent

How far would you go to kiss a ram's head? Okay, not an actual ram's head, just a large block of stone-mining debris with a picture of a ram's head painted on it? Well, if you're taking part in the Hardrock 100 Mile Endurance Run, to give it its full title, you will, perhaps rather obviously, run 100 miles, at the end of which, instead of crossing a finish line, you will kiss the head of said ram to mark the completion of your race. Failure to 'kiss the hardrock' is the equivalent of not stepping over the finish line and means you won't have officially finished the race.

However, this is not just some pointless piece of propaganda to make the race different from other 100-mile races: it is actually rather meaningful in that the run is held as a salute to the toughness and perseverance of the Hardrock miners who lived and worked in the area of Silverton, where the race starts and finishes. In deference to those miners, one of the rules of the race is, 'No whining'.

The race itself is held on a loop course on four-wheel-drive roads, dirt trails and cross-country in southern Colorado's San Juan Range in the USA, and covers extremely rugged terrain including steep scree climbs and descents, snow packs (ski poles are a necessity in some parts as the snow is so deep), river crossings (ropes are provided to assist runners as they wade through thigh-high rushing water) and boulder fields.

Photo by Tim Adams

Passing through the ski resort of Telluride, the city of Ouray and a ghost town called Sherman, it crosses 13 major passes in the 3,700–3,900m/ 12–13,000ft range, meaning competitors will be racing at that elevation for much of the race. As the organisers put it: 'The competition is against the mountains more than each other.'

In between towns, the runners will be self-supporting, although they may have support crews and can use pacers for part of the race; if aged over 60 they may employ them for the duration.

Considered by established ultra runners to be one of the toughest traditional 100 miles out there (the race has been going since 1992), the Hardrock 100 provides extreme challenges in altitude (which may cause sickness or oedema – excess of watery fluid collecting in cavities or tissues of the body), steepness and remoteness, and requires mountaineering, wilderness survival and wilderness navigational skills – skills that according to the race website are as important as your endurance, particularly when combined with the very real threat of fire, intermittent thunderstorms and rain.

Starting at 6am means that anyone completing the race in more than 40 hours will see the sun set twice before the finish. It is hardly surprising, therefore, that flashlights and headlamps are mandatory during the night sections of the race, particularly as there are portions of trail that are adjacent to steep drop-offs.

It is also hardly surprising that there is a qualification process for entry into this race, including taking part in a qualifying race as listed, and carrying out eight hours' service for an ultra race within 12 months of the event. In the same vein, runners are encouraged to help with the course-marking prior to the race to familiarise themselves with the route and acclimatise.

Perhaps more surprising is that despite limiting the number of runners to 140, the organisers receive around six times this number of hopeful applicants every year and there is actually a waiting list for acceptance.

Of course it may not be just the race they are keen to take part in, for the scenery they pass through is beyond breathtaking in its wild and rugged beauty and may even provide them with sightings of bears, foxes, elks, coyotes and mountain lions!

Who would do this?

Tim Adams is a 38-year-old construction project manager, who also works for British Military Fitness and is an outdoors fitness instructor. Tim took part in the Hardrock 100 in 2012 and will be taking part again in 2014. Thanks to Tim for the following account.

The experience of Hardrock is partly down to the organisers adhering to the ethos of the event, the course and tough-ness of the terrain, and the weather element, as well as the smallness of the race and number of participants within a wilderness setting.

The two weeks preceding the event were taken up with helping mark the course and acclimatising. It was a good way of getting to know the other runners so by the time we started, it felt like a family event.

Tim takes on Hardrock

102

At the prize giving ceremony the DNF [Did Not Finish] runners were honoured first and the race director, Dale Garland, takes the time to give a funny anecdote about every single runner.

The funniest thing I heard though was when one of the competitors was complaining to his wife about it being tough, cold, the middle of the night, etcetera. His wife, who was crewing for him, replied, "Well, you wanted this, so you just suck it up, Princess..."!

Mental Miscellany

- The average finish time of 41 hours, 10 minutes, 15 seconds is longer than most 100-mile average finish times due to the high elevations.
- The cut-off time is 48 hours.
- Records for the Hardrock 100 as of 2012 are 23 hours, 23 minutes (men) and 27 hours, 18 minutes (women).
- The first race in 1992 was won in approximately 42 hours.
- In 1992 there were 42 starters – 42 per cent finished; in 2010 there were 140 starters – 71 per cent finished.
- The youngest competitor so far was 25, the oldest 73.
- The average age of the runners in 1992 was 38.5, in 2010 it was 50.
- The 2002 race was cancelled due to forest fires.
- All finishers receive a stunning print of a photo of the American Basin.

For further information, please visit: www.hardrock100.com

RONDA DEL CIMS
ANDORRA

170km/106 miles – 12,100m/40,000ft of ascent

Considered one of the toughest mountain races on the ultra running calendar is the Ronda del Cims, which takes place in Andorra, through the Pyrenees, and boasts an ascent equivalent to one-and-a-half times the height of Everest!

Taking place on the longest days in June in the light of the full moon, the race sets out from Ordino town centre at 0700 on a Friday morning, finishing back at the start on the Sunday.

Following a giant route renowned for its long, steep climbs, which circumnavigates the whole of the principality of Andorra, including the highest point at Comapedrosa at 2,942m/9,650ft, the 170km/106-mile course takes in a total of 12,100m/40,000ft of elevation gain and loss, and a total of 15 peaks or passes, all at an average altitude of 1,981m/6,500ft.

And if that doesn't make you breathless, the panoramic views most certainly will, for the race passes through the most spectacular scenery imaginable with high mountain meadows, thick forests, fast-flowing rivers, glacial lakes and mineral zones. And then of course there is the ethereal beauty of a full moon against a clear night sky, the glory of a rising sun emerging through an early morning mist, and the wonder of running on land that is above the clouds.

Given that this is a mountain race, the weather is predictably unpredictable, with the potential for clear blue skies and sunshine equal to that of angry black clouds and snow.

The terrain too is extremely varied, from well-signposted tarmac roads and root- and rock-free tracks, to very irregular, difficult, slippery narrow tracks with lots of stones, roots, scree and rocks and is therefore undeniably tricky in places, with many short, sharp descents that will require some careful footwork, although the use of sticks is allowed.

There is a time limit of 62 hours and there are 13 aid stations along the way.

Perhaps unsurprisingly, given the toughness of this race, there is a qualification process for entry, which requires anyone hoping to take part to have completed this race or another non-stop 100km/62-mile race with more than 4,500m/14,760ft in elevation gain or a 165km/103-mile race with over 2,500m/8,200ft in elevation gain, within the previous two years.

Who would do this?

Anyone who is able to qualify, particularly those who are partaking in the Sky Running Series of races – a circuit of awe-inspiring mountain races across the world.

Mental Miscellany

- Minimum age for the Ronda del Cims is 20.
- In 2013, there were 315 runners.
- In 2013, the winning time was 28 hours, 41 minutes, 06 seconds (men) and 35 hours 31 minutes, 21 seconds (women).
- The average finish time is 48 hours.
- Around 50 per cent of starters will finish, but the dropout rate has been as high as 75 per cent.

For further information, please visit: www.andorraultratrail.com and www.skyrunning.com

COAST TO KOSCI
AUSTRALIA
240km/149 miles – 2,228m/7,310ft of ascent

Kosci is, in fact, short for Mount Kosciuszko, the highest mountain in Australia at 2,228m/7,310ft above sea level, and is situated in the Snowy Mountains in the Kosciuszko National Park, New South Wales.

Every December, at around 0530, a smallish group of hardy runners gather at Boydtown Beach some 240km/149 miles away from Mount Kosci's majestic peak, and begin an epic race that will take them from sea level to the very top of Australia in around 30 to 40 hours.

Starting at the beach in Twofold Bay, competitors will race along highways, footbridges, fire trails, forestry service roads, creeks, unsealed roads, cattle grids, bike paths, open farming country, plains and mountain roads, ultimately winding up at the finish at Charlotte Pass at the Summit Road Trailhead.

According to the route instructions, they will pass through such delightfully named points as Brandy Creek, Jigo Creek, Towamba River, Big Jack Mountain, Black Lake Road, Cambalong Creek, Snowy River Way, Jindabyne, Thredbo River, Sawpit Creek, Smiggins Holes, Perisher Village, Guthrie Creek – and a big dead tree on the uphill section just before Snowy River Way!

There will be six mandatory checkpoints that the runners must pass through and entrants will run with their own support crew.

With the race starting so early in the day, it's likely to be pretty chilly and again at night-time, when the temperature drops back down and more clothing will be needed. But this is still Australia and with it comes the dangerous rays of the sun, making sunscreen an absolute must.

Previous finishers have described the course as very tough and very long, with boring endless roads to conquer, and advise taking the race in bite-size pieces, adding that it's best to start slowly to allow for the distance, taking on water and energy gels and food when you can. After that, they say it's all about your own desire to finish. One runner also commented that the hill climb at Beloke Range is so steep 'it smacks you in the face', and the only way to get up it is on your hands and knees.

Aside from long, boring roads and near-vertical climbs, there are also likely to be snowdrifts along the mountain roads and trails, slippery ice-covered rocks, and falling snow and sleet, not to mention an onslaught of flies across the plains.

However, should you manage to beat all this aside, and run exceedingly fast, you will find yourself standing literally on top of Australia watching a flaming Antipodean sun rising from behind snow-clad mountains, or, if you fail to make sunrise, as probably all runners will, you will still witness the glory of a fat yellow sun beaming down upon the glorious mountains. Now that surely must be worth a 240km/149-mile run – or as 2009 race winner Jo Blake said by way of a thank you to the organisers: 'We all walk away with a life experience that so few people get to enjoy, but if you could bottle it, it truly would be priceless.'

Who would do this?

Mostly Australians but some Americans and Brits have taken part in this race. All those who have agree that, as with all ultras, the first time is quite traumatic, but once you have more experience there is less pain and anguish.

For most of those taking part, it's all about finishing, preferably with a smile, as well as searching for limits in an extraordinary place. For some it's about losing weight, improving their life expectancy or to inspire their own children.

Mental Miscellany

- The first race was an unofficial race held in 2004 and was won in 39 hours, 20 minutes (men).
- No women took part in the race until 2006 when the first lady finished in 42 hours, 53 minutes.
- 2007 saw the first official race.
- In 2012 the race was won in 27 hours, 31 minutes, 51 seconds (men) and 31 hours, 49 minutes, 21 seconds (women).
- Course records to the summit are 26 hours, 1 minute, 40 seconds set in 2009 (men) and 30 hours, 11 minutes, 25 seconds in 2011 (women).
- In 2013 there were 54 entrants consisting of 39 men and 13 women.

For further information, please visit: www.coast2kosci.com

THE ONLY WAY IS UP...

COMRADES MARATHON
SOUTH AFRICA

90km/56.1 miles over killer hills – within 12 hours

Despite its title, the Comrades race is not a marathon but an ultra run of 90km/56.1 miles on road, over numerous gruelling hills, in horrendous heat and with the most strictly enforced cut-off times anywhere in the world – the final cut-off is at 87km/54 miles, just 3km/1.9 miles from the finish, and as the final second of the final minute of the final hour arrives, the finish-line captain shoots a gun and people just metres or even centimetres from the line are prevented from officially finishing the race. Something like 50 per cent of people come in during that final hour and many are inside the stadium when time is called.

As such, the race has earned its well-deserved reputation for being one of the toughest ultras out there, despite the relative shortness in distance.

It is also one of the, if not the, oldest ultra races in the world, having been run every year since 1921, apart from the war years 1941–45.

It all began when Vic Clapham from London, a World War One veteran, emigrated to South Africa in the late 19th century. Vic had fought in the Great War of 1914–18 as a soldier with the 8th South African Infantry. Deeply affected by the atrocities suffered by his comrades but also moved by the camaraderie brought about in the men in overcoming them, Vic saw the race as a fitting tribute and living memorial to all those who had fallen in the war.

However, when he asked for permission from the League of Comrades of the Great War to stage the race under their auspices in 1918, they thought he was mad and turned him down on the grounds that they considered the challenge too strenuous even for professional athletes.

Undeterred, Vic applied again in 1919 and again in 1921; permission was finally granted and the Comrades Marathon was founded.

At that first race on Empire Day, 24 May 1921, 16 of the 34 starters finished the race. However, 10 of those would not have finished under today's strict cut-off time enforcements.

The race itself runs alternate years from Pietermaritzburg to Durban (known as the 'down' run) or from Durban to Pietermaritzburg (the 'up' run), and is a series of up- and downhills, all named, many historically, and many with a story to tell. Take 'Arthur's Seat', for example: this is a niche cut into a bank at the site of the Wall of Honour and is reputed to have been a favourite resting spot of Arthur Newton, five times winner of the Comrades Marathon in the 1920s. Then there's the Wall of Honour itself at Drummond, which marks the halfway point and overlooks the Valley of a Thousand Hills. The wall was created as a permanent landmark to commemorate the achievements of the comrades, and runners can purchase a block upon which is mounted a plaque recording their name and race number.

With the race having gained so much in popularity in recent years, numbers are limited to 18,000, although only around two-thirds of those starting will actually finish the race officially.

Who would do this?

Thirty-one-year-old, ultra runner and Ironman, James Elson, race director with Centurion Running, ran the Comrades Marathon in 2012. This extract was taken with kind permission from: www. centurionrunning.com/blog

To make the 5.30am start and beat road closures, we got up at 1.30am for a 2am departure, and it HURT.

We had our hearts set on the much-coveted silver medals given to those who complete the 56 miles in under 7 hours, 30 minutes but were accepting that we'd have to see how things worked out as we went along, and were prepared to work around that goal if it looked overly ambitious.

Initially, we ran in the dark for around an hour with throngs of people around us. On the downhills we stretched away at about 7-minute-mile pace and around 8:30 on the uphills. We were consistent but we were pushing too.

Crowds lined the streets, cheering loudly and cooking their braai's [barbeques] and, unusually, the kilometre markers counted down from 89 to 1.

James competes in the Comrades © Jetline Action Photo

As light came up at around 20km, we passed people who were standing still as they'd gone out so hard. There were aid stations every few kilometres and they were all rammed with people handing out sachets of water. The first couple I bit off big corners and doused myself, but then I got the hang of it.

The first 30k flew by, but from the start I'd felt fairly bad. A lack of sleep and some stomach issues had spaced me out a bit and I didn't feel particularly in control. Although the pace felt sustainable, I was having to work a bit too hard to stay with the schedule.

No matter, we pressed on through stinking chicken farms and round sweeping hillside roads towards halfway, following behind a massive group who were tailing Zola Budd [former British international famous for her barefoot running in the 1980s] in her first Comrades Marathon.

At this point there were two major climbs, one just before midway and one just after and they took their toll. We had already crested the highest point but the roller coaster continued and on the second climb I dropped to a walk.

About a mile on and I pushed on a little and started to have the first, and only short, stronger patch of my entire race.

With 30k to go, my energy was fading as the heat of the day rose. It maybe got to around 24°C but out there on the tarmac running hard with some heart-rate drift to boot, 7:45 minute-miling quickly became a killer.

As I came through Nedbank Green Mile there were girls hanging in enormous swings in trees outside fairly affluent looking properties, but a couple of miles later, we came to an extremely poor area with an orphanage on the side of the road. It was more than a little heart-wrenching as it was obvious life was more of a struggle for those living around that particular spot.

At around 20km to go, there was an extended, long downhill stretch. This was where I decided that 7:30 was slipping out of reach. Downhill was okay but I just couldn't keep it going on the flats and ups. I dumped countless sachets of water over *my head but just couldn't seem to keep my temperature down so ended up slowing to 9-minute miles and watching that elusive silver medal slip out of grasp.*

With around 10km to go I was slaloming across the road trying to pick the tightest lines while staying out of the sun but we'd reached a stretch of open motorway and there was no escape.

Seven kilometres to go, we hit the hammer a bit and banked a few precious seconds against the clock. The downs continued as we looked across Durban but there were a couple of stout little hills to work up.

Soon the kilometre markers disappeared down to the final two as we made our way over the flyover and down into Durban city centre. The roads were lined with people and we could see a straight shot kilometre dead ahead of us.

Turning the final corner with 1km to go we had 7 minutes to cross the line under 8 hours and we could finally relax knowing we had it. We ran under some giant showers over the road, into the stadium flanked with people in the grandstands and eventually crossed the line in 7:56. I think we were both pretty wiped. I felt overheated and a little sore, but I loved the whole experience.

As per the race motto it's a must-do race from a human spirit perspective. Whatever South African politics have held in the past, present or will hold for the future, this race brings everyone together. Never have I felt more included in the overall experience.

Mental Miscellany

- The race starts at 0530 and finishes at 1730 from gun to gun.
- If you complete 10 races, you get a green number and have that number for life – nobody else can wear it.
- In 1922 a 16-year-old finished in 11 hours, 42 minutes and retains the record of youngest ever finisher; the minimum age was raised to 18 in 1923 and now stands at 20.
- The first woman completed the race in 1923 in 11 hours, 35

minutes but was disqualified as she had been refused entry and had run unofficially.

- There are 50 doctors and interns, 20 nurses, a mini lab and a 3-bed fully equipped resuscitation area at the finish.
- The entire 12 hours from start to final cut-off are broadcast live on South African TV.

For further information, please visit: www.comrades.com

WEST HIGHLAND WAY RACE
SCOTLAND

*154km/95 miles – 4,498m/14,760ft of ascent –
within 35 hours*

The West Highland Way is Scotland's best known long distance trail and sets out from Milngavie before passing through Mugdock Country Park, Loch Lomond, Ben Lomond, Glen Falloch and Strathfillan, across Rannoch Moor, past Buachaille Etive Mor to the head of Glencoe, up the Devil's Staircase, back down to sea level, crossing the River Leven at the head of Loch Leven, before entering Larigmor and Glen Nevis and finishing at Gordon Square in Fort William. It was officially opened as a long-distance trail in 1980 and consists of lowland moors, dense woodland, rolling hills and high mountains.

Five years after it opened, Duncan Watson (a little-known athlete) challenged Bobby Shields (a very successful athlete) to a race along the Way. The challenge was accepted and on 22 June 1985 the two men set off from Milngavie Railway Station for Fort William.

By the time they reached Rannoch Moor some 96km/60 miles from the start, it was apparent that neither man was prepared to give an inch and they realised that if they carried on in the same way, mutual destruction was the most likely outcome. Fortunately, sense prevailed and they agreed to pool their resources and continue to the finish together, reaching Fort William in 17 hours, 48 minutes.

And so the race was born, although these days it is run in a rather more official manner under the auspices of a Scottish Athletics race permit with almost 200 runners toeing the line. Entrants must demonstrate an adequate level of fitness and a reasonable prospect of completing the race, and must carry certain mandatory kit including a head torch, map, compass, whistle, full body waterproof clothing and a plastic bivvy bag.

Each runner must also provide his or her own motorised support crew of a minimum of two people, one of which must be capable of running the last two sections of the course with the competitor if required and during the hours of darkness, and be capable of finding them if lost! Participants must also pass through mandatory checkpoints within strictly imposed cut-off times.

Just as in the original two-man duel, runners set out from Milngavie Railway Station but, unlike the original duel, they set out at 0100 on a Saturday in late June, and must reach Fort William Leisure Centre by noon on the Sunday, giving them just 35 hours to cover the 154km/95 miles, which includes 4,498m/14,760ft of ascent.

Who would do this?

Forty-four-year-old ultra runner and catering manager, Sandra McDougall, who says of herself, 'I never envisioned myself running ultras. I was the girl who "didn't do mud" or trails. Why on earth would you run on a bumpy bit of ground when you can have a nice flat pavement?' Sandra has run the West Highland Way race three times, most recently in 2013. This extract was taken with kind permission from: www.santababyrunning.blogspot.

One am and we're off. Running through the town centre is quite surreal, lots of cheers, flashes going off, people calling your name. But soon we're into the trails and it all goes quiet, head torches bobbing around, occasional chatter, but people are quite reflective for the first few miles till we're properly into the trail and onto the first hill.

I stop to take off my jacket as it's drizzly but very warm and clammy and I'm down to my vest. Across the road and back onto trail my shoes start nipping. I'll call my crew once I'm on the hills and get a change of shoe. Blisters at this stage would not be good.

Change shoes at Drymen, runners now spread out. Very misty approaching Conic Hill so put jacket back on. Breathtaking view of Loch Lomond.

The path at Conic has been improved but I take it easy, no point trashing my quads. The steps are still as steep and high as ever, for my wee legs anyway, and I have to jump down each one.

First checkpoint, crew sit me down, shove a roll in my hand and a cup of tea. Then I'm off again to Rowardennan, and am met by a mist of midges.

Crew check my feet, change Compeeds [blister plasters] and socks and treat sore right ankle with cold gels and freeze spray.

On my way again – have to stop to fix Compeed, midges dive-bomb me. Everyone passing asks if I'm okay; that's what makes this race special.

Next checkpoint, crew work on me, change tops, give me new dry hat and jacket, socks, food, and Red Bull.

Take off jacket, climb Poo Alley, heavens open. Leave jacket off knowing it will just stick to me and make me colder so I stick to my vest and it sticks to me!

Next checkpoint at Tyndrum, chicken soup, a roll and another Red Bull and I'm off again. Change into road shoes for bumpy ride across Rannoch Moor, not my favourite section.

Run with Nick, my crew runner; he is surprised how much climbing there is and asks if it ever has a downhill. There are a few but it seems like a never-ending albeit gentle climb.

I decide not to stop at Glencoe. Despite feeling no fear of the climb, my legs have different ideas and it feels like a long slog.

Only 3 miles now to Kinlochleven, cross Pete's bouncy bridge. Nick has taken to laughing manically every so often, saying, 'Every time I think we're at the top, there's another f...... climb!'

Eventually we reach the top; my legs feel okay. I'm glad I kept my road shoes on as they give more cushioning. Mind you, nothing's going to help after 80+ miles.

We put our head torches on as we enter the forest, which slows us down but we keep the momentum going.

I've taken to walking a few steps every mile or so. Braveheart just never seems to arrive. But then I see the gates and I choke up a bit. My other crew runner, Susan, joins us. Team Santa will finish this journey together.

I've made it – 23 hours and 11 minutes.

Sandra in training

Mental Miscellany

- Almost 200 competitors take part every year, with a 75 per cent finish rate.
- 798 people have completed the event ranging in age from 21 to 70.
- Records for today's course are 15 hours, 39 minutes (men); 17 hours, 37 minutes (women).
- The race is a qualifier for the Ultra-Trail du Mont-Blanc race (see page 95).
- A glass goblet is presented to all finishers.
- The race doctor's website page warns of 'Exertional Syndromes', ie. limb injuries, ankle fractures and collapse from post-exertional low blood pressure.

For further information, please visit: www.westhighlandwayrace. org

LAKELAND 100
UK

161km/100 miles non-stop trail –
6,300m/20,669ft of ascent

According to its website, the Lakeland 100 Ultra Tour is the most spectacular Lake District trail race, with a circular route, along mainly public bridleways and footpaths, that circumnavigates the whole of the Lakeland fells and includes 6,300m/20,669ft of ascent.

But don't let the word 'spectacular' lull you into thinking that the beauty of the area outperforms the toughness of the race, for, after publishing the results, the website adds: 'For those who did not finish, congratulations for being brave enough to attempt such a challenge...'

This sentiment will be gratefully received by the 50–60 per cent of starters who were defeated by the numerous and heart-banging climbs (how else would you get the spectacular views?), as well as the knee-wrenching descents, rugged ankle-turning terrain, not to mention the darkness and the often supremely difficult navigation. The majority of those who fail to finish do so through lack of sufficient preparation and the finisher's medal is therefore one of the most treasured.

The race itself starts at 1800 hours on a Friday evening in July at Coniston, and heads south. It then takes in the lesser known valleys and fells, such as Dunnerdale fells, Eskdale, Wasdale, Buttermere, Keswick, Matterdale and Haweswater before returning via Kentmere, Ambleside and Elterwater to finish back at Coniston.

As this is a non-stop race which must be completed within 40 hours – runners must be finished by 1000 hours on the Sunday or be disqualified – there will be little, if any, time to stop for a sleep or rest, although all runners must visit the 14 manned checkpoints en route.

Generally, lead runners finish in around 23 hours and the race may be run solo or as part of a two- or three-man team, with teams remaining together at all times throughout the race.

The organisers provide a list of mandatory kit, which includes full waterproof body-cover top and bottom, head torch and spare batteries, a whistle and an emergency foil blanket or bivvy bag.

It is recommended that runners visit their GP a week or so prior to the race for a general health check, and there is a race doctor/ultra runner on hand who is qualified in sports medicine, plus a local medic who is a clinical skills educator/Ironman, triathlete/mountaineer. Prior to the race all competitors will be weighed (to assist medics if required later) and after the race will be asked simple questions and weighed again. If the medic is concerned, he will ask the runner to complete an assessment.

The organisers also warn of potential injuries connected to this challenge, such as blisters, sprains and strains, tendonitis, trauma, dehydration, hyper-hydration and hyponatraemia (too much fluid), hyperthermia (raised body temp) and muscle tissue damage. They go on to state that anyone considering entering the race should be experienced ultra-distance runners with excellent navigation skills and with enough speed to meet cut-off time limits, who should take full responsibility for their own health, fitness and wellbeing on the course.

They go on to recommend that before entering, all potential runners should consider the preparation, the hours and what it takes to complete the Lakeland 100, before finally stating, 'If it was easy, it wouldn't be an achievement.'

Should the above deter entrants, however, the organisers offer an alternative – the Lakeland 50 – but insist this is not an easy option, being run over the second half of the 100-mile course, on the same rough terrain, and with 3,100m/10,170ft of ascent.

Who would do this?

Twenty-seven-year-old Liz Tunna, who, at the age of 25 (in 2012), became the youngest woman in the UK to run 100 marathons, took part in the Lakeland 50 in 2011.

The Lakeland 100 is notoriously hard. I did the Lakeland 50 a couple of years ago, which is the second half of the Lakeland 100, and it definitely remains one of the hardest 50-milers I have done. I can only imagine what that would be like after already having done 50 miles before you start this bit of the course, and I know for a fact that the first half is much steeper and much tougher.

I know a number of people who have attempted the 100 race year after year and still haven't completed it due to missing cut-off times or badly mashing up their feet on the tough terrain.

Mental Miscellany

- The first Lakeland 100 race took place in 2008.
- In 2013, there were 124 finishers from 274 starters.
- In 2013, the race was won by a 50-year-old.
- In 2013, the winners finished in 22 hours, 17 minutes, 15 seconds (men); and 24 hours, 15 minutes and 6 seconds (women).

For further information, please visit: www.lakeland100.com

LAUGAVEGUR ULTRA MARATHON
ICELAND
55km/34 miles – 1,900m/6,234ft of ascent

Swimwear is probably not the first item of clothing an ultra runner might think to pack in his bag, especially not when heading for the distinctly chilly climes of Iceland, but for anyone attempting the Laugavegur Ultra Marathon, it comes highly recommended, not for use during the race but for afterwards, when there is a hot tub available for anyone crossing the finish line!

The 55km/34-mile race, held every year in July, starts at around 600m/1,968ft above sea level with an immediate 500m/1,640ft climb from Landmannalaugar and follows Iceland's most famous hiking trail all the way to Húsadalur in Thorsmörk at just 200m/656ft above sea level.

In between, runners will face around 1,900m/6,234ft of climb and 2,200m/7,218ft of descent, passing through numerous areas of outstanding natural beauty while negotiating a wide variety of challenging terrain from sand, gravel and grass to snow, ice, rivers and streams.

The course is well marked with wooden markers and organisers have thoughtfully positioned ropes to aid runners at the steepest descents and at river crossings, where the water is not only mind-

One of several ladder crossings

numbingly, bone-chillingly cold, but can be as deep as one metre in places.

While this race may at first glance appear to fall into the 'not-too-difficult' category, and the outstanding natural beauty of its surroundings may well add to this belief and undoubtedly offers a welcome distraction, the Laugavegur Ultra is, in fact, considered tough enough to rank as a qualifier for the awesomely tough Ultra-Trail du Mont-Blanc and its organisers remind competitors: 'This is not a street race, but an ultramarathon that takes place in a mountainous and uninhabited area'. As such, there are doctors and nurses on hand as well as numerous race officials from the local running club and mountain-rescue teams who assist runners if necessary on the sands and at rivers.

Furthermore, the organisers stress that this is not a race for beginners and anyone entering the race must not only be in very good physical shape, having trained to a standard that will ensure they are capable of covering the whole distance, but they must also produce a medical certificate to prove this.

Aside from remembering your swimsuit, gaiters are also recommended as useful protection against snow and gravel, as well as a windproof jacket and ski band or head-buff for the high-altitude parts of the course.

With an average temperature of around 7°C/45°F, variable weather and high altitude, hills so steep most will resort to walking up them, as well as strictly enforced cut-off times, and bearing in mind that hikers usually take three to four days to walk the same route, any idea of this being a 'soft' option should be sensibly dispelled.

Who would do this?

Fifty-five-year-old accountant and ultra runner, Chris Heaton, who in 2013 ran 30 marathons in 30 days in hilly Cumbria to raise funds for the Brathay Trust (www.brathay.org.uk), took part in the Laugavegur Ultra Marathon in 2008.

A very spectacular race, covering mountains, volcanoes, wading through fast-flowing icy rivers, crossing glaciers and ice fields, one over 1.5km long depending on the weather.

By far the most stunning event I've ever undertaken. And not easy.

The descent to Alftavatn

Mental Miscellany

- The first Laugavegur Ultra Marathon took place in 1997.
- In 2013, the race was won in 4 hours, 48 minutes (men) and 5 hours, 28 minutes (women).
- Course records currently stand at 4 hours, 19 minutes, 55 seconds (men) and 5 hours, 0 minutes, 55 seconds (women).
- The race is open to teams as well as individuals.
- Some of the hills are so steep that the organisers recommend power-walking training sessions prior to the race.
- Once a runner is granted entry to the race, he or she is considered to have promised to safeguard the environment and abstain from littering, and is given a 'litter bag' to be worn around his waist for this purpose.
- Prizes are made by the renowned glass artist, Sigrún Ólöf Einarsdóttir.

For further information, please visit: www.marathon.is/ultra marathon

HARDMOORS 110
UK

177km/110-mile non-stop trail race –
within 36 hours – Yorkshire

The inaugural Hardmoors 110 challenge took place in May 2007 and has since become synonymous with hardcore trail running at its best, with entrants having to qualify to take part by providing proven experience of completing other named ultra races of a minimum of 40 trail miles (64km) or 50 road miles (80km). Indeed, so tough is the ultramarathon considered that the organisers insist that no unsupported runners will be allowed to drive home directly after finishing – they will be too exhausted and would be a danger not only to themselves but to other road users.

Taking place against a backdrop of some of the best that Britain has to offer by way of dramatic scenery, the race takes place along the beautiful Cleveland Way National Trail, circumnavigating the glorious North Yorkshire Moors and the imposing Cleveland Heritage coastline.

Starting out at 0800 from the market town of Helmsley on a Saturday morning in May, competitors have a time limit of 36 hours to complete the 110-mile trail race, and will pass through some of Britain's hilliest, roughest and rockiest terrain at Saltburn,

Runswick Bay, Staithes, and Whitby (made famous by Dracula), Robin Hood's Bay (made famous by smugglers), Ravenscar and Scarborough (made famous by Punch & Judy), before finishing at the town of Filey.

Such is the toughness of the course that it acts as a qualifier for the Western States 100 race and gains four points for those wishing to enter the Ultra-Trail du Mont-Blanc race.

Of course, taking place in England, runners will not only have to contend with 177km/110 miles of difficult terrain, they will also have to deal with with the fickleness of the weather, which can range from hot and dry with temperatures in the high seventies, to wet, windy and even snowy, with temperatures hovering around freezing.

Apart from the Hardmoors 110 race, there are also Hardmoors 15-mile/24km, 30-mile/48km, 55-mile/88km and 60-mile/96km challenges, as well as a new challenge, which started in May 2014 entitled the 'Ring of Steel' – a 160-mile/257km single stage ultra with more than 7,000m/22,965ft of ascent, to be completed within 48 hours.

Who would do this?

Twenty-seven-year-old Liz Tunna became the youngest woman in the UK to run over 100 marathons in 2012; during that time she has taken part in numerous ultras, including the Hardmoors 55, which she completed in 2010 in 15 hours, 48 minutes.

The terrain is technically very difficult and rocky in places with over 2,700m of ascent, and the weather is unpredictable. The year I completed this, it rained almost non-stop and there was a thick fog up on the moors which made it almost impossible to see where you were going.

I have also failed to complete this 55-mile course on another occasion due to getting briefly lost and missing the cut-offs. However, it gets tougher because there is also the Hardmoors 110, which follows this first 55-mile route and then carries on along the Cleveland Way towards Scarborough. I attempted this a few years ago and only made it approximately 45 miles through the night section; I just hadn't prepared enough.

Mental Miscellany

- In 2013, the 110 race was won by joint winners in 21 hours, 13 minutes (men) and 22 hours, 10 minutes (women).
- In 2013, there were 55 starters in the 110 race; 19 did not finish.
- Current records for the 110 stand at 20 hours, 58 minutes (men) and 22 hours, 10 minutes (women).
- The 110 race can be run as an individual or as part of a relay team.
- Records for the 55-mile race stand at 8 hours, 27 minutes for the men and 9 hours, 10 minutes for the women.
- There is a 1000 Club for anyone reaching 1,000 Hardmoors miles – rewards are 1000 Club fleece, trophy, certificate and a race number, which only you can use at Hardmoors races.
- There is a Hardmoors Grand Slam consisting of running all four Hardmoors races, and in 2014 a new Triple Ring Challenge rewards those who complete three Hardmoors Ultra Races, one of which must be the 110 or 160.
- There is also a Hardmoors 26.2 Trail Marathon Series.

For further information, please visit: www.hardmoors110.org.uk

PICNIC MARATHON
UK

Marathon – climbing 1,829m/6,000ft – North Downs

When is a picnic not a picnic? When it's the Picnic Marathon of course! At least that's what the race organisers claim on their website; they also claim this to be the toughest marathon in Britain, advising competitors to add 40 per cent to their personal best marathon times for an estimated finish time.

So why is it called the Picnic Marathon? Well, apparently there are several reasons for this, the first being because the race starts at Box Hill, the summit of the North Downs in Surrey, famous for being the picnic scene in Jane Austen's novel, *Emma*. The second is because the poet George Meredith lived at Flint Cottage, which is directly opposite the start of the race and he had a donkey called 'Picnic'. The third reason is that the race honours a group of Italian prisoners who broke out of a British prisoner-of-war camp and climbed Mount Kenya, about whom a book was later written entitled: *No Picnic on Mount Kenya*!

While not the longest of races, the Picnic Marathon, held every other June, has undoubtedly earned its reputation as one of the UK's hardest, with a course profile that resembles a cardiogram printout of the victim of a severe heart attack, with its 1,829m/6,000ft of ascent and descent (the equivalent of running up and down Snowdonia

twice), carried out over one of the hilliest areas of Britain, the North Downs.

Not only are there grassy hills to run up and roll down, there are also steps – lots of them, and tracks so rough you're likely to twist an ankle, fall over and/or cut yourself on the sharp stones. There's also a lovely, peaceful river – with stepping-stones – which sounds rather pleasant for a Sunday stroll on fresh legs, but not so much during a marathon on lactic legs and with crushed lungs.

The race, which takes in stunning views over some of England's finest landscape, starts halfway up the Burfoot slope of Box Hill. Continuing upwards for around 120m/394ft it then descends to the stepping-stones, climbs back up to the top, descends the south face of the North Downs on a narrow path, before climbing back up again along a rutted track.

The route then passes through some woods before opening out to some particularly spectacular views, before descending, re-ascending, descending, and then climbing the many, many steps.

On arrival at the top, there are more woods to trot through, and another hill to climb, followed by a crippling descent. This is the halfway stage, where runners will turn around and repeat the route in reverse, running back up Box Hill before finally enjoying a long run down to the bottom of Zig-Zag Road and the finish.

The race director offers a couple of helpful tips to participants – namely, to run the slopes and walk the steps, and to use pace judgement, leaving something for the second half.

In keeping with its name, the Picnic Marathon offers nuts, bananas and fruitcake, plus a few sandwiches – short of a full picnic, of course.

The race, organised by a company called Trionium, who also organise other similar events, is held every two years to allow runners a chance to recover and train for the next one, and raises funds for the charity MIND – 'for good reason', according to its website! Trionium also support Rianna's Fund children's charity (www.riannasfund.org).

Who would do this?

Forty-one-year-old project manager and ultra runner, Paul Ali, took part in the Picnic Marathon in 2009.

The event was well tough, with some great views, though the run itself was brutal to start with, with a large hill to start followed by many, many steps going up and down, but settled down into more gentle slopes – before another range of steps followed by a few more hills.

Despite our lack of preparation, we paced ourselves over both loops and finished the event in about 6 hours, 30 minutes (the start was at 2pm, so we finished at about 8.30pm). The quicker runners took about 4 hours, which gives you some idea of the impact of the course itself.

All finishers received a hat, T-shirt and medal. All in all, it was a great event to complete.

Paul Ali mid-race

Mental Miscellany

- The first Picnic Marathon took place in 2005.
- The course record is 3 hours, 39 minutes, 54 seconds (men) and 4 hours, 37 minutes, 58 seconds (women).
- In 2012, a special edition race called the Olympicnic Ultra – approximately 48km/30 miles with over 2,133m/7,000ft ascent/descent – took place to celebrate the Olympics – and raised £1,000 for MIND (www.mind.org.uk).

For further information, please visit: www.trionium.com

LYON URBAN TRAIL RACE
FRANCE
6,000 steps – 2,000m/6,561ft ascent – 36km/22 miles

Think of a trail race and you automatically picture lush if muddy countryside, rolling if steep and sometimes mountainous hills and, well, trails – usually of grit, sand, dirt or stones. However, in among the rural races and included within the series of trail races that make up the Trail Running Championships, is one very unusual race that takes place slap bang in the heart of a city – the city of Lyon in France to be precise.

Unlikely as it might seem, every year the city of Lyon plays host to runners taking part in what has become recognised as one of the hardest trail races in existence, incorporating as it does nearly 2,000m/6,651ft of ascent up 6,000 steps, covering a distance of 36km/22 miles, all of which is run around the city centre.

To give you some idea of what 6,000 steps are like, consider the 1,576 steps of the Empire State Building, then add in the 1,665 steps of the Eiffel Tower, and finally put in the 2,909 steps of Burj Dubai, the tallest tower in the world at 828m/2,716ft, and you have just about cracked it! And remember, external, aged city steps are not the same as the nice, evenly-spaced, symmetrical, architecturally-designed steps of an internal staircase; these are steps that are weathered and worn with age, made slippery with the passing of time and millions of feet, chipped, damaged, sunken, left to degenerate over potentially hundreds of years.

So, how on earth did such a race come into existence? Well, back in 2007, having used the city steps for training sessions in preparation for summer trails, it became apparent that these same steps offered the potential for a trail route to be realised within the city of Lyon and so, in 2008, the first Lyon Urban Trail race was held in November.

At that time, the distance was set at 40km/25 miles and remained so until 2011 when the course was slightly changed so that it could stay right in the heart of the city, ultimately reduced to 36km/22 miles.

Remarkably, 1,900 runners turned up for that pioneering event in 2008 and the race has grown in popularity year-on-year ever since, with nearly 7,000 runners taking part in 2013.

The race date has also changed from November to April and a 22km/14-mile and 12km/7.5-mile race have now been added and are equally popular races.

There are three checkpoints with supplies approximately 10km/6 miles apart and cut-off times are strictly enforced.

To enter the race, all runners must produce a current medical certificate and carry a minimum of 500ml (17.5fl oz) of water with them at all times between checkpoints.

The website also says that you may wish to carry money – 'and do your shopping on the way (this is one of the advantages of an urban trail, that you will find shops open on the course!)'.

Who would do this?

Chris Heaton, a 55-year-old ultra runner and accountant, who ran 30 marathons in 30 days in hilly Cumbria to raise funds for the Brathay Trust (www.brathay.org.uk), took part in this race in 2011.

It's a very unusual race but, in fact, the hardest race I've ever done. What makes it especially difficult is nearly 2,000m of ascent, mostly up steps. And then a descent of the same amount – also on steps. It can get very hot too.

Chris tackles the gruelling steps

It's usually a round of the Trail Running Championships too, so the runners at the front tend to be professionals from teams like Salomon, which makes it very competitive. Other races in the Championships are held in the Alps and Mont Ventoux, so this gives you an idea of just how tough it is!

Mental Miscellany

- The 36km/22-mile race starts at 0715 to avoid the hottest part of the day.
- The race organisers recommend taking the steps two-by-two if you walk them, or one-by-one if running – up and down – and recommend practising this on your stairs at home.
- The 36km/22-mile course record is 2 hours, 31 minutes, 59 seconds.
- Many of the competitors are mountain racers.

For further information, please visit: www.lyonurbantrail.com

STEEPLECHASE RACE
UK
34km/21 miles – with 1,400m/4,593ft height gain

New in 2012 came an original take on the steeplechase race, taking the 'steeple' quite literally out of the word, with runners racing across the rugged hilly terrain, fields and woods of the Peak District in four stages, from church steeple to church steeple.

According to its website, all runners require to take part in this race is 'good old-fashioned British determination, guts and spirit', plus, of course, the fitness to run around 34km/21 miles up hills, giving a total height gain of 1,400m/4,593ft.

With a maximum limited field of 500 competitors in only the second year of the event, toeing the starting line in Castleton in 2013 there seemed to be plenty of people who felt they possessed such qualities and were eager to prove it by taking on this unusual challenge.

But it is not just the chasing of literal steeples that marks the uniqueness of this event, for this is a knockout race, whereby once competitors have been split into male and female categories with each category being set off five minutes apart, each category then starts all together, racing against each other rather than the clock.

With four steeples to reach during the 34km/21-mile race, the first three steeples are treated as elimination points where the slowest third of the race field in each category will be removed and eliminated from the race, so that ultimately only 40 runners in total will reach the final steeple at Castleton.

This concept is designed to test runners both physically and mentally, as they will have to pace themselves not only to cope with the distance and challenging terrain, but also to ensure they remain in a good enough position throughout the race to avoid elimination.

The race organisers stress that this is a continuous race and, as such, if a runner makes it through a checkpoint, they should continue running and not wait for other runners to complete that section.

For those runners who are eliminated, buses are provided to take them back to the finish at Castleton, as well as a towel so they can dry themselves off should it be wet, and a hoodie so they can keep warm.

The race itself starts from Castleton at 0930 (men), 0935 (women), and passes through Bamford, Hope and Edale in the Hope Valley, finishing back at Castleton. Not surprisingly given this is the Peak District, the course is not only extremely hilly, but is a combination of gravel tracks, hard pathways, grass, mud and dirt tracks, with numerous stiles and gates to negotiate as well. There is also a river to cross via large stepping stones and, as one might expect of the Peak District in October, the potential for a lot of rain creating a lot of underfoot mud, and wind bringing a significant chill on the tops of peaks.

The organisers therefore sensibly recommend the wearing of trail shoes, and taking a long-sleeve windproof running top and a whistle in case of injury or other problems. In the case of extreme weather conditions, a long-sleeve windproof top and trousers will be mandatory.

Who would do this?

Ultra runner Dan Cartwright took part in this race in 2013.

This extract was taken with kind permission from: www. therunningman-hibar.blogspot.co.uk

The course starts on a steep hill and goes immediately up the side of Mam Tor, the view from the ground was described to me by Kelly, my wife, as like watching 500 multi-coloured ants climbing a mountain.

The top revealed miles of rolling hills and peaks and after a run along a broken trail for a good mile and a half it descends into grassy slopes and exposed rock trails. The scenery was stunning and at times breathtaking – stepping stones across secluded rivers, sun-dappled woodland, and trails alongside a huge reservoir.

Stage one totalled 8 miles with 580m of climb and initially I thought I'd made a mistake even turning up. But I didn't rush on the big climbs at the start and found the run at the top comfortable.

The exposed rock became my targets for small jumps and

Dan takes on the course

the steep descents with long wet grass became my slides as I first fell, then slid along them. Overtaking runners using a lot of energy to slow down, I opted for gravity to do the work and cruised the downhills.

After 8 miles I felt spent and proud that I was well inside the cut-off and allowed on to stage 2.

I set off with a massive smile on my face. The 4 miles of stage 2 ascended 310m of climb, the majority on Win Hill. I was running on a heady mixture of adrenaline, endorphins and Red Bull. And I was overtaking people. I was running hard and trying to gain every place I could.

At the start of the descent was a checkpoint which showed I had a mile to go and the guys on the post told me I had 20 places to make up to make the cut-off. Looking down the hill, all jagged rock at ankle-twisting angles and single-track trails leading to lower grass banks, I turned to the guys and said, 'That's too tempting not to try.'

A third-person view would probably show me as a grinning idiot, all flailing arms, little balance and moving slowly down the hills. But in my mind, I was a gazelle, leaping from launch point to launch point, legs like springs, arms there to counter-balance, using body weight to shift and land lightly before instinctively launching to the next. I overtook people into the cut-off, knowing I wouldn't make it through but knowing I'd given it everything.

When I stopped I was exhausted, had more than a few grazes and was thirsty as hell. But I was happy, genuinely; huge-smile, talking to strangers, climbing up the walls happy.

A coach collected us and took us to the finish line, and I walked away with a medal, a nice top, a cool towel with a map of the race on it and the start of a mild Red Bull addiction.

But more importantly, I let go of a lot of stress on those hills. I realised how much I'd lost sight of the fun you can have when you're training. It doesn't make you a better or worse athlete, but it makes it a lot more enjoyable.

I only got halfway through the race and spent a significant

amount of my time with either my arse on the grass or both feet in the air.

This is a reminder to myself of the importance of enjoying what you do and doing what you enjoy. Next few races for me will be prepared for and approached differently. Goal number one will be to have fun!

Mental Miscellany

- The first Steeplechase Race was held in 2012.
- In 2012, the race was won in a time of 2 hours, 48 minutes, 18 seconds (men) and 3 hours, 37 minutes, 03 seconds (women).
- In 2013, the race was won in 2 hours, 35 minutes, 59 seconds (men) and 3 hours, 19 minutes, 2 seconds (women).
- The race is sponsored and organised by Red Bull, who supply race drinks.

For further information, please visit: www.steeplechase.redbull. co.uk

FELL RUNNING:
AN OVERVIEW

Fell running is as old as the hills the sport requires you to run up! It is a sporting activity with roots that can be traced back hundreds of years to a time when, by way of entertainment, country shows incorporated races, often with bets, to see who could run to the top of a hill and back down it the fastest.

The actual term 'fell running' arose from the fact that most of these show races occurred in the hilly northern parts of the UK and most specifically over the fells of the Lake District.

Like many running-based endurance events, fell running has increased enormously in popularity over the past decade, and is likely to increase further as entry fees for town and city road races continue to rise, while fell race fees maintain a modest low.

Very little specialised kit is required to take part in fell running; it has been known, actually, for runners to sometimes take to the fells naked and with bare feet, but most conform to the idea that wearing at least a good pair of fell shoes is to be recommended!

Most races today will conform to the rules and regulations set up by the Fell Running Association, the governing body for fell running in the UK. These include the carrying of certain kit, such as full body cover, ie: trousers and jacket – preferably water- and windproof, a map of the route, a compass and a whistle.

In some longer races, runners will be required to carry not only their known required food, but extra emergency rations, which will be checked at the end of the race to ensure the rules have been adhered to. Failure to comply with these can result in disqualification.

Fell running is suitable for all ages and abilities, although it is recommended that participants should have some mountain navigational skills.

For further information, please visit: www.fellrunner.org.uk

UK & IRELAND ROUNDS

Individual Fell Running Challenges over
UK & Ireland's highest peaks

BOB GRAHAM ROUND – ENGLAND

Born in 1889, Bob Graham was a quiet, modest gentleman who ran a guesthouse in Keswick in the Lake District. He would probably have died in the same quiet, modest manner in which he lived, and been forgotten about (apart from by his loved ones, of course) through the mists of time had it not been for the fact that in 1932 Bob Graham set a record that was so remarkable it took another 28 years before anyone was able to break it – and even then it was only broken with Bob's encouragement and assistance.

That record was for the number of Lakeland fells traversed in 24 hours – a staggering 42 – Bob's age at the time he completed the awesome, self-imposed task, which took in all four of the 914m/3,000ft peaks of Skiddaw, Helvellyn, Scafell and Scafell Pike.

Bob's achievement, which comprised running a total of 106km/66 miles with 8,230m/27,000ft of ascent and descent containing 42 of the highest peaks in the English Lake District all within 24 hours, was to set the standard for what has now become known and is officially recognised as one of the most demanding tests of endurance for an amateur athlete or mountaineer. It is aptly named the Bob Graham Round.

To date, nearly 2,000 fell runners have emulated Bob's achievement and can claim proud membership of the Bob Graham Club. Formed in 1971, it is a club that maintains a low-profile policy in the spirit of Bob Graham's quiet reputation, and concerns itself primarily with keeping records of attempts and successful rounds, while encouraging and supporting all contenders by providing information about the route, terrain, weather conditions and any other pertinent factors.

Depending on the line taken, the official route is between 101km/63 miles and 106km/66 miles with approximately 8,230m/ 27,000ft of ascent and descent. As it is not a race but a personal challenge, the attempt can be carried out alone or with a supporting runner. However, for acceptance into the Bob Graham Club, the attempt must be made with a supporting runner who can attest to the contender's successful bid.

Unsurprisingly, most attempts are made around mid-summer for maximum daylight hours, although some rounds have been done in the dark and 23 have been run as a winter round. No matter what time of year runners tackle the course, they may choose for themselves in which direction to run it – clockwise or anticlockwise.

In order for a runner to break the existing 24-hour fell record in accordance with the Bob Graham Club rules as published on their website, he or she must either traverse the same peaks as the current record holder in a faster time, or traverse the same peaks plus at least one additional peak. For these purposes a peak must be over 610m/2,000ft high, be at least 0.25 of a mile (400m) away from the nearest other peak on the round and involve at least 76m/250ft of descent/re-ascent from the nearest other peak. The round must be completed within 24 hours and must start and finish at the same place.

Who would do this?

Ultra runner, Paul Navesey, took part in the Bob Graham Round as a pacer/buddy runner overnight.

He said: 'From my experience with the runner, I learned that it is a relentlessly brutal task on some of the best running trails the country has to offer. It looks perfect!'

Mental Miscellany

- Fastest rounds to date: 13 hours, 53 minutes (men) and 18 hours, 12 minutes (women).
- Record number of peaks traversed: 77 in 23 hours, 47 minutes (men) and 64 peaks in 23 hours, 15 minutes (women).
- Emulating Bob Graham's 42 peaks at the age of 42, renowned fell runner Joss Naylor traversed 70 peaks at the age of 70, covering more than 80km/50 miles and ascending more than 7,620m/25,000ft in fewer than 21 hours.
- The double (twice round non-stop) has been done twice.
- The round is a qualifier for the Ultra-Trail du Mont-Blanc race.

For further information, please visit: www.bobgrahamclub.org.uk

RAMSAY ROUND – SCOTLAND

The Ramsay Round is the Scottish equivalent of the Bob Graham Round and covers 24 Munros (summits at least 914m/3,000ft), over a distance of 90km/56 miles, with 8,534m/28,000ft of ascent.

Like its English cohort, the name originates from the first man to complete the challenge – Charlie Ramsay from Edinburgh.

Setting out from Glen Nevis Youth Hostel just before noon on Saturday, 8 July 1978, Charlie Ramsay, accompanied by several support runners, proceeded in a clockwise direction on to the Mamores mountains. Twenty-three hours and 58 minutes later, he reappeared alone running down the slopes of Ben Nevis, the final Munro of the 24, to the finish line where his family and friends were waiting to greet him.

Checking his watch, Charlie then sank to his knees with exhaustion, elated by the culmination of his dream of circuiting all the Lochaber Mountains in a single day. Behind him a trail of exhausted bodies littered the route – these were his support runners who had simply been unable to maintain the fierce pace set by Charlie.

And so, Scotland's classic mountain ultramarathon was created, with Charlie's record standing for nine years.

To date, a further 74 people have successfully followed in Charlie's footsteps, including three ladies. Of those, 61 have run the course the opposite way round to Charlie in a clockwise direction, starting with Ben Nevis, while the remaining 13 have run in an anticlockwise direction, finishing with Ben Nevis, just as Charlie had.

A few diehards have even completed the round in both directions in winter conditions, challenged not only by the Munros themselves but also by the weather, battling against blizzards, snow, gale-force winds and torrential rain.

Mental Miscellany

- Course records are 18 hours, 23 minutes (men) and 20 hours, 24 minutes (women).
- In June 1984 Philip Tranter followed a different course and covered all 24 Munros in 57km/36 miles with 6,278m/20,600ft of ascent.
- The Ramsay Round was a low-profile event until Chris Brasher (Olympic gold medallist and organiser of the London Marathon) visited Edinburgh seeking information about the round, which he had attempted himself in 1977.

For further information, please visit: www.ramsayround.com

PADDY BUCKLEY ROUND –WALES

There are several notable differences between the English and Scottish rounds and the Welsh version. Firstly, Paddy Buckley devised the course with the assistance of Chris Brasher (in a pub) but has never actually completed the round himself; secondly, the first person who did complete it was a woman – Wendy Dodds, who did so in 1982 in a time of 25 hours and 38 minutes; and thirdly, the time of Wendy Dodds's round has meant that no 24-hour limit has ever been set.

Despite that, the first sub-24 hour round was set in 1985 by Martin Stone who completed it in 23 hours, 26 minutes, and these days most contenders aim also to finish in a sub-24 hour time.

The round itself is a circular route that can be started from any point and followed in any direction, and takes in the peaks of Snowdon, Glyderau and Carneddau. Continuing with this rather more casual approach, the summits to visit are pretty well arbitrary and no rules appear to apply in their selection. However, generally the route will take in all the major peaks of ranges being crossed and any minor peaks, and the terrain is rough and rocky with steep climbs, rocky descents, grassy knolls and woodland.

By and large, the Paddy Buckley Round is considered a very unofficial race with no actual records of how many people may have completed it. It has the reputation of being harder than the Bob Graham Round, but without the application of a 24-hour time limit.

Mental Miscellany

- The only record times known are: 17 hours, 42 minutes (men) set in 2009, and 19 hours, 19 minutes (women), set in 1991.
- The Paddy Buckley Round is also known as the Welsh Classical Round.
- Despite the lack of officialdom, the Paddy Buckley Round is still recognised as one of the UK's Big 3 Mountain Challenges, the other two being the Bob Graham Round (England) and the Charlie Ramsay Round (Scotland).

There is no official website for the Paddy Buckley Round but details can be found at: www.gofar.org.uk

THE BIG 3 MOUNTAIN CHALLENGE – ENGLAND, SCOTLAND, WALES

The Bob Graham Round, the Charlie Ramsay Round and the Paddy Buckley Round, make up the Big 3 Mountain Challenges.

Only one man, Mike Hartley, is known to have completed all three challenges in three consecutive days in a total time of 3 days, 14 hours and 20 minutes, running a total of 300km/187 miles with 25,298m/83,000ft of ascent, including 113 tops.

Four people have completed all three rounds in one season and just 33 have completed all three in their lifetime.

WICKLOW ROUND – IRELAND

A recent addition to the three UK Rounds is Ireland's Wicklow Round. This is a looped course starting and finishing in Wicklow, taking in 26 peaks, covering 96km/60 miles, with over 6,000m/19,685ft of climb. It must be completed within 24 hours and runners must visit 29 nominated points in their specified order, which includes the 26 peaks. The round may be run solo or in groups, but each runner must carry their own gear and no pacing or navigational support is allowed.

The organisers stress that anyone considering attempting this challenge should have the resources and skills necessary to survive in a mountain environment for the duration; they make clear that this is a personal challenge, not a race, taking place at the runner's own risk with individuals fully responsible for their own safety, support and equipment.

The round was first completed in 2007 on a slightly longer course in a time of 33 hours, 56 minutes and 48 seconds, but due to popular demand and feedback of those wanting to take up the challenge, this was shortened in 2009, bringing new course times of 17 hours, 53 minutes and 45 seconds for the men, and 22 hours, 58 minutes and 30 seconds for the women.

The Wicklow Round serves as a qualifier for the Ultra-Trail Mont-Blanc race.

For further information, please visit: www.imra.ie/wicklowround

WHILE DOWN ON THE FLAT...

THE THAMES RING
UK

399km/248 miles – longest non-stop foot race in the UK

When Dick Kearn, a committee member of the Trail Running Association, turned up at a committee meeting one evening in 2008 and produced a map of the Thames Ring (a boating circuit taking in the Oxford Canal, the Thames and the Grand Union Canal) with the suggestion that it might make a viable ultra run, the idea was considered ludicrous. It was 399km/248 miles long for goodness' sake; it would take four to five days to complete, at best three if anyone was able to maintain an average speed of 4 miles per hour, but then when would they sleep? Sure, Dick's brother-in-law had cycled it for charity in 60 hours, but that was on a bike, nobody had ever attempted it on foot. It was out of the question. 'We could just ask around, see if anyone's interested?' Dick persisted.

The following year, on a Wednesday morning in July, 33 runners toed the start line at Streatley to set off on the first ever Thames Ring ultra trail marathon, and so the longest foot race in the UK was born.

The race now takes place every two years, starting on a Wednesday at 9am, finishing by 1pm on the Sunday, allowing runners just 4 days, 4 hours (or 100 hours) to complete the challenge, and is run in an anticlockwise direction. This is in order to offer a different perspective for runners who have partaken in the Grand Union Canal race and also to allow them to negotiate the more difficult section of the Thames canal path approaching London, before they are too fatigued.

Along the route there are 9 checkpoints, 25 miles apart, which provide food, water and rest. Support crews are mandatory and cut-off times are strictly enforced.

Runners who manage to finish do so in somewhere between 60 and 100 hours and for their efforts will receive a finishing plaque.

Who would do this?

Paul Ali is 41 years old and works as a project manager. He ran his first ultramarathon in 2009 and describes himself as a 'fun ultra runner'. Paul finished the 2013 Thames Ring race in seventh place in 82 hours, 41 minutes. This extract was taken with kind permission from: www.ultraavon.com

I left Streatley at 9am on the Wednesday to run the 27.3 miles to Reading. The first thing that happened was my friend dropped his water bottle into the river, so I got some guy in a boat to fish it out for him.

The terrain was pretty straightforward and the weather was cool, although there was a light shower. Then I ran past my office where my wife also works and she and 20 colleagues were waiting for me!

At Henley it was the regatta and the path was so busy I had to walk through all these well-groomed people in my sweaty running kit.

At the first checkpoint I had a slice of pizza and some energy drinks. Then the weather warmed up and I couldn't maintain my pace so I started doing a stop-start thing. I think

I was tired from running the Grand Union Canal race (145 miles) five weeks earlier.

I arrived at the second checkpoint at Chertsey at 8.10pm, had some food and drink, put on an extra layer and a head torch. I also changed my socks as I knew it was important to look after my feet. Despite that my feet started to get sore through the night and I was glad to reach checkpoint three at Yiewsley [in the London borough of Hillingdon] at 4am. I slept for an hour on the pavement in a sleeping bag.

When I left the checkpoint my legs felt stiff and my knees and feet were sore. By the time the weather started warming up, I was hardly running and was really glad to reach Berkhampstead and the next checkpoint where I had a bacon sandwich and a massage.

From then on it was really just a fast walk to Milton Keynes and I refilled my water bottles from the lock taps. I reached Milton Keynes at 7.45pm and ate pizza and ice cream, I tried to sleep under a bridge but it was too noisy with traffic.

I set off again at 9pm to Nether Heyford. It was now a march through the evening gloom along the dark, narrow, lumpy wet path. I tried to grab some sleep under a bush using a foil blanket for a bed and set my alarm for one hour, but the ground was too lumpy and uncomfortable so I just lay there staring at the stars; I got up again, put my backpack on and trudged on.

I reached the next checkpoint at Fenny Compton at 5.30am. I'd now covered 183.1 miles. I ate some breakfast and grabbed an hour's sleep, then I patched up my blistered feet and set off again at 8am. It was already warm so I applied sun lotion.

Knowing I only had 75 miles to go, the whole thing began to feel like an adventure, but then the bit from the Grand Union Canal to the Oxford Canal felt too long. I'd relied on my Garmin [GPS], but the checkpoint didn't appear when I expected it to at 26 miles. I ran out of water, but finally hit the checkpoint at 29 miles. It was late afternoon and my knee was swollen, so I put some ice on it, refuelled, changed my socks and patched up my feet. I didn't bother trying to sleep, as I wanted to make the most of the daylight so I continued on to Lower Heyford.

I realised then that I hadn't spoken to anyone apart from at the checkpoints for 36 hours. Ultras are a lonely business.

I reached Heyford railway station checkpoint, and immediately fell asleep on a chair, using ear plugs to block out the railway noise. I managed to get two hours sleep and was surprised when I woke up to realise I was still mentally alert. Then I had a bacon sandwich and tea, and set out for Abingdon and the final checkpoint.

The grass was wet with dew. I suffered lacerations from thorns, bushes and stinging nettles. My knees were sore and my feet were blistered. When I reached Oxford I had a hot pasty and a drink.

At the final checkpoint I refuelled again, dumped unnecessary gear and set off for the final 19 miles to the finish. I'd had 4 hours sleep in 75 hours.

The day became quite hot and I'd forgotten to put on any sun cream so I borrowed some from a picnicking couple. I had to get extra water from loch taps as I'd been taking Ibuprofen for a few days to dull the knee ache and my sore feet. I don't normally do this but it had become a necessity.

The path ran close to the River Thames and people were swimming, so I walked into the river to soak my sore feet and aching legs. Then I had two ice lollies at a café and a coke.

I was into the last 8 miles when I came across a lady who was stuck in the river unable to get up the high bank in her flip-flops and dress, with a cigarette in one hand and a bowl of water for the dog in the other. As I walked passed she slid down the bank into the river and got covered in mud. I pulled her out, then continued on my way.

Minutes later, another lady with a dog bounding ahead of her were coming straight for me. I stood still to let the dog pass but it careered straight into my 'little soldiers' winding me for a while and leaving me with that uncomfortable stomach ache type feeling. The woman barely apologised.

Then suddenly Streatley Bridge came into sight. This was

the one moment I didn't want to end. After a long, hard, tiring, solitary slog, enduring physical discomfort and sleep deprivation, I was nearly there and I could enjoy arriving at the finish and finally sitting down.

Someone insisted on taking a photo of my feet to be hung in the photo gallery with the others. I was reluctant to do this but having since viewed the gallery mine were not the worst.

Completing the race

Mental Miscellany

- In the inaugural race in 2009, there were 33 starters and 12 finishers.
- In 2013 there were 34 starters and 14 finishers.
- The winning time in 2013 was 66 hours, 49 minutes.
- The recommended time for boats to complete the circuit is three weeks.

For further information, please visit: www.tra-uk.org

GRAND UNION CANAL RACE
UK

233km/145-mile non-stop canal path race – within 45 hours

First held in 1993, the Grand Union Canal Race (GUCR) was until very recently hailed as the toughest, longest non-stop ultra in Britain and, even now, there are only a handful of races that surpass it.

At that inaugural race, the race director himself, Dick Kearn, ran and finished first of the 20 runners who took part, although only five, including Dick, actually completed it within the 45-hour time limit.

Held under UK Athletics rules and with permission of British Waterways, who award special trophies for the winning male and female, the race, which is held in May, starts at 6am from Gas Street Basin, Birmingham, and follows the waymarked Grand Union Canal Towpath all the way to Little Venice, London.

With no medical backup or first-aid provision, runners must carry a foil 'space' blanket, a mobile phone and cash, and organisers strongly recommend that competitors bring their own support crews, who will play a vital role not only in offering physical support by providing fuel and fluids, treating blisters and minor injuries, but also, and perhaps more importantly, in giving mental support. For although the flatness of such a race may suggest an easier option compared to a mountain run, it is that very apparent advantage that has many runners almost crying in despair as the miles drag on in seemingly endless monotony.

Despite that, the race has an almost unparalleled reputation for good organisation and camaraderie, the like of which sees competitors returning year after year.

Who would do this?

Twenty-seven-year-old ultra runner, Liz Tunna, who in 2012 at just 25 became the youngest woman in the UK to run 100 marathons, took part in the Grand Union Canal Race in both 2012 and 2013. This extract was taken with kind permission from: www.lizogical. blogspot.co.uk

We arrived at the start in plenty of time with me still mulling over the loss of my sports bra. I hadn't yet had my morning coffee so I was delighted to see hot drinks being offered to runners from a van – for free! So I fuelled myself up on coffee, although, unlike last year, I was feeling pretty wide awake, even though I hadn't slept much at all.

Everyone was happy and excitable, gearing up to go. I noticed a lot of runners were facing the wrong way, which is easily done. Fortunately, for once, I was sure of my direction.

The first bit of towpath is narrow and not the prettiest. I wasn't going out fast, so I stood to the side to let the speedy ones go in front and positioned myself near the back – 145 miles is a long way and my instinct tells me to hold back and play it cool and block out how fast anyone else is going. My approach would probably be more refined if I trained hard for these things and was really fit.

Me and Jon [another runner] settled into a comfortable pace and chatted away, enjoying the cool but sunny morning. Then, suddenly, this relaxed atmosphere was shattered. While running underneath a bridge, Jon took a painful fall when he hit his head on the low wall/roof. He hit it really

hard and was on the floor. At this point I saw just how kind the running community can be.

Other runners provided assistance and handed over tissues for the cut Jon had sustained to his head. Fortunately, everything turned out good and there were no more bridge-head-banging incidents.

Approaching the Mile 10 checkpoint, we were pretty much at the back. I kept telling myself not to worry, there is always a high dropout rate and I would not be on that DNF [Did Not Finish] list. The field had gone out pretty darn fast, we literally saw no other crews for maybe 30 miles or more. It can be mentally hard when you just don't see many other supporters out there for so long. Your head starts to play silly mind games with you and you start to question your game plan.

My game plan was slow and steady. I was also very focused on refuelling often, making sure I took in enough electrolytes and fluid. It was shaping up to be a scorcher of a day and I didn't want to get into any tricky territory of feeling or being sick.

Time is weird during long ultras. Before you know it, hours have passed and you've reached a milestone and then another. Then, when you're in pain, the miles suddenly become much longer and time slows down completely and every step seems to take an eternity. The first milestone for me was getting the first marathon done. We met our crew at a lock and refuelled with cola and Pringles. And my amazing crew had found my sports bra! So I shuffled over a lock gate and changed in the back of the van.

The next section was quite difficult. I was starting to feel a bit frazzled by the sun and my arms were burning. I started to have negative thoughts. We were around 37 miles and I kept thinking we had run a small ultra but had almost 110 miles left. It felt so impossible.

My food strategy was to eat small bits early and often, but the sunny weather suppressed my appetite and made me not want to eat too much. Pringles were my rescue food, so easy to eat and full of salt and calories, perfect! And we found a little canal-side shop selling ice lollies.

As darkness fell, I felt sleepy, but at least it wasn't raining. The canal bends and bends and goes on and on at this point. You think you're nearly at the bridge and then you're round a corner and there isn't anything there. Then you see the orange lights and you've made it to another milestone.

Heading towards Milton Keynes and nearing the 80-mile mark, my head became muddled with negativity. I was so tired. I was struggling to keep awake. Seeing all those cosy narrow boats became a sort of sleep-deprived torture. I just wanted to snuggle down in the warmth. I sat myself down on a bench and gave myself a talking-to. I also downed a mini bottle of full-fat Coke and got out my mp3 player. I needed to stimulate my brain somehow. Listening to music really helped me stay on track and alert during this sleepy tough section. I may even have done a little singing to myself.

There were these swirling clouds of foggy mist on the water. It was spooky, surreal and beautiful all at the same time. It was also incredibly difficult to see where you were going. If I'd taken my head torch off and aimed it at the ground, it would have helped, but I was just too tired to take it off my head, so I just plodded on.

Daylight – phew. I can't describe that feeling of making it through a tough night section and into the light. It's such a great feeling, a new day and you've covered a big chunk of distance.

The Sunday morning seemed pretty darn chilly, but it made me move faster and woke me up. Before I knew it, we were approaching 84-ish miles and I was so happy to see the orange glow of lights signalling the checkpoint. It was now around 4.15am and the checkpoint didn't close until 7am. I was chuffed. I'd made up some time.

As time ticked away and we moved further forwards and past the 100-mile marker, my feet really started to hurt. The uneven towpaths and gravel and stony tracks had tenderised my feet. I could feel every little bump and stone or bit of grit.

My feet were too far gone to be helped by any medication. All I could do was keep putting one foot in front of the other and getting this thing over with sooner rather than later.

Then, just after 120 miles, I felt a sharp pain on the sole of my foot. Sure enough a rough patch of sharp gravel path had caused a blister to burst. I sat down on a bench to examine my feet. I had a huge blister the size of a two-pence coin on each heel. I rummaged around in my waist pack for something sharp to burst them with. I didn't care that you're not supposed to burst them; they needed draining as the pressure was quite irritating due to their size, but I didn't have anything sharp enough so I'd have to wait until I caught up with my crew.

Fortunately, my crew weren't much further along and had some sterile needles. I drained the blisters and patched up the most painful one.

The upside of this was the pain made me run faster, setting myself goals to run to certain narrowboats or trees or bridges. Walking had become too painful because it put too much pressure on the sole of my foot.

It's sort of crazy – I think that sums up my thoughts in the latter stages. I was now feeling more optimistic and actually pretty emotional, a bit teary eyed. My mobile phone had run out of battery and I hadn't had contact with the outside world since Saturday evening and it was now well into Sunday evening.

I was also getting emotional because I had thought about reaching checkpoint mile-133 during every tough bit I encountered. Getting to this point would mean I had made all the cut-offs and reached the last official checkpoint.

It was nearing the last checkpoint that I started to see a few things. I thought trees and bushes were people, just the usual visions really.

Ultimately, the last bits were filled with super highs and tough lows. Highs included the kindness of strangers: men on a barge clapped me, I heard a father tell his kids, 'Next time you complain about going for a walk, these people have

158

come all the way from Birmingham'; some guys that were fishing had a nice chat with us and offered us some beer. Also, the hallucinations were quite entertaining, just faces and heads and people and things.

Lows included increasing foot pain, I had to keep stopping to itch and relieve my feet. Every mile was really dragging and the last 13 were the longest of my life. But eventually, persistent forward motion led me to familiar territory and I knew for certain we only had a few miles left; I recognised the towpath from last year.

And then there were smiles and I was able to run. And somehow I had made it and was able to sprint across that finish line in 43:13:00.

Mental Miscellany

- Any runner stopping for longer than 40 minutes at any one time will be disqualified.
- Runners are allowed to sit in a vehicle for rest, food, drink, etc, but if the vehicle moves the runner will be disqualified.
- Running 'buddies' (support runners) are allowed to accompany competitors for the final 70 miles.
- The race allows for a maximum of 90 starters – on a first-come, first-served basis.
- The course records are: 25 hours, 37 minutes (men); 28 hours, 1 minute (women).

For further information, please visit: www.gucr.co.uk

24-HOUR RUNNING
WORLDWIDE
Run for 24 hours – without stopping

Twenty-four-hour running pretty much does what it says on the tin. You have 24 hours to see how far you can run – not in a Forrest Gump kind of way, but more in a round-and-round-in-circles kind of way.

This type of ultra-running generally takes place on a 400m track or round circuits of one to two miles and top athletes will usually cover somewhere between 209 and 290km/130 and 180 miles, depending on the conditions.

Participants may use a support crew who will keep them supplied with fluid and fuel or changes of clothes or shoes and, of course, much needed words of encouragement. Alternatively, runners may choose to simply set up camp themselves near the start of each lap, setting out all their gear and supplies so they will be easily accessible as and when they need them.

Running around in circles for 24 hours is potentially likely to challenge a person's mind more than their body and it may be advisable to build up to this sort of event gradually by entering a 6- or 12-hour event first. Equally, if 24 hours seems too easy, there are also 48-hour events available.

Believe it or not, there are even European and World Championships for these types of events, which are organised by the International Association of Ultra Runners (IAU).

The IAU, which has been in existence since 1984, was granted patronage by the International Amateur Athletic Federation (now the International Association of Athletics Federations) in 1988, and today is responsible for over 1,000 ultra races around the world, with more than 100,000 runners. They also organise world championship races for 100k, 50k and trail running.

Who would do this?

Twenty-six-year-old former outdoors study tutor turned endurance athlete and coach Robbie Britton ran his first marathon in 2009. Four years later, Robbie pulled on a GB vest for the first time and represented his country in the 2013 24-Hour World Championships in Steenbergen, Netherlands. This extract was taken with kind permission from Robbie's blog at: www.robbiebritton.co.uk

I'd run about 100 miles and food wasn't going down too well but I was still munching some oranges and Clif Shot Bloks [energy bars], while vomiting every now and again. Morning was coming and it would soon be business time, time to get my act together and start pushing on!

About 19 hours in, fuelled by plenty of flat coke, I was feeling good and started to put in some quicker laps. It was at this point I considered the gamble. I felt good, so should I pace it out steadily until the finish, still some five hours away, and hope that it all held strong, or should I smash the hell out of it now, in the present? My legs haven't been an issue in races, just my fuel, so I could move quickly and decided to go for it.

Robbie dons the GB vest

The next few hours were wonderful. I was lapping people and I felt real strong. I even posted my fastest laps of the race about 22 hours in! Could I keep this up until the finish?

Alas, it wasn't to last. I keeled over halfway round a lap and threw up about 2 litres of Coca-Cola, much to the delight of the nearby photographer who was snapping away.

The last two hours were just a situation of hanging on and moving forward.

I had the pleasure of running my penultimate lap with a wonderful American runner who helped me when I was feeling low, in return for the encouragement I had given during the race. A real moment that reminded me why I loved ultra-running so much. We're all in this pile of s*** struggle together, we'll get through it.

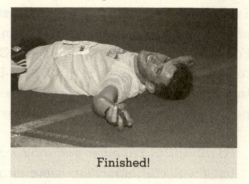

Finished!

Robbie finished 19th and ran 239.635km/148.902 miles, the equivalent of almost six marathons in a day.

Mental Miscellany

- Men's world record for 24-hour 400m track running is 303.506km/188.590 miles (= just over seven marathons in a day).
- Women's world record for 24-hour 400m track running is 255.303km/161.126 miles (= just over six marathons in a day).
- Mami Kudo of Japan has run 255.303km/158.112 miles in 24 hours and 368.687km/229.161 miles in 48 hours.
- Giorgio Calcaterra of Italy has been the 100k world champion three times with a personal best time of 6 hours, 23 minutes and 20 seconds.

For further information on this event, please visit: www.iau-ultramarathon.org

ARE WE THERE YET?

LOS ANGELES TO NEW YORK FOOT RACE
USA

3,200 miles/5,150km – average 45 miles/74km a day – for 70 days

It is pretty much universally accepted that the best way to see any country is on foot. However, when it comes to a country the size of the United States, most people would probably beg to differ.

If you find yourself at odds with this second statement, then you may be interested in partaking in a jolly little jaunt that takes place every year from June to August, which crosses America from west to east coast, taking in a total of 14 states and 5,150km/3,200 miles, with an average daily distance of 74km/45.7 miles; the shortest day being day 65, with a mere 42km/26.4 miles, and the longest on day 29 with a blister-inducing 96km/59.7 miles. Maybe this explains why the race is also popularly known as the 'Bunion Derby'.

It is a race whose origins go as far back as the Great Depression of 1928 when endurance events such as dance marathons, week-long flagpole sitting (yes, really) and ultra-swimming were extremely popular as a means of lifting people's sagging spirits, and a certain Mr C C Pyle, a showman and promoter, saw it as a good way to make some money – marketing the race as 'The Greatest Show on Earth'. It was also held partly as a promotional effort to market the new Route 66 from Los Angeles to Chicago.

The structure of the race itself back then was based on the Tour de France, with times being recorded for each stage and rankings being awarded accordingly. With a prize pot of US$25,000 the race saw 199 starters, 55 finishers and was won in 573 hours, 4 minutes and 34 seconds – or 84 days – with an approximate average of 74km/46 miles being completed each day (the course then measured 5,510km/3,423.5 miles).

It is hard to say whether it is surprising or not, but the next race didn't take place until 1992.

Today, the race still starts in Los Angeles and crosses California, Arizona, Oklahoma, New Mexico, Missouri, Illinois, Indiana, Ohio, West Virginia, Pennsylvania, Maryland and New Jersey, finishing in New York. The minimum pace for the race is 5.6km/3.5 miles per hour in order to meet the cut-off times and, just as with the inaugural race, all stage times are added together to find the ultimate winner. Failure to meet the cut-off times results in disqualification, but participants are allowed to continue in the race, although they will not be officially ranked.

Naturally, covering such a vast distance and crossing so many states, participants will face a huge diversity of terrain, environment, weather and other challenges. These range from asphalt and gravel roads to uneven sidewalks and rocky trails, sandy deserts to mountainous climbs ascending from sea level to 9,500ft and back again, skin-burning heat to bone-chilling cold, flooding rivers, thunderstorms, earthquakes and even the threat of hurricanes, not to mention the frustrations of being delayed by busy state intersections, all hampering progress and eating greedily into precious time.

Due to the high temperatures and weather conditions of the

first 13 days, all participants must provide their own support crew and car for that period, but it is not mandatory for runners to have a support crew for the remainder of the race. In such circumstances, unsupported runners tend to group together and share a vehicle or stay close to a runner who has one and who is willing to share the vehicle and services.

In addition to personal support crews, the race organisers have a vehicle that goes back and forth along the route with water and food that guarantees to see to runners at least every hour, but they will not make any additional special trips for individual runners, hence the mandatory rule stating all runners must carry 1.5 litres of water at all times, as well as US$10, head torches and fluorescent vests.

The last race, which was held in 2011, was only the ninth race ever and mustered up just 16 runners. Apart from Americans, there were representatives from six other nations, including Dutch, French, German, Italian, Japanese and the UK.

Who would do this?

Thirty-three-year-old data analyst, ultra runner, infamous blog and book writer, James Adams, who describes himself as someone who likes running a long way slowly, took part in the LA to NY race in 2011. This extract was taken with kind permission from: www.runningandstuff.squarespace.com

It was dark when we gathered at Huntington Beach for the start, and halfway took a long time coming; LA is so huge. By 35 miles I had a blister on my little toe.

It got much hotter entering Norco, a funny town made for horses. I walked a bit, feeling a little dehydrated and light-headed.

Finished the day with usual Achilles tightness, headache and left hip pain.

Day 2 – 48.9 miles – Around 20 miles we were out of town heading for impressive looking mountains and a 1,000m climb. Around 35°C in the valleys.

Day 3 – 47.4 miles – old Route 66, 44°C into the Mojave desert, the sun and straightness messed with my head.

Day 6 – 39.7 miles – I am handling the 40°C+ heat so well I am told, 'James, you are from London, you should run like a penguin but you run like a Kenyan.' I am confident this is the first and last time my running will be compared to a Kenyan. I am also confident that it's not the last time it will be compared to a penguin.

Day 8 – 51.3 miles – First time we crossed a state, from California into Arizona. Hideous chaffing, no more running like a Kenyan.

Day 9 – 42.3 miles – For the first time I think the size of the task overwhelmed me. First 20 miles a bit of a slog, straight up a road into the mountains.

Day 10 – 45.9 miles – 1,500m climb to high plains of Arizona. To put a positive spin on everything, my shin hurts no more than yesterday. On the negative side, this has now stopped being fun.

Day 11 – 30.7 miles – A very different and beautiful landscape unfurled. It had flowers and trees; barren and beige rock and plants were now wonderful scatterings of green on brown and gold, and the chainsaw noise of bugs was now singing birds. Clouds? I have not seen you for over a week. I could have been running through the English countryside in the summer.

Day 13 – 40.3 miles/Day 14 – 53.1 miles – Up and up to around 2,400m. First few miles is always a strain but I have learned to ignore it and carry on. I think I am mentally beating it now after a few days of letting it poison me.

Day 15 – 41.4 miles – started in starlight. With no clouds and light you can see all the stars. We are now deep in the Navajo desert, impressive rock formations and what look like volcanoes. Not as hot as Mojave but more beautiful. It has just started to rain, the first rain I have seen for two weeks.

Day 16 – 47.9 miles – I've known ultra-running take you to the extreme of your emotions. Euphoria, depression, anger, pride. Within a race you may hit several peaks of various emotions. *I am in for two more months of these euphoric highs and crippling lows. I am not entirely looking forward to it.*

Day 17 – 44.5 miles – Struggling to stay awake and feel sick again, the sun got to me.

Days 18–23 – 250 miles – I've hit a rough patch, have had diarrhoea for five days after the vomiting episode; went to hospital to see if it was bacterial, it isn't. I'm starting to recover now.

Day 24 – 37.1 miles – Lovely downhill stretch. Started at the highest point of the race, which in theory means it's now downhill to New York.

Day 25 – 53.6 miles/Day 26 – 54.8 miles – Today is the kind of day that made me wish I'd taken up golf to get my excitement quota, not a lot of it in the plains just short of Oklahoma. Long straight roads, wobbling up and down slightly so you can't see more than a couple of miles ahead.

Day 27 – 49 miles – Hello Oklahoma. The weather forecast is easy to remember, 100°F for all the time we're there.

Days 28–32 – 250 miles – It's international news now that America is gripped by a heatwave.

Days 35–36 – 95 miles – We left the worst motel so far in the USA at 5am, it was 85°F. It never cools down here.

Day 37 – 37.9 miles – I have now run for nearly 400 hours.

Days 38–39 – 90 miles – Around halfway we entered Joplin, a town devastated by a tornado in May. The view from then on was an upsetting shock, miles of rubble, the town had been razed; with that harrowing few miles everything else seemed to fade, minor pains in my legs didn't really matter anymore.

I saw a sign that said 111°F.

Days 40–41 – 97 miles – Thunder storms and the temperature dropped, 20 minutes of beautiful rain.

Days 42–46 – 207 miles – Generally, I am getting slower.

Day 47 – 44.7 miles – The scenery was spectacular, rolling hills, trees and little houses. If the houses were not made of wood then I could imagine I was in the Cotswolds. I miss England.

Day 59 – 55 miles – The sunrise was the best I remember, the glowing sun sat at the end of a beautiful corridor of trees making it look like they were on fire.

Day 62 – 51.1 miles – Mountain stage. I was hardly king of the hills today but I loved them. Actually if Budweiser are allowed to call themselves King of Beers then I am going to call myself King of the Mountains anyway.

Day 63 – 50.6 miles/Day 64 – 46.2 miles – This is the 'last Sunday' of the race. No more running on Sundays after today. This time next week I won't have to do any running, etc. It really lifts spirits to be able to say things like that, to say to a passer by who asks, 'Yeah we started two months ago in LA but this is the last week'.

Day 65 – 48.8 miles/Day 6 – 26.9 miles – We were expecting 26.2 miles today but there was a diversion so it was 26.9 miles. My chances of a marathon pb [personal best] are slipping.

Day 67 – 50.5 miles/Day 68 – 51 miles – I'm 3,100 miles into a 3,200 mile race, but all I can think is how it sucks to only be 17 miles into a 51-mile day. I can't get myself into New York mode for some reason; all I can focus on is the next horrible mile.

Day 69 – 47.4 miles – Hurricane Irene is due to hit the east coast late tomorrow after we have run. The problem is New York is closed, and Washington Bridge may be too.

It's possible the bridge will close before noon; in that event the race will end at the start of the bridge, in New Jersey. So I will have run the LANJ race. Does not sound quite as appealing.

The finish has been changed. Central Park is closed so we will finish on the seventh floor of the Novotel [Hotel] in Times Square, emerging from an elevator, soaking wet. That is, of course, if we even get into New York.

Tomorrow was meant to be a nice stroll to glory but now it has become a headache. Damn nature interfering with our ultras.

Day 70 – 35.2 miles – I felt a little down today; we discovered it was very unlikely the bridge would be closed but that did not change my mood. I just felt so empty. There was no excitement or anticipation anymore, very little emotion.

I had been warned to expect a two-week funk after the event while I try to adjust back to normal life, and wake up to the reality that the incredible thing you are doing is now done and in the past. Could it be that I have started suffering the post-race depression before the race has actually finished?

As I left the river to head onto Broadway towards Times Square, it got a bit better. I have run for nearly 800 hours and I have about 20 minutes left.

It was a great atmosphere at the finish, with some runners and all the support crews there. The organisers wanted this to be a low-key race, which is why there was no media coverage or fanfare in the places we went. Every now and again someone would find out about the race and make a noise, but on the whole we crossed the USA unnoticed. The organisers said if the media had been at the finish, they would make it look like it was all about one moment, crossing the line. It's not; it's about 70 days of unique experience that only the 16 of us would really understand. I still feel a bit down about it now, but I know it will sink in soon and I will realise the magnitude of what I have done. Right now my brain is just an empty space unable to really think about anything. My loved ones are a bit worried about my silence but they need not be. It will pass.

I have just run across the United States of America. I just need to say that to myself a few more times and then perhaps I will believe it. And then my emotions should come back.

Mental Miscellany

- The only man to run the route in both directions is Harry Abrams, who ran the race in 1928 and then ran it in the opposite direction in 1929.
- The average age of participants today is 48, compared to 1928 when most were in their twenties.
- Stages start at 0530.

- There are no rest days.
- Apart from vomiting, heat exhaustion and cramp, the organisers also warn of snakes.
- There is no beer at the finish as it is generally illegal to drink alcohol outdoors in the USA.
- There is also a Trans-Europe foot race of 4,000km/2,700 miles, in 64 stages, over approximately 2 months, usually from August to October.

For further information, please visit: www.lanyfootrace.com

JOGLE ULTRA
UK

1,397km/868 miles – in 16 days –
John O'Groats to Land's End

When the first ever JOGLE [JOGroatstoLandsEnd] ultra race took place in 2010, race director and renowned ultra runner Rory Coleman remarked: 'At one stage we were worried that no one would finish'.

He had good reason to worry for by day two of the 16-day race, four competitors failed to finish, on day four a further two failed to finish and one failed to start, on day five another one did not start and on day eight yet another runner failed to finish. By day nine, just over halfway, there were only three runners left in the race.

Luckily for Rory, however, those three runners made it all the way to the finish, covering a total of 868 miles from the north-eastern tip of Scotland all the way down to the most westerly point of England, having run an incredible average of 58 miles a day between 30 April and 15 May.

By 2012, the number of participants had changed very little, with just 12 hardy men and women daring to take on what must surely be one of the most testing ultra-running challenges in the UK, a claim borne out by the fact that this time only one person managed to complete the epic feat.

The race, which has checkpoints every 10 miles via a van providing food and drink as well as encouragement and advice, travels from north to south via Brora, Beauly, Spean Bridge, Tyndrum, Paisley, Moffat, Penrith, Garstang, Tarporley, Ludlow, Chepstow, Taunton, Bow, Lostwithiel and Penzance, with a short final run of around 10 miles to the finish line at Land's End.

As a result, the route, which is a mixture of road and trail, takes in the highs of rugged Scotland, the lows of the lush valleys of Wales, as well as the unexpected undulations of England. Taking place in April/May, when the weather is at its most unpredictable, the runners may face anything from snow, hail, sleet and gale-force winds to balmy sunshine and gentle breezes.

Who would do this?

Forty-one-year-old, Mark Cockbain, electronics engineer, ultra runner and company director of Cockbain Events (www. cockbainevents.com), took part in the inaugural event in 2010 – mainly because the race was his idea in the first place! This extract was taken with kind permission from: www.markcockbain.com

A while back, I pitched the idea of running from John O'Groats to Land's End as an actual race to race director Rory Coleman. He agreed it was a great idea and in June 2010 myself and 11 other ultra runners were on our way to John O'Groats on a big purple sleeper bus (rock-star style), which was to be our home/base for the next two weeks. We were all assigned our own bunks and had an on-board cook called Anne.

Day 1 – John O'Groats to Brora – 63 miles. There's nothing but a signpost and a start/finish line painted on the ground at JOG [John O'Groats].

The weather and coastal scenery are fantastic but at around 40 miles there are some very long steep inclines and my right ankle feels strained, causing my tendons to inflame. This triggers shin splints, one of the most painful injuries you can get.

I try stretching it out over the next long uphill but it worsens.

Around 50 miles I remove my shoes and cool the strain in a puddle, but it's just a brief relief and with over 800 miles to go I decide to walk the last 10 miles.

I find some ice and cool the leg overnight, knowing the injury won't go away; it will be just a matter of how much pain I can take.

Day 2 – Brora to Beauly – 58.5 miles. Up at 5am, I hardly slept for worrying about my leg. My shin is still swollen and painful, so I decide to run slowly to limit the damage and am accompanied by Mike, who has similar problems and a sense of humour.

We shuffle up and down hills. I put emphasis on my left leg to compensate, but every now and then I get a sharp, shooting pain reminding me not to overstretch. I don't take painkillers, as I prefer to know if it's getting worse.

Again, the weather is perfect as we edge down the east coast towards Beauly. There are fantastic views of ruined castles and cliffs overlooking the sea. It's flatter today in the early stages but then there's a huge hill at around 45 miles. Still, it's good to finish the first 100 miles, although a few of the runners dropped out today.

Day 3 – Beauly to Spean Bridge – 54.4 miles. Again, I team up with Mike and we try to limit the shin pain; we even try going backwards down some steeper slopes! We make slow progress but I just want to finish and I don't care about stage times.

Mike's problems worsen and I have to leave him behind.

I quite enjoy running on my own, just absorbing the nature around me, and the fantastic lochs. The sun is shining and I feel pretty good, managing to keep my feet fairly flat and not irritate my shin too much.

Day 4 – Spean Bridge to Tyndrum – 55.8 miles. It's a hilly run today, winding our way through Glencoe with views of Ben Nevis. The views are amazing but the traffic is heavy and we need to be alert, as some drivers seem intent on knocking us down!

After 50 miles there's a steep downhill which sends sharp pains up my shins forcing me to slow right down.

I see a nice little stream and remove my socks and shoes and dip my legs into the water. It feels great and with the sun overhead I could spend hours here, but with less than seven miles to go I set off for the bus, taking it nice and slow as the pain is still bad.

Everyone struggled with the hills today and more have dropped out, including Mike.

Day 5 – Tyndrum to Paisley – 57.7 miles. There are now just four runners left. Most of today's run is along the shores of Loch Lomond. It's a beautiful summer day and the views across the blue water are stunning. The route is flat, which relieves the pressure on my ankles, and the lunch-time checkpoint van is right next to the water's edge, so I take off my shoes and socks and cool my aching feet in the water. It feels like heaven.

Loch Lomond seems to go on forever but as we approach Glasgow the rush-hour traffic is heavy. There's only 14 miles left but my right shin is so painful I can hardly walk on it.

At the next checkpoint I ask Rory to give my shins some physio but all he can do is give them a hard rub, which is very painful but loosens them up for a short time.

I take my first painkillers as I head towards Paisley. They kick in and I'm running fast, which is just as well as the area is a bit rough!

I catch up with a couple of other runners just before the Clyde Tunnel. It's dark and full of graffiti and I'm glad there are three of us!

We are completely lost when we came out of the tunnel and so tired we cannot read the map properly and have to call Rory for instructions. We eventually find the bus at Paisley Golf Club at 11pm.

Day 6 – Paisley to Moffat – 58.2 miles. I can barely put my right foot flat on the floor as my right shin has swollen so badly. I begin to think running another 500 miles will be impossible, so I decide to run with Colin and take it really slow.

We set off early and get lost straight away by running up a hill in the wrong direction!

It takes about 20 miles before we're back in the country lanes. My shin is causing me major problems and I lay down on a bench in a village square while Rory works on it and I swear with the pain. I realise it's not going to get better and I might as well just let the pain reach its maximum and put up with it; hopefully eventually I'll be able to shut it out.

I catch up with Colin and we stay together, but in our tired state we find ourselves running down the hard shoulder of the M74, which we thought was the A74!

I don't realise this is illegal until a highway agency worker pulls up behind us, so we climb over a wall to get off the motorway just as blue flashing lights appear. Two police officers jump out to question us. We try to stay cool and tell them the truth and that we're running for charity. Mentioning charity defuses the situation and they end up being very helpful driving us to the opposite side of the motorway onto the parallel road, no distance gained or lost. I think they're glad when we get out of their car: the smell coming from us is embarrassingly bad as we have not washed for six days!

We finally reach the bus at around 11pm.

Day 7 – Moffat to Penrith – 58.4 miles. I haven't slept due to the pain in my shins and I wonder if it's going to be physically possible to move forward.

I try taping the bottom of my foot and ankle for extra support. It doesn't work and I rip the whole thing off. To my surprise, it's a flat route and it gives my shins a break. I start running at a decent pace again. It's a very hot day as we run through Gretna Green, the last Scottish village before we reach the 'Welcome to England' sign.

As I leave Carlisle at around 40 miles, I feel weak. I haven't been eating enough and my shin splints are painful again. It's dark and I have another 10 miles to go. I walk the hills and don't reach the bus until just after midnight. I have low blood sugar and start to shiver, feeling light-headed. I drink a sugary cup of tea, which improves me slightly. I hardly eat anything, which is stupid of me, and go straight to bed.

Day 8 – Penrith to Garstang – 60.1 miles. After another restless night we head out of Penrith. Eventually I get moving and join Neil and Dave for the long climb up Shap, one of the highest passes in the Lake District. I actually feel quite good today.

After Shap, it's a nice long downhill into Kendal. It's another red-hot day and as we reach Lancaster we get stuck on a one-way system, which takes us on a lap of the city, which we didn't need. It's now late in the day and dark as we come out the other side of Lancaster, but I feel very strong. Colin drops out of the race today.

Day 9 – Garstang to Tarporley – 58.4 miles. There's just three of us left in the race now, the three amigos, and the days have become a blur of road, food, road, food.

We leave Garstang just after 6am and work well as a group, taking it in turns to pull each other along. It's one of the hottest days so far as we head into Wigan and I get a touch of heatstroke and drop behind. I stumble in a daze through the town centre but keep drinking to try and stay cool. I eventually catch up with the team as the sun starts to go down and it gets a little cooler. I am over my wobbly patch for now. 'Only six more days of serious leg pain to go,' I joke to Rory as we make it to the sleeper bus at around 11pm.

Day 10 – Tarporley to Ludlow – 53.3 miles. My shin problems haven't got any worse and the weather is red hot again as we head through Shrewsbury and into Wales. I feel more confident as I know my injuries, however painful, will not stop me moving forward.

It's now mid-afternoon and I'm having some strange sharp shooting pains in my right knee. I ignore it, and try a walk-run combo and a few painkillers. As it gets darker the pain increases until around 9pm my knee just 'goes'. I cannot run. I only have about 10 miles to go but as soon as I try running it just locks up. I try to shuffle on at a slower pace and knock back more painkillers.

A few miles from the bus and I just cannot moved forward. We agree to call it a day and add the few miles onto tomorrow's run. Rory takes us to the van in the bus. I'm panicking and get ice straight on to my knee, take more anti-inflammatories then go straight to bed after some food.

Day 11 – Ludlow to Chepstow – 53.7 miles. I slept like a log but I can't bend my knee. I think my over-tight quad muscles have knocked my knee out of alignment. I will need to run alone today, I will be far too slow for the others – or I will not be able to run at all.

Rory drops us where the previous day's leg ended and I run/limp with one straight leg…hop, hop, hop.

I pop into a garage to use the toilet and catch sight of my reflection in the mirror. I look like an unshaven tramp and I laugh at my self-inflicted predicament.

The thought of seeing the Severn Bridge tomorrow spurs me on; people say if you can make it that far, you can make it to the end, and anyway, I am now prepared to crawl.

I force myself on, my mind beating my body hands down, and eventually catch up with the team. My knee has loosened.

We stick together, and run all day and late into the night. We're on a mission. Down dark country roads in silence we run like zombies. On and on until we slow to a shuffle. We are exhausted. Dave lies down in the middle of the road. We agree not one more step today. We mark the route then go to the bus and straight to bed.

Day 12 – Chepstow to Taunton – 59 miles plus a few from yesterday. We have over 600 miles in our legs now and hobble for the first five miles or so until our muscles warm up and our minds adjust to the background pain.

We run across the Severn Bridge and leave Wales behind and head towards Bristol and Devon, running at a steady pace. Staying awake is a problem for us all now.

The A38 is a terrible up-and-down road that causes my shin splints to blow up again. For some reason I'd gone ahead of the group earlier, now I'm paying the price. The group splits and I'm annoyed, even though it's my fault for going faster earlier. My anger gives

A low point

me a boost and I put on a pace just ahead again. I think we are all just going a little crazy! It is soul destroying. At around midnight we finally get to our bus.

Day 13 – Taunton to Bow – 54.7 miles – We struggle to stay awake and pop into several garages on our way out of Taunton to buy Red Bull to keep us from drifting off. I think I feel okay, I'm running anyhow. It's a long day of trudging.

Onwards we go as the weather changes and we're soaked in our first rainstorm. It's a pleasant distraction and we put our heads down and move forward along the side of the road. We can taste the car fumes now.

I shuffle to the bus around 10pm.

Day 14 – Bow to Lostwithiel – 52.1 miles. Everything changes as Neil decides he wants to head out alone today. Dave's not bothered either way and I say I will just run behind and listen to some music, so we all agree to do our own thing to start with.

I feel good and ready for a long day, my legs work fine and the miles go by and the sun is out. There's no pressure to keep with the group and I plan extra rests for myself at the roadside.

I head off across Exmoor National Park and suck in the amazing scenery. I run smoothly for hours and hit that rare moment when everything just works. It feels easy, amazing; I am strong, I'm in the ultra 'groove'.

Then I get badly lost and head the wrong way down the A38. Luckily the sponsor team spot me and send me back in the right direction to the checkpoint, only for me to go off again in the wrong direction. It's very frustrating but eventually I'm back on track the other side of Liskeard.

I am the last man home today at around midnight; the other two are already in bed, but I don't care, tomorrow is the last full day. I have this now.

Day 15 – Lostwithiel to Penzance – 52 miles. We're up at 6am for our penultimate day; spirits are high. We all know it will be done.

Cornwall though is bloody hilly and it's a real slog. It's a dangerous game to relax your mind before the finish.

The roads are very steep and narrow with some pretty hair-raising blind corners, the traffic is really heavy and dangerous, and at one point a car bumps into the back of another car that has slowed down to watch us. We glance at the chaos, see no one is hurt and continue plodding on like machines.

We are all just trying to keep it together, one step at a time nearer our goal. We've helped each other through the ups and downs and had one hell of an adventure.

With night falling, Dave slows and Neil goes ahead a little as we turn the corner to see St Michael's Mount all lit up out to sea. Penzance is near.

We arrive at the bus around 10pm for one last celebratory meal of Cornish pasty and chips!

We decide to run the last 10-mile leg to Land's End in the morning so we can celebrate in daylight and have our friends and family meet us. We are going to make it!

Final Day – Penzance to Land's End – 10 miles. So, this is it. We're up early and raring to go. There's talk of 'sprinting' it in from Neil and Dave, but I'm going to savour every last mile. Neil goes off like a rocket. He's already won the race with his cumulative stage times. Dave goes off second, he will finish second, and I am guaranteed third, as no one else is left.

The last 10 miles is an undulating country lane that will lead me to the completion of one of my life-long goals, to run the length of my country. It would be a lie for me to say that I had not enjoyed every high, every low. We had worked well as a team, but ultimately we all wanted it more than anything and we were prepared to finish at all costs.

As I turn the final corner to see the white buildings of Land's End, I have a lump in my throat, the enormity of what I am about to achieve hits me. What a journey!

Mental Miscellany

- The JOGLE is the longest foot race in Great Britain.
- Only four people have ever completed the JOGLE as a race, although it is believed that others have run it as individuals.
- It is believed that Mark Cockbain is the only man ever to have both cycled and run from John O'Groats to Land's End.
- Race organiser Rory Coleman holds 9 Guinness World Records, has run 10 Marathons des Sables, run from London to Lisbon in 43 days, and has taken part in more than 190 ultramarathons.

For further information, please visit: www.ultrarace.co.uk

IDITAROD TRAIL INVITATIONAL
ALASKA, USA
1,609km/1,000 miles – along frozen sled-dog route

Claiming to be the most remote and longest winter ultra race in the world, the Iditarod Trail Invitational race takes place in February along one of the most famous sled-dog trails in the world.

Indeed, the human-powered race itself was born out of the sled-dog races when a man named Joe Redington Sr, who was responsible for the original idea of a dog-mushing race from Knik to Nome along the trail in 1973 at a time when dog mushing was fading, actively encouraged human-powered races on the trail with a mind to keeping the trail alive.

As a result of his efforts, the first snowshoe and cross-country ski races took place in the early 1980s, with a 322km/200-mile bike race being added in 1987, giving birth to the Iditabike race, before the further addition of a foot race in 1991, although at this stage the race for all three disciplines covered a mere 161km/100 miles.

Then in 1997, a new 563km/350-mile event was brought in named the 'Extreme', taking racers from the start in Knik all the way to McGrath over the Alaska Range. This event continues today running alongside the 1,609km/1,000-mile race, named the

'Impossible', which started out in the year 2000 with just 12 racers making it all the way to the finish in Nome.

Since 2002, the Iditarod Trail Invitational, which was formed by a man named Bill Merchant who has been involved with the race since 1998 as competitor, trail breaker and race director, having completed the 350-mile race eight times in all three disciplines, as well as completing the 1,000-mile course with his wife, Kathi, in 2008, has become an event that is synonymous with total autonomy, thanks to Bill and several veteran racers agreeing that race support should be kept to a minimum. Aside from the distance and remoteness of the race, it is this that sets it apart from others, allowing racers to make decisions for themselves about what to carry, when to rest and when it is safe to travel. There are no designated or marked routes, only mandatory checkpoints that racers must pass through.

In order to explain the reasoning behind this, Bill Merchant quotes the words of one of the legends and winner of the early sled dog races, Joe May: 'Sometimes when you offer too much support you cheat the true adventurer out of a big part of why they are on the trail. They come to race, to confront and hopefully overcome whatever is thrown their way. To solve problems for them diminishes the experience.'

Both the 350-mile and the 1,000-mile races start at Knik and follow the Iditarod Trail to McGrath, with the 1,000-milers continuing up the trail to Nome.

The only support provided during the races are three snow machines, which stay ahead of the leaders as far as McGrath, and seven checkpoints where food and lodging are available. There are also three food drops along the route. Other than that, the website states: 'Between checkpoints the racers have each other'.

For those continuing to Nome, they will do so along lengthy stretches of uninhabited trail completely on their own, except for one food drop provided between McGrath and Ruby/Shageluk at a place perhaps prophetically called 'Cripple'. Village stores and post offices (where packages may be sent ahead of the race) are used to re-supply with food and fuel for stoves, while schools are often the only places racers will find to spend the night.

Who would do this?

Over the years, participants in this race have come from the USA/Alaska, Italy, the UK, Slovenia, Canada, the Czech Republic, Germany, Netherlands, France, Austria, New Zealand, Switzerland and South Africa, and from all different walks of life, but they all have one thing in common – a sense of adventure.

As Bill Merchant puts it: 'This race is not for everyone. A mistake at the wrong time and place in the Alaskan winter wilderness could cost you your fingers, toes or even your life. At times, the only rescue will be self-rescue.'

Mental Miscellany

- Applicants have to qualify for this event and must go through an interview process with the race organisers.
- Final cut-off times are 10 days, 23 hours, 59 minutes and 59 seconds for the 350-milers, and 30 days, 23 hours, 59 minutes, 59 seconds for the 1,000-milers.
- All entrants (except previous finishers) must pay a refundable bond, which will be used if help is requested from the Iditarod Trail Crews during the race (except in life-threatening or serious-injury situations).
- The 1,000-mile foot record as at 2012 stands at 20 days, 14 hours, 45 minutes (northern route) and 20 days, 7 hours, 17 minutes (southern route).
- There is no prize money in this race, although the first overall male and female winners and first male and female runners in the 350-mile and 1,000-mile races will receive free entry for the following year.
- The race is worth four points towards qualification for the Ultra-Trail du Mont-Blanc race.
- American Tim Hewitt has finished the 1,000-mile race at Nome seven times!

For further information, please visit: www.iditarodtrailinvitational. com

MASOCHISTS APPLY HERE...

PIECE OF STRING FUN RUN
UK
Keep running until you're told to stop

The Piece of String 'fun run' could probably be best described as diabolic in nature. According to the *Oxford English Dictionary*, 'diabolic' means 'of the Devil; devilish, inhumanly cruel or wicked'. The run is also, according to its website, 'The world's most pointless race'.

Dreamed up by a man who has run 3,200 miles to cross the United States, to name but one of his many ultra-running achievements, James Adams came up with the idea of a race with no known end when he realised that during every race he ran, he reached a point where he just wanted it to finish and would ask himself, 'How much further have I got to go or how much longer must I endure this pain?' A glance at his watch or a well-positioned mile-marker and he had his answer and a level of comfort knowing the end was if not in sight, at least a finite distance or time away and with that knowledge he could persuade himself to hang in there, knowing relief would be his within the next however long or however far.

But what if he didn't know how long or how far? What if, at the point when his big toe nail had just fallen off or a blister had just burst or his lungs and legs were screaming for mercy, he had no idea how much longer he must live with the pain and had to just keep on going no matter how bad he felt? There would be no comfort to be found if there was no answer to the question, just a continuing battle of mind over matter. And that, in a nutshell, is what the Piece of String race is all about, as much a psychological challenge as a physical one.

Runners who choose to accept this open-ended challenge, which is held at the end of November, do so in the full knowledge that they will have no idea as to how long they will be running and therefore no idea of how to pace the race; neither will they have any idea how much kit will be required or how much food to carry. Without such knowledge, they will not have been able to put in any specific training or preparation for the race beforehand.

What they will know is that the course will consist of various loops around Streatley (a town which sits on the River Thames at a point where the water cuts through the Ridgeway – an 85-mile chain of hills and high ground stretching from the west of England almost to the capital), where they will be given a new 'route' every time they arrive at HQ; they will also know that the routes will vary from 'x' miles to 'xx' miles; and they will further know that they must keep running these routes until the race director puts his hand on their shoulder and says, 'Congratulations, you have finished'. They will also know from the deliberately vague race data supplied on the website that it will be cold, there is likely to be rain, there will be some elevation, and the terrain will range from easy to brutal.

Some reassurance may be derived, however, from the knowledge that at least the two race directors know how long the race will be before it actually starts, although the specific race configuration will only be known once one of the runners selects an envelope from one of five – each containing a different race configuration. Whichever one that runner picks is the race.

Further reassurance may be taken from knowing that there will be cut-offs, although the runners won't know what the cut-offs are until the day arrives, and will be informed along the way how close they are to each one. There will also be aid stations – spaced at approximately every 10km to 100 miles – bag drops and food. However, no support crews are allowed on the grounds that this would, 'make things less miserable'.

In order to enter the race, runners must submit a paragraph about why they want to take part, as well as a photo displaying their own abject misery. Such pictures are then displayed on the race website, and currently offer an attractive array of bloodied toenails, blistered feet, cracked teeth, broken limbs and swollen knees, giving the appearance of a line-up of extras for the TV drama *Casualty*.

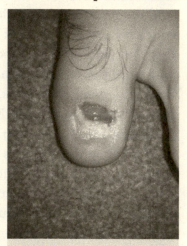

The 'experimental' inaugural race, which took place in 2012, unfortunately coincided with the worst flooding the Thames had seen in many years, causing river banks to collapse into its wildly thrashing waters. With Streatley sitting so low on the river, the 10 fearless runners who took part in the race were faced with negotiating

Not for the fainthearted

exceptionally muddy and flooded riverside paths, as well as the challenging hills, forests and trails that rise up and surround the town.

In the end, the two competitors who finished the 2012 race ran for more than 30 hours and covered a distance in excess of 100 miles.

Who would do this?

Sam Robson, a 31-year-old cancer research bioinformatician (someone who looks at large amounts of biological data with a computer to try and spot patterns), and ultra runner, participated in the Piece of String Fun Run in 2012 and 2013. Sam was one of the two finishers in 2012. This extract, about his experience of the

2012 race, was taken with kind permission from Sam Robson's blog: www.constantforwardmotion.blogspot.com

The main idea here is psychological. The only information we'd been given was to be in Streatley at midnight on Saturday. We had no idea what kit we needed or how to pace ourselves.

My approach was simply not to think about it and I went into the race expecting to run a really, really long way at whatever pace felt comfortable. I didn't use my Garmin [GPS], aiming instead to run on feel alone. And I had about 60 hours' worth of audio books to keep me entertained – my brain is not a place I want to be for a long period of time with nothing to distract it! As for kit, I just took everything I owned.

A few people pulled out of the race, so there were 10 of us at the start. The weather had been terrible all week and the Thames had burst its banks in several locations.

As the start time of 00:01 approached, we had our race briefing – 'Please don't die out there' – and were assigned our fate – by me. I had a choice of five envelopes, one with a ball of string, one with a g-string, one with a science-y string-theory image and two other string-related images that I can't remember. I went for the science-y one.

With a sudden lack of fanfare, we were told to 'get going', and headed out into the night along the Ridgeway until we found the checkpoint where we would be given our next instructions.

My one and only game plan at this point was to be first into the first checkpoint just in case that would be the end of it!

I found myself running with Wouter Hamelinck and we kept a good pace together. After crossing under the A34, we saw car lights ahead. A slightly cheeky sprint meant I made it there first – but this was not the end. Not by a long shot! I topped up my water and we turned round to re-tread our steps back to Streatley.

I decided to hold back a bit now I knew we could potentially

be in for a long haul. Racing this type of event is odd because if you want to win your only option is to always be in front. But there's no point being in the lead if you don't finish. It's a toughie. From here on in, I was on my own.

Our next section was a pleasant run around the Chiltern Valley Way – hills, woods and trails. The wooded sections were difficult to follow at night, though arrows painted on the trees helped keep us on track. At one point I went off-track but could just make out the road, so set my compass to make sure I was going in the right direction.

Our next task was to run the same section again. I returned to find quite a few people had already pulled out.

Next we ran a section incorporating both the Thames Tow Path and the eastern side of the Ridgeway. Despite a diversion to avoid the worst of the flooding, there were several sections where getting through involved wading knee-deep through the Thames. Wouter and I ploughed straight through but some of the runners chose to find diversions.

It was around this time that the weather started to worsen. It started with just a drizzle but it got worse as the day progressed.

Our next little jaunt followed the start of the Chilton Valley way before diverting off northeast onto the eastern section of the Ridgeway again. This was good fun and involved some surprisingly tough hills. Navigation outside of the woods was going well and I was plodding along quite nicely. I'd started the day feeling quite tired and as if I was going down with a cold, but my legs felt great, and while my chest ached it didn't feel any worse than when I'd started.

I arrived at the aid station, had a chat then headed back out for the return leg.

By this point it was getting dark and the lack of sleep was catching up with me. I decided to sacrifice a bit of time and lay down for half an hour to recharge. I was also soaking so changed my clothes to a fresh set. It's amazing the difference this made and when I left for the next section I was feeling really positive again.

Unfortunately, this section was bloody tough – firstly because it didn't follow a particular named path so it was easy to take the wrong footpath and end up off course; secondly, we were back to running through woods in the dark for long periods of time; and finally, the weather was particularly horrendous by this point, turning most of the forest routes into an unrunable bog. Between having to check and re-check my navigation and being constantly stopped dead in my tracks by the sludgy mud, running was almost impossible. This led to me getting colder and colder and more and more miserable. I was not having fun.

When I came into Nuney Wood, I was having difficulty working out my precise location. I had my iPhone with me so used the Maps app to try and pinpoint where I was. Unfortunately the app does not automatically orientate itself to North, as I found out after running the wrong way trying to find the path I should have been on. By this point I was cold, tired, pissed off, wet and generally not having fun. Annoyingly my legs were really not tired at all; I just felt like I couldn't use them.

I phoned James Adams [race director] to let him know I was thinking of pulling out and he told me a few of the others had gone off course so this section was going to be a bit of a write-off. He said that if I wanted to carry on, I could head back along the roads. Two of the aid station crew kindly drove along with me to make sure I wasn't taken out by a car along the way.

Once I got going I started to feel good again. I was still wet and tired but was able to move and keep my body temperature up. In fact, I was moving better than someone who had just run over 80 miles had any right to, a nice fast pace that got me back into Streatley in no time. There was only one small moment where I nearly fell asleep on my feet but luckily the oncoming traffic woke me up.

I arrived back at the Streatley checkpoint and saw Wouter sitting with his shoes off. This was it! I'd made it to the end. And not a moment too soon as the lack of sleep was really taking its toll and I wasn't sure I could go on for another loop.

Yeah right! As if it would be that easy. Wouter was just taking a breather before heading back out again back along the Ridgeway. I had some soup and tried to psych myself back up again to get back out there.

So off I went back along the Ridgeway with a disturbing sense of déjà vu having run this exact route more than 24 hours ago. But now the weather was much worse. I have never encountered winds as strong.

Annoyingly, it was a headwind, making running into it very tough going. It was also very rainy, but as long as I kept moving and avoided cooling down it was fine. Unfortunately, between the wind and the churned-up bog that had resulted from runners going back and forth along the route and my increasing inability to ignore the fact that I hadn't slept in 48 hours, I was finding it difficult to do anything more than a zombie shuffle towards the next checkpoint. One problem with being able to see the checkpoint from a distance is that you never feel like you're getting any closer to it!

I arrived at the checkpoint and took a half-hour break before running a 10km loop through Compton village. While only a small village, finding my way along the exact footpaths was difficult with the scale of the map.

Next I had to continue along the Ridgeway for two miles to the next checkpoint. As I ran under the A34 again and saw the lights in the distance I again had that weird déjà vu feeling. It was tough going with the wind and slight incline making me feel as if I was getting nowhere.

As I approached the checkpoint, the wind was so loud I couldn't hear a thing and with all the head torches I couldn't see anything either. I ran right up to the van to get out of the wind and was finally able to take in my surroundings. James Adams was there. 'I guess you know what this means, don't you?'

Actually no! Since I'd started falling asleep on my feet, I'd arrived at every checkpoint hoping it was the end, but this was the one checkpoint I knew wasn't the end. Shows what I know.

Yes, indeed, after more than 30 hours of running, I had survived the inaugural Piece of String Fun Run.

The main thing that kept me going no matter how I felt was the knowledge that if I pulled out only to find there were only five miles to go, I would be really pissed off. More to the point, my wife Jen would be pissed off because I wouldn't be able to shut up about it!

I think I had the right mental attitude – just run! I wasn't thinking about times or distances and was planning on it being stupidly long so that if it was short, it would be a nice surprise. I think this is probably the most important mental aspect. Get comfortable and run until somebody says stop.

In some regards, I might even say this is the most pure form of race. No pacing strategies. No timings. No GPS. Just running to the best of your abilities for as long as you can.

All things considered I had a lot of fun.

Mental Miscellany

- The 2012 race started at 00:01.
- 16 runners started the 2013 race.
- England was considered the ideal location for something different, to challenge people who'd already been challenged conventionally, with no mountains, jungles, deserts or tundra – just the British winter to contend with.
- The website course map is a map of the world.

For further information, please visit: www.centurionrunning.com

THE BARKLEY MARATHONS
TENNESSEE, USA

100 miles of nature's most gruelling obstacles –
within 60 hours

Waking up to the sound of a conch shell being blown sounds romantic – until you realise that the sound signifies just one hour to the start of a race that hugs its reputation for hardness and likelihood of failure to its chest like an undersized bra.

The fact that none of the runners in the race know what time the conch-shell blowing or the race start will take place, other than some time between 11pm and 11am, means that anticipation will have kept most of them awake all night so they will stand on the start line already sleep-deprived. Indeed they may be so sleepy that they will miss the lighting of the race director's cigarette, which indicates the start of the race.

That race director, Gary Cantrell, who incidentally has never completed his own race, says of this event: 'All other races are set up for you to succeed; the Barkley is set up for you to fail.'

He does not lie, even gaining entry into the race is a mystery, deliberately so, increasing mental stress before the race even begins, with no website, and no course map or directions supplied until just hours prior to the start of the race; even then the directions are notoriously hard to follow.

Should hopeful competitors actually manage to find a way to enter, they then have to complete a bizarre questionnaire before their entry is accepted. They also have to bring a licence plate for Cantrell's collection, which he displays next to the yellow starting gate, and write an essay on 'Why I should be allowed to run in the Barkley'.

The field of around 35 is then selected from those who have fulfilled the above requirements and completed the race before, or athletes with impressive ultra-running credentials and veterans, plus one sacrificial virgin.

Cantrell's inspiration for such a unique race stemmed from hearing about Martin Luther King junior's assassin, James Earl Ray, escaping from the Brushy Mountain State Penitentiary and making only 13km/8 miles after running for around 55 hours in the woods. He was found lying face down in a pile of leaves, scratched to pieces and utterly defeated by the terrain. Cantrell apparently said to himself, 'I could do at least 100 miles', and hence, the Barkley was born. The prison closed in 2009 and now forms part of the course.

The uniqueness of the event lies not only in the difficulty of entering, nor the fact that all the obstacles are natural – such as vertical hills that can only be conquered by running up them or suffer sliding back down and meeting flesh-ripping, head-high briars and thorns, and impossible-to-cross streams, all of which have been given appropriate names, such as 'Testicle Spectacle', 'Big Hell', 'Rat Jaw', and 'Bad Thing' – but also in that each runner must find between 9 and 11 books (the number varies each year), which are hidden around the course, and remove the page corresponding to their race number from each book as proof of completion.

As if all that isn't enough to contend with, temperatures range from freezing cold to blisteringly hot on the same day, cut-off times are strictly enforced, and the only prize is getting to stop.

Every time a runner gives up (which is often), Cantrell, who sits by the yellow starting gate with his dogs, smoking Camel cigarettes and drinking soda throughout the race, plays 'Taps' on his bugle in homage to the triumph of nature over man.

On the plus side, the entry fee is a mere US$1.60 – representing one penny for each mile of the 100-mile race plus the 60-mile fun run (seriously), held at the same time.

The race itself is held in Tennessee's Frozen Head State Park in late March/early April and consists of a 32km/20-mile loop with no aid stations except water at two points, which the 100-milers must complete five times, with loops three and four being run in opposite directions and loop five being the runner's choice. Each loop must be completed within the 12-hour cut-off time. Sixty-milers run three loops, and each loop must be completed within 13 hours, 20 minutes, the whole within 40 hours. There is a total accumulated vertical climb of 16,500m/54,200ft.

The race instructions give the terrain of each section and categorise it as one of three types – 'candy ass trail' (soft option), 'real trail' (harder option), or 'what?' (hard-as-nails option). Runners can then choose which of the three options to tackle at each section.

Who would do this?

Thirty-three-year-old, data analyst, ultra runner and writer, James Adams, took part in the Barkley in 2012. This extract was taken with kind permission from: www.runningandstuff.squarespace.com

I never really sleep before the start of a race, I'm too paranoid. However, I have not set an alarm for this, it will be done for me. Every noise in the campground startles me; this is no way to rest for a race.

It gets light around 7am and I decide not to bother trying to sleep anymore, it's too frustrating. Then there's a dull and distant sound of a conch shell. It's 8.11am.

I make my way uphill to the start at the yellow gate. The race director tells us there are 60 seconds till the start and that this is the time when most race directors give some good advice, but since we are here we clearly never listen to good advice anyway, so he won't bother. Everyone watches

carefully for him to light the cigarette that signifies the start. It is lit and we are off.

I wear calf guards at the start to stop my calves from being ripped open by the briars, but they're screaming from the off, so I pull the guards down. That does the trick, and I'm in for a day of laceration.

I take the candy ass trail and follow some guys who know where to go for the first book. Getting there feels like a landmark.

After the first book, Barkley really starts; without any clue or landmark people just seem to throw themselves down a ravine covered in dead trees. I follow. After some bushwhacking we hit a stream and get a second book.

Back on the candy ass again and a chance to run a bit. Back up to the top of a peak and the third book.

We're about halfway through the loop and have completed about 5,500 feet of ascent and descent.

Climbing out of a ditch and navigating some barely noticeable trail, I collect the sixth book in some rocks and turn a corner, to see one of the most intimidating sights I've ever seen: the Testicle Spectacle, 800 feet of climb in 0.58 miles, and it's not even in the top five of the big hills here.

It's getting hot and the climb is exposed. Heading up the 'real trail' at some points, the climb is more than 45 degrees. I slip around all over the place in inadequate shoes and grab a triangular rock to use as a pick-me-up, delighting the camera crew at the top looking for evidence of suffering.

From the top it's straight back down the other side via some arse sliding.

Pig Head Creek – this is even harder than the Testicle. I stagger and grab onto trees and rocks to stop myself falling back down. It's the first time ever my mind has given up before my body.

A huge 40-degree lump of earth shoots up in front of me; this is Rat Jaw. There's a cable that can be used to help climb, but it goes over some of the worst parts, so instead it's another hands digging in the ground slog to the first bench (a temporary flattening of a hill). I think I'm at the end when I head up through a crevice, which takes me to the second half of the climb. At least it's been cleared of briars, well at least the six-foot-tall ones. It's vertical. I grab hold of clumps of something to give myself balance. At the top is the seventh book. Two-thirds of the way in, nearly there, right? Wrong.

Going back down Rat Jaw is almost as horrendous as going up, tripping over thorns; if I properly fall I'm not stopping till the bottom.

There follows a vertical drop of about 10m leading to the road by the prison. The briars are head high, but eventually I reach the tunnel under the prison. There's a stream running through it; I could avoid getting wet if I balance along a short beam that runs along the middle but I just splash through.

I choose to get out of the stream by wading through deeper water onto a bank, rather than climb over a 7ft wall, the only other option. Book eight is hanging outside the prison.

In every other race, hills can be made easier just by going slower; here, standing still means sliding down, like being on a reverse escalator. I leap from tree to tree, taking about 10 steps up and clutching hold of something as I climb my own height one feeble stutter at a time. My heart feels like it's going to rip out through my body. This isn't even about hills anymore; it's about my fitness. I'm nowhere near in [good enough] shape to do this properly. My legs and lungs are okay, but my heart is making a desperate attempt to leave my body.

To make things worse, some of the trees I leap for snap in my hands, they're dead. I try not to look up, just head down and keep crawling. It must take an hour to get to the top of Bad Thing; finding the book is easy.

I don't know why the name Big Hell seemed less intimidating than all the others; if I had only two words to describe what I now climb the first would be 'big', the second would be 'hell'. This is the steepest yet and it's starting to get dark. It's cooled down some too but the sweat drips from my head every time I look down.

Barkley is also different in that in other races groups of people get together for combined strength, helping each other through the low times: here when people get together if one person decides to quit, everyone else will follow.

I put my head torch on before reaching the top and find the last book. I'm going to miss the 12-hour loop cut-off to stay in the 100-mile race but can stay for the fun run. For me though it's over; I'm not tired, but the thought of ripping my heart out at all those hills again and in the dark is unthinkable.

What I really wanted from this race was to reach the end of my physical limits and say this race beat my body but not my mind. That didn't happen; I quit long before my body was done. My legs could have gone on, I just didn't want to. This race beat me in ways I've never been beaten before. So now I have a new obsession: I want to finish this race, or die trying.

Mental Miscellany

- The inaugural Barkley Marathons took place in 1986.
- Since its inception in 1986, only 14 out of approximately 800 runners have completed the 100 within the official 60-hour cut-off.
- The first person to complete the 100-mile race was a Brit, Mark Williams, in 1995 in a time of 59 hours, 28 minutes.
- A new course record of 52 hours, 3 minutes was set in 2012.
- Since 1986, more than 30 runners have failed to reach the first book.
- Cut-off times are 12 hours per loop for 100 miles/13 hours, 20 minutes per loop for 60 miles.

For further information, please visit: your own initiative!

GET DOWN –
AND DIRTY...

LA TRANSBAIE
FRANCE

Race away from an incoming tide – Somme Estuary

When people think of the Somme in northern France, one of two things most likely come to mind – first, and most sadly, the World War One battle in 1916 when more than a million soldiers were wounded or killed; second, and rather more happily, the beauty of a bay which claims membership to the exclusive 'Most beautiful bays in the world club' and is famous for its vast expanses of open water, marshes and dunes, making it one of the best places on Earth to spy on migrating birds.

What probably does not spring to mind, however, is the vision of almost 6,000 runners, many wearing fancy dress, slipping, sliding, or in some cases actually running, across the muddy bay in a race that will take them from Saint-Valery-Sur-Somme to Le Crotoy, and back again.

The race, which began in 1989 as the result of a challenge between friends to see if they could make it out across the bay and back before the tide turned and swept them off to an untimely and watery death, takes place every year on a Sunday afternoon on varying dates, usually in June, when the tide is low enough.

Due to its unique geological aspects, the course is set out by teams of voluntary stakers, who carry out terrain analysis over a two-week period immediately prior to the race and mark out the course accordingly – a process known as 'marking the bay'.

Starting at low tide, the runners will face a mixture of terrain from asphalt paving stones, road, water, sand (some wet, some soft, some hard) and holes (created by the tide), to mud – mostly mud – thick, deep, sticky, energy-sapping, trainer-sucking, inglorious mud! As the website rather charmingly puts it (although the order and exactness of words may differ slightly in translation): 'It is the return run on the double mandatory passage that is often the location of falls and loss of shoes ... what makes beautiful shared laughter of the audience and viewers' – yes, that's right, the whole event is filmed live by French TV!

In short, the course is approximately 16km/10 miles (dependent upon the route across the bay), but is considered to be the equivalent of a half-marathon owing to the difficulty of the terrain and, according to the race organisers, it requires both physical and psychological endurance qualities – most particularly because in the middle of the bay there is no possibility of abandoning the race.

That said, they do have helicopters on standby for those not making it back before the returning tide swallows them up, although the tide is relatively slow and the helicopters tend to be used more for ill or injured runners rather than those in imminent danger of drowning.

Who would do this?

John Wellington is the managing editor of the *The Mail on Sunday*. He was 52 when he took part in the Transbaie race in 2008.

It was a one-off. I had a friend with a holiday home in the local village; he'd seen the race and said it looked fun, so we decided to give it a go.

At the time I was looking for a way to raise money for charity and thought this was an excuse to do the race.

It was about nine miles, but they say it's the equivalent of a half-marathon due to the difficulty of the terrain – mud, hard and soft sand and waist-high water at the deepest point.

You get covered in mud. I'd never done anything like it before. Just one London Park Run of 5km, and after La Transbaie I did a 10-mile run at Haywards Heath. I did do a bit of training for the race – about three miles each week around the local reservoir.

It was fun. I would recommend it.

John not only completed the run without getting caught by the tide, he also raised enough money to build a school library in Thailand.

Mental Miscellany

- In 2013, there were 5,921 runners.
- The 2013 race was won in 58 minutes, 04 seconds.
- The winning time is usually around one hour, with stragglers not caught by the rising tide finishing in around three hours.
- Year-on-year results and performances are difficult to compare as the course changes according to different parameters such as the terrain, tides and weather.
- Medical certificates are required to enter the race.
- The race organisers describe the race as: 'Better than a spa, a rejuvenating experience in a beautiful landscape. A unique experience guaranteed.'

For further information, please visit: www.transbaie.com

THE GRIM
UK

A series of filthy dirty races + a duathlon –
in daylight and at night

From Army-vehicle testing tracks to motocross circuits, the GRIM series of events are, at least according to the website, 'tough but fun'.

The series consists of four events, the first of which falls in May and is known as the 'Beast in the East'. Held at the motocross circuit at Swanley in Kent, competitors will run two laps of the (approximately) 5.6km/3.5-mile circuit, which comprises a mix of mud, sand, hills, trails and grass, as well as the motocross circuit itself. The course is labelled as 'extremely tough', boasting downhills that are as arduous as the ups and for which the organisers recommend specific pre-race hill training. The race starts at 1030, averages a finish time of around one hour and has a limit of 1,500 runners.

Next on the GRIM series calendar comes a combination event consisting of a duathlon known as the 'Grimathlon' or Grim Duathlon, which is held during the day, and a run of approximately 10km/6 miles, known as 'Blackout', held at night-time. Competitors may choose to enter one or both events, which are held at the British Army's vehicle testing circuit at Aldershot, Hampshire in October.

The Grim Duathlon is billed as one of the toughest short-course duathlons in the country, with the run section taking in trails, hills, mud, water, cammo nets, moguls and the sand dune on the vehicle testing circuit, while the bike section, consisting of two 10km/6-mile circuits, offers a widely varied, mainly wet, terrain of rocks, sand dune, sandy paths and a hill circuit, some of which will necessitate competitors carrying their bikes. The race has a limit of 1,000 competitors and starts at 1030, with finishing times ranging from one-and-a-half hours to more than three.

Should the Grimathlon leave you wanting more, however, there is the option to follow on with the 'Blackout', which starts at 1900 on the same day and is described as 'dirty, dark and wet'. The race itself consists of running two 5.6km/3.5-mile loops in the dark with only a head torch and LED course-markers to light your way through the ghostly woods and help you negotiate the sand dune, rocks, large 'puddles' and bog. Teams are recommended for this event, though individuals are also welcome if they are brave enough to face alone what is described as a 'daunting, disturbing, spine-chilling, grim blackout'. The race is limited to 1,000 runners.

The final race in the GRIM series falls in late November/early December and is such a popular event that due to the limited numbers able to run at once, it is now held over two consecutive days; runners may choose whether to race on the Saturday or Sunday.

Entitled simply the 'GRIM', this race takes place again at Aldershot's Army-vehicle testing tracks and is around 12km/8 miles long with a mixed terrain, mainly wet and boggy with the addition of trails, hills, nets, moguls and that all-testing, calf-stressing sand dune. The race starts at 1030 each day and is limited to 3,500 runners.

The race organisers offer the same advice for all of their races, namely not to wear brand-new white trainers, or spikes – the paths are too stony and they might endanger other competitors when crawling under netting!

Who would do this?

Wannabe soldiers and motocross racers – and anyone who likes getting down and dirty.

Mental Miscellany

- Competitors must be aged 17 or over.
- All races are open to teams or individuals.
- It is recommended that anyone considering entering any of the GRIM races should be able to comfortably run 8km/5 miles without stopping.
- The winning times for the GRIM in 2012 were 50 minutes, 51 seconds (men) and 54 minutes, 04 seconds (women).
- The winning times for the Grimathlon in 2013 were 1 hour, 32 minutes, 27 seconds (men) and 1 hour, 53 minutes, 41 seconds (women).
- The winning times for the Blackout in 2013 were 49 minutes, 50 seconds (men) and 59 minutes, 41 seconds (women).
- The winning times for the Beast in the East in 2013 were 41 minutes, 45 seconds (men) and 52 minutes, 49 seconds (women).

For further information, please visit: www.grimchallenge.co.uk

AND DIRTIER STILL...

OBSTACLE MUD-RUNNING
AN OVERVIEW

Following hot on the heels of the running boom of recent years and all the 5ks, 10ks, half-marathons and marathons, the latest craze to hit the popularity stakes in both the States and the UK is mud-running.

Not to be mistaken for cross-country running, which is a serious matter of running as fast as possible from the start to the finish and beating all your rivals, mud-running is a combination of fanciful fun and physical endeavour put together in the form of a military-style assault course and run on an old-fashioned cross-country course – the type used in the years before TV demanded courses resemble horse-racing tracks with man-made hillocks and the occasional water jump, rather than wooded trails with real hills, mud that came up to your elbows and wildly thrashing icy rivers.

For those bored with running the streets of famous cities or churning out the miles on a treadmill, mud-running brings its own unique style of racing and training, with competitions often held in beautiful parts of the countryside or in the grounds of national parks or stately homes. Not that you'll notice the scenery as you plunge into a skip full of icy water that makes your brain freeze, or fall face-first into a mud bath.

For the essence of mud-running is not so much about the mud and the running as it is about the obstacles – of which there are many and various. The obstacles are all given descriptive names that are pretty much self-explanatory, such as the delightful sounding 'ice enema' and the rather shocking 'electric eels'.

In short, mud runs usually consist of a run of around 10km/6 miles over a muddy countryside course interspersed with obstacles. Obstacles to be overcome, as well as the aforementioned brain-freezing iced bath and the shocking electric eels will have participants scaling 8-ft walls, skinning shins while climbing ropes, bloodying knees on cargo nets and singeing ankle hairs on gasoline-soaked flaming logs or hay bales. Although obstacles can be missed out if a participant finds them too difficult, they will incur penalty points as a result.

Participants may enter a mud race as individuals or as part of a team – some companies use mud races as a team-building exercise for employees.

For some reason these sort of events seem to hold an almost magnetic appeal for those who have taken up some form of running in recent years, with the larger events, such as the Spartan Race, the Warrior Dash and Tough Mudder, all American-born races which hold a series of races throughout the year in both the States and the UK, seeing annual participation levels rise from the low thousands to almost one million in three years. The same meteoric rise is true of the UK event, Tough Guy, which started out 25 years ago and was undoubtedly the forerunner for this type of event, describing itself as the toughest survival ordeal in the world.

But the real heart of these events is the camaraderie – it is not about winning, it is far more about helping your fellow man – and should any participant require assistance during the race, they are encouraged to ask another participant for help rather than a race official.

Despite this, or maybe because of it, participants need to be reasonably fit, not just for the running part of the event but in order to be able to help others, for example hauling someone over the top of a high wall or pulling themselves up a rope, both of which will require a reasonable amount of upper-body strength. Circuit training is therefore recommended preparation for a mud race.

It is also about fancy dress – or lack of it – with many men choosing to take part wearing nothing more than a pair of thongs – apparently it's easier to wash mud off skin than it is material!

This may explain why many of these events attract a lot of spectator support!

More recently, longer and tougher races based on the original shorter versions have been set up, which offer greater and far longer challenges, testing a participant's mental strength and physical endurance to its limit. These have been labelled, 'Death Races', and carry the logo: 'Every man dies, but not every man lives'.

The races are billed as being for 48 hours plus – they have actually been known to last for more than 70 hours – and claim to break participants physically, mentally and emotionally. They also claim that 90 per cent of participants won't make the finish. All Death Races are unsupported.

The summer challenge, which takes place in June in Vermont, comes with very simple rules – don't cut the course and don't litter; likewise the winter challenge, also in Vermont, but this time in January/February. The winter race also comes with a cold-temperature warning.

Organisers claim that Death Races will present participants with the 'totally unexpected and the totally insane'.

In addition to the summer and winter challenges, there is also a 'Team Death Race', which has not yet been set up but promises to be brutal once it is, together with a 'Travelling Death Race', whereby the organisers transport the participants to an unknown destination to partake in the race. The rules for this race state simply, 'Do not die. Do not get left behind.'

For further information, please visit: www.youmaydie.com and www.peak.com

TOUGH GUY
UK

A demanding, one-day, military-style
survival ordeal – Staffordshire

In the bleak mid-winter on his 600-acre farm in Staffordshire, England, gentleman and former British soldier, Billy Wilson (also known as 'Mr Mouse'), dons a scarlet military jacket complete with off-white, scrubbing-brush-size epaulets that are almost a perfect match for his off-white, scrubbing-brush-sized moustache and prepares to welcome around 5,000 men and women on to his land to voluntarily partake in an event that claims to be the most demanding one-day survival ordeal in the world.

It is an ordeal that will require them to cover a mud-based distance of around 12km/8 miles and overcome up to 25 obstacles, during which they will suffer electrocution from live wires, negotiate barbed wire, run through searing flames, climb mountainous walls, scramble down netting, dive into a freezing lake and crawl through water-filled tunnels, among other things.

Prior to the event, each participant will be required to sign their own 'Death Warrant', which will act as a disclaimer against the organiser should injury or death occur. Indeed, in the 25 years the event has been running, there have been two fatalities;

aside from death, there are also warnings of risks such as burns, dehydration, hypothermia, acrophobia, claustrophobia, electric shocks, joint dislocation and broken bones.

And yet, ever since Billy Wilson came up with his idea for the event, the number of people wanting to literally risk life and limb has increased year-on-year and the event itself has been the precursor to a number of other similar military-style, obstacle-based survival events now being held throughout the world.

So, what can Mr Wilson's guests expect in return for their apparent willingness to amuse and entertain their host and enliven an otherwise potentially dull and boring winter in the countryside?

Well, held in January in the worst of England's wintry weather, the so-called Tough Guy Winter Challenge gets underway with the deafening firing of a cannon gun, which sends the runners racing, often on their backsides, down a steep, muddy hillside and across boggy countryside until they reach the first obstacle.

To add to the fun, marshals dressed as commandos fire amphibious tank gun blanks and release exploding flares and smoke bombs over the heads of the competitors throughout the race, causing chaos and confusion.

Every year, the 25 obstacles are varied to incorporate a different range of tortuous tests designed to push competitors to test their mettle to its absolute limit. To give you a taste of what these might entail, here are just a few of the imaginatively named obstacles that might be on offer:

'Fiery Holes' – series of muddy water ditches followed by burning bales of hay.
'Vietcong Torture Chamber Tunnels' – underground tunnels created from Vietcong.
'Stalag Escape' – a 20ft mud crawl beneath barbed wire.
'The Anaconda' – series of large concrete pipes with overhanging electric wires.
'Jesus Bridge' – a bridge of barrels and planks of wood.
'Viagra Falls' – a steep, muddy hill slide beneath overhanging electric eels.

'Dan's Deceiver' – a vertical cargo net followed by a declined cargo net.

'The Tiger' – a 40ft A–frame crossing through hanging electrified cables.

'Brandenburger Gate' – a 40ft vertical wall climb.

'Torture Chamber' – a dark, partially-flooded tunnel, with hanging batons and electric cables.

It is worth noting that to this day Mr Wilson is proud to claim that there has never been an actual winner of the Tough Guy event, stating that although there may have been 'a first person to cross the finish line', they would have been disqualified for not completing every single discipline in the appropriate or correct way – at least according to Mr Wilson's interpretation of his own rules!

However, he does go on to state that the event is not so much about winning, but more about camaraderie and overcoming one's personal fears.

Given the growing numbers of participants every year, it would seem that those two facets alone are all the motivation people today need to voluntarily face the types of torture that soldiers in the past were forced to endure during combat.

Who would do this?

Adam Seldon, a 21-year-old student, has taken part in the Tough Guy competition twice. Thanks to Adam for the following account.

In my final year at school I drifted in to signing up for an upcoming tradition in my House – sending a group of us to Tough Guy. In a school where a male culture still dominated, my lack of stature meant I was unable to flourish in the prime forum of masculinity, namely rugby. Tough Guy was thus a time to show my credentials on a different stage.

Despite the seemingly exclusive title, 'Tough Guy' is any-thing but. You certainly do have to be tough, but you don't need to be a guy. Many women take part, as do many men who don't consider themselves one of the 'guys'. So it's not just for the aspiring alpha-male like myself. Many of the 5,000 who take part each year choose to run it in standard cold-weather gear, but many others will face the challenge clad in fluorescent dresses, a Borat-esque 'mankini', or almost totally naked. I conservatively went for the former approach on the now two occasions that I've done it (I got a team together at my university last year).

I was given ominous accounts about people dying every year and up to half not completing it. In fact, I would hazard that around 1/6 don't complete it and only two have died in the history of Tough Guy, so technically that makes it 'safer' than the marathon.

That's the only way in which Tough Guy could be described as 'safe'. The first part of the course, the cross-country, is fairly leisurely – perhaps to lull you into a false sense of security. What follows the cross-country is a series of obstacles, which get progressively worse.

On the two occasions I've done it, it's been winter. Upon my arrival the first time, the ice was being broken up for the anticipated contestants. It's the cold that stops you from finishing – in 2001, 700 contestants suffered from hypothermia; ambulance crews in bright yellow clothing line the course, with silver sheets at the ready for those who can't take the cold any longer. I'm not sure whether I found their presence reassuring or unnerving.

The race climaxes with the 'Killing Fields', with the most infamous obstacles, such as the underwater tunnels, where you have to go fully underwater on several occasions, and the one I most squirm at, the 'Horror Chamber', where crawling contestants have to try and avoid electrically charged wire in the pitch black.

I will take part in Tough Guy again. Despite the worries that linger within, there's lots to look forward to. There's the fun of training as a team; jumping into rivers, rolling through snow, to prepare yourself for the water. Then on the day itself, there's the running with other members of the team. On both occasions I've run in a team of three and on the first occasion one part of our motley crew was fundamental in ensuring the others made it round.

The camaraderie with strangers is striking too. As people run, trip, slide over a series of steep hills, hundreds thunder together anthems such as, 'Oggy oggy oggy! Oy oy oy!' There are countless occasions on the course where you require assistance from others – a leg over the wall, a hand up after you've slipped over in the mud. Often, people flag towards the end, when the cold means you can't feel your limbs, you're violently shaking and your mind is numb, 'that time in the body when the blood stops flowing through the brain', as Mr Mouse [Billy Wilson] puts it. The encouragement of strangers, both on the sidelines and from fellow contestants, is a sight to behold.

Tough Guy tests the limits of the human mind. Because of this, witnessing and participating in Tough Guy is an affirmation of the depths of the human spirit.'

Mental Miscellany

- Minimum age is 16, no maximum age.
- Up to one-third of participants fail to finish in a typical race.
- Since 1998, Tough Guy has also held a summer challenge in July called 'Nettle Warrior'. The course is essentially the same as the winter challenge, but incorporates two laps of an area known as 'The Killing Fields', which contains extra-strength, armpit-high, stinging nettles.
- Tough Guy also organise a triathlon event and events for kids aged 10–16, called 'Tough Tykes'.

For further information, please visit: www.toughguy.co.uk

TOUGH MUDDER
WORLDWIDE

19km/12 miles– Special Forces-designed muddy obstacle race
+ 24-hour Tough Mudder World Championships

Okay, so you've run a few races over a variety of distances and terrain and now you're looking for something new, something different to further test your physical and mental ability.

Enter Tough Mudder – a company co-founded in 2010 by friends, Guy Livingstone and Will Dean, two Brits living in New York, following Will's original concept developed while at Harvard Business School which culminated in the setting up of a company specialising in hardcore obstacle courses designed by the Special Forces to test all-round strength, stamina, mental grit and camaraderie.

And so the first Tough Mudder event was held in May 2010 at Bear Creek ski resort near Allentown, Pennsylvania, attracting more than 4,000 participants. By 2013, there were 53 events held in the USA and four other countries including the UK, and in 2014 there are 60 events planned in the States, Australia, New Zealand, South Africa, Canada, Mexico, Asia, France, Switzerland, Austria, Germany, Belgium, Poland, Netherlands, Denmark and Sweden, as well as the UK and Ireland.

In May 2013, just three years after its inaugural event, Tough Mudder announced that it had received one million registrations for its events. So, you see, you are not alone.

The Tough Mudder website claims its events are all about the challenge rather than the race; it doesn't matter if you finish first or last: '... finishing equals satisfaction and helps us to find out what we're made of'.

In order to reach that pinnacle of satisfaction, participants will have to run approximately 19km/12 miles, passing through, over or under around 20 obstacles, as well as copious amounts of mud, water, fire, ice and live electricity.

Distraction may be found in the imaginatively yet perhaps self-explanatory names accorded to the obstacles. For example, the following:

'Arctic Enema' – a dumpster (skip) filled with 32–36 tonnes/ 70–80,000 pounds of ice and water with a temperature of 1–1.5°C/34–35°F, which you dive into from a 4.6m/15-ft high plank. Once in, a barbed-wire covered plank will force you to duck your head beneath the water causing such severe shock to your system your brain will freeze and you will become completely disorientated, and without the assistance of other competitors shouting instructions, you would be unable to work out how to escape. This is what they call 'camaraderie'; or, as someone who has done it rather eloquently describes it, 'It's like eating ice cream while being kicked in the balls'.

'Everest' – a 4.6m/15-ft tall, 10.7m/35ft-wide arced obstacle made from plywood with fibre-reinforced panels on the front and such a high degree of arc and slippery surface (vegetable oil is also sometimes smeared over the surface for extra fun and spectator entertainment) that the only way to conquer it is to take a really hard, really fast, run at it and hope there is someone (anyone) at the top waiting to help haul you over the top. Assuming there is, this will, apparently, restore your faith in the kindness of strangers.

'Electroshock Therapy' – cruelly situated just two minutes from the end with the finish line in sight – this final obstacle consists of 1,000 live wires each containing 10,000 volts of electricity powered by multiple controllers to ensure even distribution. The wires are suspended from a man-made structure covering an area 6 x 13.7m/20 x 45ft, and participants must run through its muddy water clambering over strategically placed hay bales that raise them upwards to the suspended wires. Everyone will receive shocks; the designers have made sure it's impossible not to. Word on the street is, 'It doesn't tickle'.

But it does at least lead to the finish line, where you can now collect and wear your special bright orange headband with 'Tough Mudder' printed across the front in bold black letters. You can also, if you so choose, receive a 'Tough Mudder' tattoo, which can be personalised with the event date and location, and which can be added to should you decide to repeat the experience elsewhere at some future date.

Tough Mudder events also offer prizes to all finishers and a post-race party with a bar, a DJ and an awards ceremony, as well as food and drink. Oh yes, and a chance to rinse off all that mud!

Of course if all the above sounds just too easy, then there's always the World's Toughest Mudder championships to find the world's 'Toughest Mudder', which describes itself as an extreme competition, putting hardcore Tough Mudders through a gruelling 24-hour challenge.

Starting between 0800 and 0900, there is no set finish time limit but if you haven't reached halfway by the designated time, you will be shown a modified route.

Spectators are encouraged to attend with these winsome words on the web: 'Watch someone run through 10,000 volts of electricity, make their way through fire or jump off a 15ft plank into freezing cold water.'

Masochists and sadists of the world unite!

Who would do this?

Joel Richardson, a publishing assistant, and Aideen Carroll, a medical student, both aged 21, took part in a Tough Mudder event in May 2013, having decided in January that they needed to improve their fitness. Thanks to Joel Richardson for this account.

There was initial optimism of a full and intense four-month training programme, but the combination of work and study meant it was all rather squished into the last month, with runs across London and the serious consideration of whether shoving fingers

Thick mud

into plugs would constitute training for the electric shocks.

The start-line environment is incredible, with a warm-up man who almost makes you feel like you might be capable of finishing, and the chanting and chest-bumping certainly gets you pumped up.

The event itself was, predictably, tough. The early obstacles come thick and fast and, as the distance racks up, the crowds dissipate and the weight of mud stuck to your body starts to increase, so it all starts to feel a bit more like hard work.

Then there was the Electric Eel. This obstacle involves commando crawling through mud, with a forest of electrified wires hanging down. I led the way, to show how it was done. Two seconds later I was squealing in pain and, far more worryingly, the woman in the next lane was screaming that she couldn't feel her legs. She was pulled out and recovered enough to continue the race. The pain is absolutely horrible but disappears quickly and with many a scream we made it through.

The other 'highlight' was the famous mud miles. Whereas we'd been aware of the electricity, this was surprisingly the real killer. Alternating lakes of mud and un-climbable slippery mounds with repeated face plants. Luckily we'd fallen into company with an enormous rugby player, who was heroically lifting people over the worst of the climbs. And if that was bad, the state of the Portaloos that came immediately afterwards was something else.

The second half was exhausting, our lack of training

definitely told and we dropped further and further back. Even the simplest tasks took on strange new difficulties: climbing frames are fun until your arms are too weak to bear your weight. The great thing, boringly clichéd as it sounds, was the ability to help each other along.

By the time we came to the finish, muddied and bloodied, we'd dropped to the very back of the field. As we approached the home stretch though, the announcer came out to meet us stragglers and coordinated everyone into cheering us through the last obstacles. One final run through Electroshock Therapy and we were home – there were tears.

Overall, we couldn't recommend it enough. The sense of teamwork was brilliant, and the shocked fascination of our fundraising friends was worth almost every inch of pain. Not the electricity though. That was horrible.

At the finish

Mental Miscellany

- Only 78 per cent of participants finish a Tough Mudder event.
- First aid and drinks stations are available at all TM events.
- Teams as well as individuals may enter a TM event.
- TM events support Help for Heroes by offering a £20 refund of the entry fee to anyone raising more than £120 for the charity.
- TM has an online boot camp offering specific training for their events.
- Participants must be aged 18 or over to enter a TM event, but there is no maximum – people over 75 have been known to participate!

For further information, please visit: www.toughmudder.co.uk

X-RUNNER MUD & WATER SERIES
UK
Extreme obstacle races + open-water swimming

The X-Runner series consists of four muddy obstacle races per year, but there is one fundamental difference between these and other similar races and that is the rather more generous use of water, including open-water swimming and the use of water slides.

All races are made up of 5km/3-mile laps and competitors can choose to complete one lap or two on the day of the race, depending on how they feel.

The first ever X-Runner race took place in 2009 and is known as the 'Mad Monk' race. Located within a World Heritage village and set within picturesque parklands along the banks of the River Derwent in Derbyshire, each lap contains numerous obstacles, including tightropes, tunnels, high hurdles, giant walls, cargo nets, spiders' webs and Jacob's ladder, and the course contains mud, water and an assault course, plus a 50m/164ft open water swim which takes place in the river.

The 'Mad Monk' takes place in May and is recommended for beginners and hardened obstacle racers alike, although there is a limit of 5,000 runners.

Also taking place in Derbyshire in stunning parkland that

forms the old grounds of Osmaston Manor, is the so-called 'Wild Run'. This particular event comes without a swim but contains more obstacles with 30 per 5km/3-mile lap, including balance beams and monkey bars, as well as the more usual tunnels, fire, giant walls, cargo nets, high hurdles, tightropes, not to mention an assault course.

The 'Wild Run' is limited to 4,000 runners.

'Water Wipe Out' is the imaginative and potentially self-explanatory name accorded to the third in the series of X-Runner's four races and takes place at the National Watersports Centre in Nottingham in June.

As its name implies, this challenge is more about the water, in particular the water slides, and will have its contestants climbing, crawling, swimming and running, as well as facing 25 obstacles per 5km/3-mile lap.

The race boasts of being perfect for runners and triathletes, with 'oodles of oozing mud and loads of lakes' (for dunking contestants in), and promises participants that they will never again be so wet or muddy!

The race has a limit of 7,000 competitors and takes place over two days.

The final event in the X-Runner's calendar falls in September where back once more in Derbyshire, this time at Wild Park, contestants will face the challenge of running along trails through undulating fields, woods, water and mud. Again the course will consist of one or two 5km/3-mile laps, and obstacles with names like 'The Swamp of Doom' and 'Muddy Mayhem', as well as water slides, tunnels, tightropes, quicksand and giant walls to negotiate.

Again, there is a limit set at 7,000 competitors over the course of two days.

Who would do this?

Middle-distance Olympian, World Champion and former World Record holder, athlete Steve Cram took part in the 'Water Wipeout' event at Nottingham in 2013. Steve was joined by family members and his personal assistant to form a team, and together they completed two laps or 10km/6 miles, overcoming 50 obstacles and the giant 15m/50ft waterslide. During a video of Steve's performance, he said that the idea was to have fun and that he intended to 'attack it'.

Steve finished the race in a time of 1 hour, 24 minutes 08 seconds, coming in 283rd out of 1,366 competitors.

Mental Miscellany

- The minimum age for any X-runner event is 15 – although anyone under 18 must provide written parental consent.
- The runners set off every 30 minutes in waves of 250.
- Eighty per cent of runners opt to complete two laps.
- Included in the entry fee is an X-Runner gym bag, a technical T-shirt and a finisher's medal.

For further information, please visit: www.xrunner.co.uk

SPARTAN RACE
WORLDWIDE
5km/3-mile–20km/12-mile muddy obstacle race

Inspired by the film *Death Race*, wherein inmates of a prison are used as players in a gladiator-type game, Spartan Race was the brainchild of a group of ultra athletes, mountaineers and former Royal Marines who designed a series of muddy obstacle-style races at escalating distances ranging from 5km/3 miles to 20km/12 miles.

The real difference with Spartan Race events as opposed to other muddy obstacle-type races is that the obstacles are different every time and there is no course map, forcing competitors to think on their feet when confronted by the unknown.

The other major difference is that Spartan Race have developed a ranking system which takes into account standards and times, which are then transformed into points. Consequently, a Spartan Race is just that – a race – that is as much against the clock as it is against the opposition on the day.

With the first race taking part in Vermont in 2010, the popularity of the Spartan Race has seen an astonishing rise so that by 2013 it was anticipated that one million people would have taken part in a Spartan Race at various venues throughout the world, in particular the United States, Canada, Mexico, the

UK, Slovakia, the Czech Republic, Germany, France, Australia and South Korea.

The ideal of the Spartan Race team was to make adventure racing more accessible to everyone by meeting the needs of all differing levels of ability. As a result, they introduced three different levels of racing, starting with the Spartan Sprint – a minimum of 5km/3 miles with a minimum of 15 obstacles; the Super Spartan – a minimum of 13km/8 miles with 20 or more obstacles; and the Spartan Beast – 20km/12 miles or more and a minimum of 25 obstacles. Additionally, they introduced the Spartan Trifecta – the completion of all three Spartan distances within one calendar year anywhere in the world and the right to claim membership of the much-coveted Spartan Trifecta Tribe, which comes complete with the honour of the member's name being inscribed on the Spartan Trifecta Tribe wall and an official Spartan Trifecta patch to wear.

Although there is no map and the race organisers claim that each course is unique so nobody ever gets to run the same course twice, they do admit that there are some 'staple' obstacles, as well as some that are venue-specific or terrain-inspired. What they will also reveal is that competitors can expect there to be fire, mud, water and barbed wire, and should a competitor fall off or fail to complete an obstacle, they will have to drop and perform 30 burpees (squat thrusts) before going any further.

Spartan Race also offer coaching, claiming this to be not just about the race or its obstacles but about sharing the exhilaration of fitness and reaching goals, applying this to everyday life and improving ourselves as human beings.

According to the event organisers, a Spartan Race is designed to 'rip you from your comfort zone', and will test your resilience, strength, stamina, quick-decision-making skills and ability to laugh in the face of adversity, whatever your level. They also say that it's an event of pure primitive craziness that you'll never forget and promise you the 'adrenalin rush of your life'!

Who would do this?

Anyone competitive, quick-thinking, with good navigational skills and a desire to laugh at themselves.

Mental Miscellany

- Teams of four plus, as well as individuals, may participate in Spartan Race events.
- Special discounts are available to teams – the larger the team, the greater the discount.
- Finishers receive medals and a T-shirt; there are other prizes for winners.
- 'Elite' runners (those wanting to be as competitive as possible and race against the best), start in the first wave of 250 runners at 1000 hours; the rest of the field follow in half-hourly waves also in groups of 250.
- The minimum age for a Spartan Race is 14 in the United States and Western Canada and 15 in the UK and Eastern Canada; the maximum stated age is 99.
- There are Junior Spartan Adventure Races in the USA for children over four years old, 'to have fun in nature, learn a few things and receive a medal...'
- The website states: 'If you need a road map for each step of the way, then maybe this isn't the race for you'.

For further information, please visit: www.spartanrace.com

TIME TO CLEAN UP YOUR ACT...

SWIMMING
AN OVERVIEW

Open water swimming is considered a wild and free, almost primal, sport in that there is no reliance on technology or machinery – it is simply the swimmer and nature. Like many sports, it is on the verge of becoming immensely popular with the masses. There are many races available over varying distances across the world. These range from mass participation events to cold water swimming and solo-supported events. Some great examples are the NYC Manhattan Marathon, the Lake Zurich Marathon, and the British Channel.

Open Water and Sea Swimming Races

Most open water events have two categories – wetsuit & non-wetsuit. There is a distinct advantage in wetsuit swimming due to the lower resistance a swimmer gains from the use of a wetsuit. Wetsuit swimming is more about power rather than technique, as the suit can vastly assist swimmers with less advanced technique and stroke ability. Hence the two categories are clearly split and non-wetsuit swimming is often seen as the ultimate non-assisted true challenge.

Distances are wide and varied, ranging from one mile to 10km up to 21 miles and above.

The majority of open water events are mass start (non-wetsuit and wetsuit) and tend to spread out quite quickly due to the varying abilities and the two categories.

Swimmers may start a race anywhere within the pack, although some races set swimmers off according to their age ranking, and competitors will be given a number-marked thin hat to wear, but many take their own additional hat to wear underneath.

Race times are taken from the gun to the finish. Some races do provide ankle chips for personal timing. Routes vary from point to point and circuits – finishing in the same place as the start.

Safety is the real issue with open water swimming. Usually races will provide three layers of support or marshalling. Firstly, there is an inner layer of kayaks that follow the packs of swimmers and provide one-to-one immediate assistance and, on longer distance races, will also provide swimmers with water and occasionally food. If a swimmer is in difficulty, a simple hand in the air will gain assistance; a second layer of cover in some races is provided by larger boats/jet skis; and a third final emergency cover may be supplied by lifeguards, who can react to any immediate danger a swimmer may find himself in.

Cold Water Races

Cold water races are usually confined to outdoor pools or lidos because of the safety risk to swimmers. These often tend to contain more of a 'fun' element and will be held as non-wetsuit events. Swimming with the head above the water is usually the rule for safety reasons and distances are also much shorter, consisting of anything from 50m to 400m. Swimmers are strictly limited to standard swim trunks or suits and events are more about the ability to race while withstanding the cold, than anything else.

Solo Swim Challenges

Solo swim challenges usually consist of events over 20k or marathon distance. Swimmers are supported by a pilot ship, which monitors, feeds and guides the individual swimmer to his destination.

The stronger tides and weather are more apparent and part of the challenge.

INTERNATIONAL SELF-TRANSCENDENCE MARATHON SWIM
SWITZERLAND
26.4km/16.4-mile lake swim –
Rapperswil to Zurich – within 12 hours

If it's watery scenery you're after, you probably can't get a much prettier place than Lake Zurich, especially during the lovely summer month of August, when the 40 x 3km (24.75 x 1.75-mile) pool of water becomes the perfectly reflected cerulean blue of the sky, surrounded by snow-capped mountains, fairy-tale castles and chocolate-box Swiss chalets.

And what better place to enjoy the views from than within the reasonably warm depths of the lake itself, which extends southeast from the city of Zurich.

The swim, which starts early in the morning on the east side of the Lake at Rapperswil, with its large dam carrying both railway and roadway, sees solo swimmers and teams from all over the world plunge into the blue abyss, which has a depth of 49m/161ft, as they set off for Zurich, some 26km/16 miles away.

For some this will be a mighty long journey taking up to the full 12 hours allowed for completion of this race; for others it may take a little over half that time.

Photo by Rachel Gillingham

Either way, with an average air temperature of around 28°C/82°F and water temperature of 24–26°C/75–79°F, the less competitive swimmers are not likely to feel in any great rush to leave the spirit-lifting Alpine scene, but may rather choose to enjoy the calming influence that exercising in fresh water among such outstanding natural beauty brings, not only to the body but also to the mind and soul.

It stands to reason that this is an aspect of the race that its late founder, the renowned spiritual guru and all-round sportsman Sri Chinmoy, would thoroughly approve of, for his belief was that sport was a natural medium for inner growth and personal transformation: he founded the Sri Chinmoy Marathon Team in 1977, as a service to the running world and to promote spiritual growth through sport. As a matter of fact, over the years the Sri Chinmoy Marathon Team has become one of the world's largest organisers of ultramarathons, triathlons, multi-events and long-distance swims, including the Zurich Lake Swim or, to give it its full name, the International Self-Transcendence Marathon Swim.

Who would do this?

Intrepid grandmother and chiropodist, 60-year-old Ann Richardson learned to swim in the River Thames and didn't use a swimming pool until she moved from her native Channel Islands to England in her teens. Once a competitive swimmer, Ann now contents herself with swimming longer distances and in unique environments. Ann has taken part in the Lake Zurich swim twice, once in 2004 and again in 2012. With thanks to Ann for the account that follows.

I first decided to do this swim after several tough times in the [English] Channel – sometimes with great success and also learning that the Channel can be a cruel place.

The Zurich swim offered the chance to tackle a long swim where the conditions would be more predictable. The scenery surrounding the lake is beautiful and the lake temperature is surprisingly warm. The distance is 26.4km [16.4 miles], but because it is fresh water the lack of buoyancy is noticeable, especially as you tire towards the end. The race can be swum solo or in a relay

Ann reaches the finish line

team, wetsuit or – as I always feel true swimming – without a wetsuit.

It is organised by the Sri Chinmoy Team – a group with a strong belief in meditation. You certainly get plenty of time to think life through when you are face down in the water for miles of swimming!

Each swimmer has a boat to accompany them, so you always feel safe. You organise your own feeds and drinks, preferably with a friend on the boat to help with all that. There are many nationalities taking part and the Sri Chinmoy Team really look after you.

The first time I swam the race was in 2004. The weather was perfect and the lake flat calm at the start, but there was a slight chop towards the end of the swim.

I am not the fastest swimmer, but long distance really appeals to me. It was great not having to swim laps and to feel like it was a journey. When I stopped for a drink or feed it was great to look around at the scenery and also try to spot other boats that were accompanying swimmers. There is a generous allowance on time allowed to finish, but there is a halfway point that must be reached in a given time.

I was tempted back in 2012 and again the conditions were good. A bit of rain near the start but then the sun broke through. It's an amazing feeling standing there looking down the lake for miles, swimmers all around greasing up and chattering nervously. The early morning light makes it all eerie, but once you are in the water the journey starts.

Although it is a race, like all tough challenges it is only about you and your goal, and when you complete it the feeling of self-worth is amazing.

You can see the finish from quite a distance and it does feel like it is never getting closer, but when you finally wobble up on to the platform you are greeted by clapping, big smiles and a garland of flowers. There is food, drink and a real carnival atmosphere that makes a perfect end to the day.

Mental Miscellany

- In 2013, 50 solo swimmers and 24 teams from all over the world took part in the Lake Zurich race.
- In 2013, the solo race was won in 6 hours, 56 minutes, 36 seconds.
- In 2013, the team event was won in 7 hours, 9 minutes, 50 seconds.
- In 2013, seven solo swimmers and two teams did not reach the cut-off times or retired from the race early.
- In his younger years, Sri Chinmoy (1931–2007) was an accomplished footballer, volleyball player, sprinter and an outstanding decathlete. Later, he became a long-distance runner, played tennis almost daily and set records for calf-raises and one-armed weightlifting. He has written extensively about the importance of sport as a path for spiritual growth.
- A quote famously attributed to Sri Chinmoy is: 'What gives life its value, / If not its constant cry / For self-transcendence?'
- The *Oxford English Dictionary* defines self-transcendence as '…the overcoming of the limits of the individual self and its desires in spiritual contemplation and realisation: the logic of self-transcendence is based on humility, and respect for the mystery we did not create'.

For further information, please visit: www.ch.srichinmoyraces. org/veranstaltungen/zhlake (Lake Zurich swim) and www. srichinmoyraces.org (other events)

VIBES & SCRIBES
LEE SWIM
IRELAND

2km/1.25 miles – tidal river swim – Cork

In theory, a swim of just over a mile or two kilometres in a river in southern Ireland during the lovely summery month of July doesn't sound too arduous, but when you learn that the river is actually tidal and that there is a time limit of 1 hour, 15 minutes to complete the swim, you realise that maybe the theory doesn't quite reflect the practical.

The Lee Swim, which takes place, perhaps unsurprisingly, in the River Lee which runs through the centre of the city of Cork, was actually started as long ago as 1914, although it wasn't until 2005, when the city was designated the European Capital of Culture, that the event was officially relaunched, a relaunch largely facilitated by the agreement of Vibes & Scribes, Book and Craft Shops of Cork, to be the title sponsor of the event. The Vibes & Scribes Lee Swim, to give it its full title, is now recognised as one of the top open-water swimming events in Ireland.

Starting just before St Vincent's Bridge, the course passes beneath a total of nine bridges, following the river downstream for 1,700m before almost turning back on itself after the sixth

231

bridge for the final 300m upstream, until it reaches the finish at Clontarf Bridge, some 2,000m later.

The river itself is unusual in that it is part saltwater, part fresh. This affects the ability to swim, with salt water offering more buoyancy than fresh, which means that swimming stroke and performance are affected and have to be adapted at the point of change.

While wetsuits are allowed, most swimmers opt not to wear them, finding the water temperature in July reasonable, and with a minimum age of just 12 and no upper limit, the race is pretty much all-inclusive, the only real bar to entry being the self-certification of swimmers in declaring themselves fit enough to complete the distance within the safety-induced 1 hour, 15-minute time limit.

In true Irish fashion, and with the swim taking part right in the city centre, the whole event produces something of a carnival atmosphere with thousands of spectators prepared to stand on the riverbank to shout and cajole the swimmers during the race, and to join them afterwards in festivities that last well into the night.

Who would do this?

Paolo De Luca, 43-year-old graphic/web designer, triathlete, 16 x Ironman, ultra runner, and member of the 100 Marathon Club, took part in the Lee Swim in 2007. This is what he had to say:

The race starts in waves, with the fastest swimmers starting last.

It's a short swim, but if you're not quick enough you can't make it under the bridges as the tides rise and you have to be pulled out.

The first part is seemingly easy because it's salt water. Then the second part you drop as it's fresh water, which isn't as buoyant, and you're swimming against the tide.

All in all, it's a fun day out!

Mental Miscellany

- At the first event since its relaunch in 2005, the swim attracted 110 swimmers; in 2011, it attracted almost 400.
- In 2011, the winning times were 24 minutes (men) and 26 minutes, 28 seconds (women).
- Many participants in the Lee swim to raise funds for charity.
- The swim is organised by the Cork Masters Swimming Club.
- Cork Masters Swimming Club also organise the Sandycove Island Challenge Swim – a 1,800m/5,900ft sea swim around Sandycove Island.

For further information, please visit: www.corkmasters.ie

CORRYVRECKAN SWIM
SCOTLAND

Swim in the world's third largest whirlpool

The Gulf of Corryvreckan lies between the islands of Jura and Scarba, about a mile apart, and hosts one of Britain's most iconic swimming challenges.

The whirlpool itself is caused partly by the tide being squeezed between the islands and, most importantly, because the seabed is scoured by deep contours and drops into a 219m basin. During the flood-and-ebb tides, the sea surrounds a pinnacle that rises to within 30m of the surface forming a giant, furiously eddying whirlpool that makes a spin cycle on a washing machine look like

the barely visible ripple on a shallow puddle after a raindrop has splashed gently into it, while the thunderous noise of crashing waves that appear from nowhere can be heard over 10 miles away.

Which is why nobody who wishes to stay alive, rather than drop to its fathomless depths never to be seen again, would attempt to swim across it at the wrong time. However, it is possible, if a little scary, to swim safely across the Gulf during slack tide when the whirlpool lies dormant and almost secret.

The safest way to do this (apart from 'very quickly' – the safe period lasts for a mere 30 minutes), is on an organised trip with a company called SwimTrek, who offer swim trips complete with a safety boat that will escort swimmers across the Gulf at the least dangerous tidal times, and who also provide a pre-swim briefing and a pre-crossing swim in a nearby bay to help participants to acclimatise. For safety reasons, the briefing and the pre-swim are both compulsory.

Tidal conditions offer two opportunities to swim through the day, one in the morning and one in the afternoon, although on some days the tide and conditions may render an attempt too dangerous; it will be entirely down to the guide and boat pilot to make what they consider the safest decision as to when and if a crossing will take place on any day.

Because of the dangerous nature of this sort of swimming, it is a requirement for anyone wishing to attempt the crossing to be able to swim a mile in 35 minutes or less – the crossing is approximately 1.5km (just under one mile) and the water temperature in August when the swims take place is between 13–14°C/55–57°F, with an average air temperature of 18°C/64°F. The trip organisers therefore recommend bringing warm clothing, including woolly hat and gloves, waterproof jacket and waterproof sun cream, as well as tinted goggles to protect against the glare of the sun reflecting off the water during the swim.

Aside from the water and weather conditions, there is one other thing to be wary of if attempting this swim – jellyfish – although the organisers state that stings are rare and they are able to treat anyone from the safety boat if necessary.

Who would do this?

Intrepid grandmother and chiropodist, Ann, who now contents herself with swimming longer distances and in unique environments, completed the Corryvreckan crossing in 2013 – the swim was an early birthday present from her friends! Many thanks to Ann for the following account.

I'd seen a film of the whirlpool on a programme about the world's largest whirlpools. The 'corry' being number three makes it pretty impressive.

It can only be swum when the conditions and the tide are right, otherwise it would be a trip to the bottom and never to be seen again! There are whirlpools and standing waves that reach massive height; it's remarkable.

Our trip was with a company called SwimTrek who organise swims across the gulf. Without proper safety it would be foolhardy.

The day we set off was cold and grey, and the sea was choppy and uninviting, but myself and my friends were so excited – that's crazy open-water swimmers for you!

We saw a dolphin just before we entered the water and an eagle flew overhead – wonderful.

I, like some of my friends, chose to swim non-wetsuit, but you really need to be used to the cold. Oh, and not afraid of the numerous jellyfish that lurk below! Nobody got stung – well not that day; we did on our other wild swim trips that holiday.

There is no time to mess about as slack tide and the safe time doesn't last too long. The water looked very strange as although the sea was choppy there were areas that looked smooth as if they had been ironed. It appeared to be doing different things all across the gulf, unlike anything we were used to swimming in.

So, it was off the boat and a swim to the rocks of Jura. We then turned and swam as a group (there was another group as well), towards the island of Scarba. It was wonderful to look up at the rock shores as we swam across. The water felt strange and we could tell it was a wild place to be. Close by is the safety boat though, so all is well.

It took about 30 minutes to reach the other shore and then it was a swim back to the boat and hot drinks and layers and layers of clothes.

I just thought, 'Wow! What can top that as a birthday present?' See, 60 isn't old anymore, it's a chance to take on new challenges.

Mental Miscellany

- According to its website, SwimTrek is the world's first open-water swimming operator.
- SwimTrek recommend bringing your own swim hats, flippers, rash vests and wetsuits, although they can supply these if necessary.
- There is a maximum number of 10 per group, with 2 swimming guides and a motorised pilot escort boat.
- The swim across the Corryvreckan was featured on British actor Robson Green's *Wild Swimming Adventure* series.

For further information, please visit: www.swimtrek.com

COLD WATER SWIMMING
CHAMPIONSHIPS
UK/WORLDWIDE

Swim in 3–4°C/37–39°F outdoors in a swimsuit in winter

In the summer of 1906 Tooting Bec Lido, originally known as Tooting Bathing Lake, in southwest London, opened to the public. It measured 100 x 33 yards, and was intended to serve partly as a communal bath as, back then, very few homes had their own bathrooms. It is now one of the oldest and biggest open-air freshwater pools in the country.

In January 2006, the South London Swimming Club, who formed within weeks of the pool opening in 1906, celebrated their centenary by holding the UK's first ever Cold Water Swimming Championships, based upon the existent World Championship format.

Both championships consist of individual races of 25m/82ft, team relays and an endurance swim of 450m (492yds).

Competitors must use one of two strokes: the first is known as 'head-up breaststroke', which is the traditional cold-water swimming event as it can be used in ice-cold conditions, with the rules stating that eyes must not go below the water level at any time during the race. On this basis, swimmers are advised to wear a warm hat, and a prize grandly entitled the 'Best Hat of the Day' is given for the most creative and original headpiece. Pictures on the website show one swimmer sporting a swim hat, topped with a cycling helmet, topped with a pineapple!

The alternative to head up and fancy hats is freestyle, which means you can use any stroke you like, although front crawl tends to be the most popular, and quickest.

For all events, swimmers are split into 10-year age groups, ranging from 19 years and under to 80 years and over.

For team events, there must be four competitors of mixed gender (at least one male and one female) who can represent their country, town, club, or be just a group of friends. There are two categories for relay races based on the combined ages of a team: over 180, and up to and including 180. Teams may choose their own names – in 2013 these included, 'Nippy Nipples', 'Ice Maidens', 'Numb Numpties' and 'Chalkwell Redcaps Brass Monkeys'.

The final race of the day is the endurance challenge. This is for experienced cold-water swimmers only, by invitation, and takes in two circuits of the lido.

Whatever race you choose to do though, the organisers recommend all swimmers acclimatise to cold water before taking part in the competition and suggest gloves as well as hats are worn.

Rules also state that swimmers must wear something on their head, fancy or not, such as a swimming cap or woollen or other warm hat, and swimsuits must be appropriate and non-transparent and must not go beyond the middle of the thigh or past the shoulder (i.e., no legs or sleeves); neither should they wear a wetsuit. Topless or swimming naked is not permitted!

The Cold Water World Championships, which started in Helsinki in 2000 and now take place every other year in various places around the world, follow much the same format as the UK Championships, although the races often take place in icy lakes rather than pools.

Who would do this?

Sixty-year-old Ann Richardson learned to swim in the River Thames and didn't use a swimming pool until she moved from her native Channel Islands to England in her teens. Once a competitive swimmer, Ann now contents herself with swimming longer distances and in unique environments. Ann has swum in both the UK and World Cold Water Championships several times. This is her account.

Now this is fun. Tooting Bec Lido, and the water temperature is just a few degrees.

The day starts early and the lido is soon packed with all ages of swimmer. Frankly, the main thing besides swimming that they have in common is being raving bonkers!

The event has grown each year and there are now food stalls, hot drinks, the opportunity to purchase kit or book a swimming holiday. They even have a hot tub and a sauna – very necessary to help thaw yourself out throughout the day.

The organisation is brilliant and they have a steady stream of races – all full. For those not keen to race, there is a lane provided for what they call 'dippers', who can just drop in and swim a breath-taking width or two.

The relays are hilarious as it seems to be a massive competition to wear the most outrageous swim hat. I mean really outrageous!

I heard of the event in 2006. I really didn't know what was involved but entered online and took a chance. I have to say I was hooked from the start. There are usually one or two famous faces, and the TV cameras and newspapers cover the event. Although many are

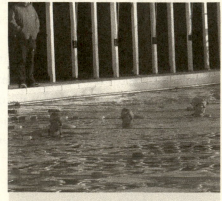

Tooting Bec Lido

really good swimmers, it is open to all and because of the nature of the event, it is all about fun. Last year I remember watching a group of ladies warming themselves up in the hot tub while drinking champagne from china teacups!

After the races there is a chance for the super crazy to do the endurance swim of 450m. Not a long way normally, but in four degrees when I swam it I thought it to be a massive challenge.

The first year I was there accompanied by some good friends we met a group of swimmers from Finland. They told us about the World Cold Water Championships that are held every two years. So, as if four-degree water wasn't enough, we all decided to make that a plan for the following year.

Arriving in Finland to a scene like a winter wonderland we wandered down to the deeply frozen lake to inspect the swim area. A 25m pool is cut out of the deep ice and laned off. The water has to be kept swirling or it will freeze.

Our first night there the temperature dropped to -35°C [-31°F]. Now that was scary. Our first race was the second night with temperatures at a barmy minus -27°C [-16°F]. I can't describe how cold that is even to stand for a few seconds in a swim costume.

Anyway, with very little messing it was a blow of a whistle then you entered the water (quickly, so not much time to panic), then on the second whistle it was shoulders under. Whistle three is go! The water was dark and swirling, the lake floodlit with spectators watching from the stands – weird and surreal.

The cold was like nothing I'd ever experienced but it was a case of getting across as quickly as possible. You are helped out at the other end. The ladders into the water are covered, as you would stick to any of the metal. Divers in dry suits

Ann getting out of the pool

241

are on standby to rescue any poor soul that can't make it; they all did.

We also swam again the following day, that time in daylight.

It all sounds crazy but as always the sense of achievement and the excitement of stepping out of the normal type of race is so exciting. I really hope to go again.

Mental Miscellany

- Tooting Bec Lido holds 30,000sq ft of water.
- The UK and World Cold Water Championships are held every two years in alternate years to one another.
- 2013 was the fifth UK Cold Water Swimming Championships and attracted 575 swimmers and more than 1,000 spectators.
- In between timed races, less-competitive swimmers can take part in un-timed swims of different distances in the Dipping Lane – 'Polar Bears' swim 60m; 'Seals' swim 30m and 'Penguins' merely take a dip in the pool.
- Hot showers, a hot tub and a sauna are available for swimmers.
- Participants in all events must be 10 years or over on the day of competition.
- The first World Championships took place in 2000 in Helsinki with 500 swimmers; in Slovenia in 2010, there were 790.
- The next UK Championships are in January 2015; the next World Championships are in March 2016 at Rovaniemi, Lapland, Finland.

For further information, please visit: www.slsc.org.uk (UK Championships) and www.visitrovaniemi.fi (World Champion ships, 2014).

242

ENGLISH CHANNEL SWIM
UK/FRANCE

Swim 33km/21 miles across the English Channel

The English Channel lies between England and France and in a straight line measures 33km/21 miles. It has an average temperature of between 15 and 18°C/59 and 64°F. The first swimmer to cross it in one go was Captain Matthew Webb, which he did in 1875 in a time of 21 hours. Since then, there have been thousands of attempted crossings, of which just 1,790 have been as successful as Captain Webb's, although many have been faster, with the quickest crossing to date standing at 6 hours, 55 minutes and the slowest 28 hours, 44 minutes.

Of course comparing times of any ocean swims is bound to be slightly haphazard, given there are so many variables that can affect any crossings, such as tides, currents, water temperature and weather conditions, to name but four. There's also the jellyfish, debris and hypothermia to contend with, and the fact that the tidal conditions and the tiredness of the swimmers will ensure that they mostly swim in a zigzag fashion rather than in a straight line, meaning that some crossings will be considerably more miles than others.

However, time is perhaps not the essence of such a challenge. It must surely be more the ability of man or woman to endure all that the ocean and its unique traits on a specific day will throw at them and how they, their physical prowess and mental strength will deal with and overcome it in order to achieve the end result.

Although a Channel crossing doesn't come in typical race format, being more a challenge to compete against time and tide rather than beat your fellow man, there are usually several crossings happening at once and the same rules apply equally to all challengers. For example, swimmers can only enter the challenge wearing a swim costume, a swim hat, swim goggles, grease and earplugs; they must have no physical contact with the pilot boat or any person; they must start by walking into the sea from dry land; and they must end by finishing on dry land.

Anyone wishing to take up such a challenge should contact the Channel Swimming and Piloting Federation (CS&PF), which is the governing body for English Channel swimming and is officially recognised and approved by both the British Maritime and Coastguard Agency and the French Coastguard, as well as being a member of the Amateur Swimming Association. Their main aim is to ensure your attempt is carried out safely, although they stress that all swimmers swim at their own risk.

With this in mind, and to ensure that swimmers are aware of the challenge they are undertaking as well as giving them a taste of what to expect, the Federation demands that anyone attempting the crossing should have completed a ratified six-hour swim at least 14 days prior to taking on the challenge, or, if attempting the crossing as part of a relay team, all members must have completed a ratified two-hour swim at least 14 days before the Channel crossing.

The CS&PF also recognise and register the pilots of support boats and through its website offers much advice and information about the best ways to prepare for swimming the Channel, such as training, nutrition (including how to manage your feeds and drinks during your swim) and health issues, taking you right through to the actual day of your swim and all that entails – and beyond.

Within its preparation and training advice, the CS&PF advise that swimmers train themselves to breathe bi-laterally so they will be able to swim on either side of the boat using the hull for shelter if the wind gets up, or to avoid exhaust fumes if the wind is blowing it towards them. They also recommend training outdoors for long periods in cold water – ideally around 15.5°C/60°F, as the body reacts and performs differently in colder temperatures and needs time to adjust.

Perhaps one of the most difficult aspects of a Channel crossing to master is the feeding, which needs to be arranged well in advance so the swimmer and crew know exactly how it is going to work. The CS&PF recommends keeping feed times to a minimum so as not to add extra time to the swim. The usual pattern adopted by swimmers is hourly feeds for the first two hours, then half-hourly feeds for the remainder, with each feed lasting less than one minute.

Perhaps one of the most nerve-wracking things about swimming the Channel is that the precise date and time of your swim can only be approximate, as these will, of necessity, be dependent upon tidal and weather conditions. As a consequence, you must wait until your pilot contacts you and tells you the swim is on!

On a note of caution, the CS&PF warns that Channel swimming is an extreme sport that requires consistent dedicated training and a good support team, adding, 'If you are not ready to swim, don't risk it. The English Channel will always be there, ensure you are ready for it.'

Who would do this?

Twenty-seven-year-old Marcus Wadsworth, an accountant with just four years' swimming experience, swam the English Channel as part of a two-person relay team in 2011, before achieving a solo crossing in 2013 in a time of 15 hours, 43 minutes, and 47,150 strokes! Marcus is also a marathon runner and triathlete. Thanks to Marcus for this account.

On 3 September 2013, I was at work when I got a message from my pilot, Neil Streeter, asking if I would like to go the next day. A wave of excitement and nerves hit me at the same time.

At around 10.30pm Neil texted me saying, 'See you in the

morning, be there for 6.30am, don't be late.' F*CK! At first I was jumping up and down with excitement, this turned to fear. I had to focus and inform my crew of the plan and then get as much sleep as possible.

I was very lucky with my crew, which was made up of girlfriend, Scarlett Little, who has supported me through everything and knows me better than anyone, Scarlett's step-dad Ian Coles, Stephen Roberts, my best friend and swim partner in 2011, and Matt Dawson [not the rugby player] and Mark Fabik, both Channel swimmers.

We arrived early at Dover. There was nobody there, no boats, no swimmers and nothing to do. I was getting nervous. All I'd been able to think about in the car was that I was heading to Dover to swim the Channel. My head was going to explode. I tried to sleep but was far too excited; I have a chance to live a dream.

Eventually, the sun rose and people started turning up and boats arrived at the harbour, and we started packing the boat.

The crew were really organised, each with their own jobs to do. They separated my kit and put it in its right place, setting up the thermos for feeds. This is important and gives control to the crew who need to know where everything is in an emergency.

My swim kit was ready, my goggles were clear and my ginger nut biscuits were on hand. I always eat three (my lucky number) before a swim; the ginger helps with sickness and the biscuits calm me.

I was very lucky with the conditions, it was a lovely hot day but misty, so the sun was kept at bay and the water was dead flat.

When we were alerted that it was five minutes to the start, Scarlett and Stephen had the envious task of greasing me up! The grease is not to keep warm; it's to avoid chaffing. I use a whole bottle of sun cream everywhere, including on the bum and inside the thighs, and then add Vaseline in the key areas. Scarlett and Stephen were lucky people.

The start of the swim was planned at Shakespeare Beach and as we were the first boat out of the harbour, I was the first swimmer to set off. This was great as all the waiting was finally over, but at the same time we were being rushed so others could get in.

At this stage, irrational fears crept in. Unfortunately, just before the swim my goggles had broken and I bought new ones for the swim. A big no-no, as I hadn't been able to test how tight to have them, and if they leaked I was stuffed.

Another concern was my hat: I always have problems keeping it on. I don't know whether I have a funny head or don't put it on properly, all I know is it comes off and I end up looking like a rooster!

Plus, I had to face my fear of jellyfish; I've never liked them, but it's all part of Channel swimming and you just have to deal with it.

I did a few stretches on the beach and took a few seconds to calm myself and set my mind. Then I raised my arm and got the okay to set off. My official start time was 4 September, 7.13am.

I had chosen to swim on the port (left) side of the boat as it is the side the pilot sits so he can see in the water more easily.

I got into my steady swim pace and focused on this being just a normal swim on a normal day and not the biggest swim of my life. I've seen other swimmers fly out at great speed, adrenaline pumping, just to burn out at later stages. I didn't want this to happen to me, so began to plod.

I had decided to swim for an hour, feed, and then feed

every 30 minutes. That first hour never seemed to end and I kept thinking if I'm struggling in the first hour, how am I going to swim the Channel?

However, the feeds went well, and, with the side of the boat not being too high and Ian Coles being 6 feet 5 inches, I could see him and the rest of my crew, which gave me this closeness to them and I could look into their eyes feeling this bond and their warmth.

A feed is a carb drink made with a product called Maxi or Maxim mixed with water, and with boiling hot water stirred in to keep the swimmer warm. Swimmers can take it from a cup or bottle. I decided to go with the bottle but was getting bloated by taking in too much air when squeezing it, so I changed to cups and that felt much better and got feeds down quicker.

You can also have food and drugs during a feed. I found flat Coke helped cramp and chocolate Swiss rolls were amazing even if they do stick to your teeth!

Mentally, the Channel is really challenging; it's a common belief that swimming it is 20 per cent physical and 80 per cent mental. As a swimmer, you break the swim up into chunks, focusing on the next feed, and this makes the Channel seem more doable.

Another way to break it up is to have the crew tell you when you reach each of the separate sections. The entire swim is 18 nautical miles: the English inshore being four nautical miles, the north-west shipping lane another one, the central separation zone two, the south-east shipping lane five, with the French inshore three nautical miles. I got my crew to do a 'Y' sign with their arms to indicate every time I reached the next section, then calculated how long I thought I had left to swim. It was stupid. I reached the first shipping lane just after 4 hours and still had 14 nautical miles to go. By my maths I was going to do a total swim of 16 hours, so I had another 12 hours – where's the comfort in that?

I also learned the hard way never to ask where you are in the Channel – you will never like the answer.

Eventually, I reached the first shipping lane and the flat water changed to a chop with the arrival of some huge boats.

I also broke the swim down into targets. First of all, I figured my work colleagues would track me till 6pm, so I needed to swim for at least 11 hours. Then Mark Fabik had swum the Channel in 12 hours, 1 minute, so I targeted to reach his time. Then I aimed for sunset at around 8pm or 13 hours into my swim. After that I focused on Matt Dawson's time of 15 hours, 6 minutes and another friend who swam for 15.5 hours.

I had also organised a drug plan to receive paracetamol every four hours and ibuprofen in between, which gave me something else to think about.

In the first shipping lane I got cramp in my arms, shooting pain up and down my forearms. There was nothing I could do but keep swimming. I did shout to my crew who organised a Coke. It made a change from the Maxi and seawater I'd been drinking for the past five hours.

Another way of passing the time was waving. Every time I turned to breathe facing the boat, I'd wave. The crew waved back; it was lovely having some sort of interaction with them.

For a solo swim, you're allowed a support swimmer after three hours who can swim alongside you for an hour, then break for two hours and then swim another hour if required, and so on. The support swimmer cannot touch the swimmer and must swim just behind him. Matt Dawson was my support swimmer but I didn't want him to join me until I reached the central separation zone, because that is where the jellyfish are!

As soon as I saw the first jellyfish my body tensed up, altering my stroke. I started looking up rather than down to spot them and my neck began to hurt. Luckily, the central separation zone is only one nautical mile and we reached the other side before Matt had to get out. I think we saw only about 16 jellyfish and I got stung once. Ever since, Matt has been my jellyfish lucky charm, the man who scared the jellyfish off for me!

I reached the second shipping lane in about nine hours. At five nautical miles, this is the longest section and never seems to end. I was still focusing on my plod and my stroke rate rarely changed. Mentally, though, I was struggling, with fights constantly going round inside my head – if I got out now I would have to do all the training again and then swim for 10 miles just to get to this stage and past the jellyfish again. I drew great confidence by conquering this and getting through to the other side.

With nerves, seawater and feeds, swimmers are often sick in the Channel. I tried not to be as the process once a swimmer's been sick is not nice. Ten minutes after being sick the swimmer is given water, then a weak tea 10 minutes later, then a weak Maxi, and, eventually, if they haven't been sick at any of these stages, a normal feed. It means you don't get a proper feed for nearly an hour. There was one stage where I ate a banana and coughed a little up. My crew took this as me being sick and on the next feed gave me water. I was not happy.

The second shipping lane was the hardest stage for me. I started looking for land. I'd build myself up swimming for 30 minutes thinking I'd be able to see land on the next feed, but then nothing. I'd been swimming for hours and was just ready for it to finish.

Then the sun began to set and I couldn't see the people on the boat, it was the first time I'd felt lonely.

In the dark my stroke was actually gradually getting faster and stronger as we went on but the crew had concerns. Sam asked if I was cold but before I could answer Mark said, 'He's fat, he is not going to get cold.' Thanks Mark! But honestly I was fine.

After about 12 hours my hat began to come off and I had to pull it back on every few minutes. My earlier concerns about my goggles weren't needed; they were actually too tight and had given me a headache from early on.

When the sun set my crew organised light sticks along the boat so it was visible. They also put some around their necks so I could make out each member. It was great to be back in contact with them again.

Twelve-and-a-half hours into the swim near the French inshore, Matt was preparing to jump into the water for the second time when I heard the worst thing a swimmer can hear, 'We need an hour of power.'

Basically, they needed me to sprint for an hour as the tide was changing and it could potentially drag me back out into the Channel or I could miss the Cap Gris Nez and add hours to my swim.

The shortest distance is from Dover to the Cap, so the pilots plot a route considering the tides and aim for this point, and the swimmer follows the boat. I was heading south at this point and was below the Cap. With the tide about to change, I could have been pushed right past it.

I didn't argue, and with Matt in the water it pushed me to swim harder, though the sudden change of pace hurt my shoulder early into the sprint.

Finally, Matt got out after the hour, and I said I couldn't sprint any more. I was struggling to raise my right shoulder and with each stroke on that side I was in agony. The drugs I'd relied on throughout the swim weren't working any more but I knew I must be close. At this stage I could begin to make out lights.

On the 15 hours, 30 minutes feed, I heard the best thing possible, 'last feed'. It meant I was within 30 minutes of swimming the Channel and making land. The side light on the boat was put on so they could spot me – and I saw thousands of little white jellyfish floating all around me! It freaked me out, but nothing was going to stop me now. I decided to swim to the front of the boat where the light wasn't visible and have an 'ignorance is bliss' approach, ignoring the jellyfish.

At this stage I enjoyed each stroke and took the whole experience in, recalling the whole day and how I was about to realise a dream.

About 10 minutes later, Stephen, Mark and Matt all jumped in to swim to shore with me. As it was pitch dark and I didn't *have the boat to follow any more, there was a torch shone from the boat pointing me in the right direction. As I got closer to land I could make out rocks and stones.*

My friends kept telling me to keep pushing. Eventually I felt a big rock underneath me submerged in the water. I'd touched land but hadn't finished the swim. I had to be fully out of the water for that. So I scrambled through rocks making sure I didn't hurt myself (easier said than done in the dark), until I finally made land.

I had one final test to do – climb on a slippery wet rock and the swim would be over. I found one, slid up it getting out of the water and stood up very carefully. Being vertical for the first time in nearly 16 hours made me feel light-headed or it may have been because I'd just swum the Channel and was giddy with emotion!

From there we all turned so the swim lights weren't visible from the boat to show the boat I'd made it. I'd swum the Channel in 15 hours, 43 minutes, arriving in France at 10.56pm-ish.

I was just relieved it was over. You swim for hours and go through so many highs and lows by yourself in the water with nothing to focus on. You may start to believe it will never happen and then suddenly you reach France, and you're just glad you don't have to swim any further.

Leaving the rock, we swam back to the boat, everything ached and I was slow. Getting back in the water was the only time I felt cold; it was bloody freezing.

I reached the boat feeling joyful, and tried and failed to pull myself up the ladder; eventually Ian had to pull me out of the water. My first reaction was to hug and thank everyone. I couldn't have done it without them.

My crew helped me get dressed and we headed back to England on the boat. I focused on drinking my protein shake but with being in the sea for so long trying hard not to be sick, it all came out. Luckily I had a bucket; unluckily, it was beginning to fill up.

On reaching Dover Harbour, I viewed my route. I had

no idea of my plot across to France but when I saw it, and depending on how you viewed it, it looked like an M or W, my initials. The radio was playing the Take That song, 'The Greatest Day'. I'm no Take That fan but was emotional when this came on at the end of the swim with me checking my route. It was meant to be.

The whole experience made me realise anything is possible if you want it bad enough and are willing to work for it.

Mental Miscellany

- To date, there have been 1,335 successful solo swims across the English Channel. Of those 911 were men, 424 were women.
- In 2013, there were 57 solo crossings and 62 relay crossings.
- The average time for swimming the Channel is between 10 and 20 hours.
- The most popular stroke used for swimming the Channel is front crawl.
- During the crossing, a swimmer's tongue and mouth will become irritated due to the salt, making chewy foods difficult to consume. Swimmers therefore eat things like Swiss rolls, bits of banana and Jelly Babies.
- Due to the intake of salt, the use of electrolytes, which are used in many other ultra sports to replace lost salt and other minerals, should be kept to a minimum or avoided; an overdose can be life-threatening.
- The Channel is used by 600 commercial ships every day.
- The CS&PF award numerous trophies for outstanding swims every year, as well as awards for pilots, crews, observers and supporters.
- The CS&PF also assist with crossing the Channel by other methods such as rowing, canoeing, paddle boarding, etc.
- Swimmers most commonly grease-up using a mixture of lanolin and petroleum jelly, available from Boots the Chemist, at Folkestone and Dover.

For further information, please visit: www.cspf.co.uk

BROWNSEA ISLAND SWIM
UK

6.5km/4-mile wild water swim –
around Brownsea Island, Dorset

Take a beautiful island, complete with majestic castle, strutting peacocks and sunset-red squirrels, set just off one of the largest natural harbours in the world, then add in a bucket-load of boys, and you have the birthplace of Lord Baden Powell's first ever Boy Scout camp held way back in 1907. For those unfamiliar with the Scouting movement, this is Brownsea Island, a delightful, peaceful paradise owned by the National Trust, sitting just off Poole Harbour in southern England and accessible only by chain-link ferry from one of the wealthiest areas in England – Sandbanks.

Not only is the island home to the first ever Scout camp and Britain's rapidly declining red squirrel population, as well as sika deer and a heronry, it is also where the Royal Life Saving Society Poole Lifeguard's annual Brownsea Island Swim has taken place every year since 1991.

Wild-water swimmers may elect to enter the full swim of 6.5km/4 miles, which will take them around the circumference of the entire island starting and finishing at the tiny sandy beach just in front of the castle, or they may choose to go halfway round, starting from the same point but finishing at the far end at Pottery Pier.

The swim, which is held in July and starts at varying times each year dependent upon tide times (in 2013 it started at approximately 0830), is open to anyone aged over 14. As it is billed as a 'wild swimming' event, it is the swimmer's responsibility to navigate their own course around the island, and even though there are boats positioned in various places en route, these are there solely for safety reasons and to encourage the swimmers on their way, rather than to act as a guide.

Strict cut-off times are applied to both distances – 180 minutes for the full distance, 150 minutes for the half, and anyone not finishing within these time limits will only be allowed to continue at the discretion of the safety officer or a member of the safety crew.

Indeed, the safety crew may at any time remove a swimmer from the water should they consider they are in danger for any reason.

Once the swim has started, swimmers may change their minds as to what distance they wish to swim. However, a half-distance swimmer deciding to complete the full swim will forfeit any right to being placed or receiving any awards in the half-swim category. Equally, a full distance swimmer finishing at the halfway point will be considered not to have finished the race at all.

Swimmers may also elect whether or not to wear a wetsuit and results are given separately for those who do and those who don't, as it is recognised that wetsuit swimming is considerably faster than non-wetsuit swimming.

All swimmers are granted free entry on to the island, and all finishers will receive a memento and a T-shirt, as well as hot soup and a bread roll at the finish, while those finishing in the first three of each category will also receive a plaque.

The RLSS Poole Lifeguard, who organise the race, are an entirely voluntary lifeguard club and a charity in their own right. As such, they encourage swimmers to raise funds for their favourite charities or for the RLSS itself.

Fittingly, the race motto is: 'Held in the spirit of self belief and madcap adventure, started by the few who wondered if they could swim around Brownsea Island; not so much a race, but a voyage of discovery!'

Who would do this?

Forty-three-year-old graphic/web designer, Paolo De Luca has taken part in the Brownsea Island Swim a total of seven times.

This is a well-established classic UK open-water swim, with around 350 swimmers taking part in both categories, swimming around the beautiful Brownsea Island.

You swim anti-clockwise around the island and catch the tides right in the first half, but then struggle back round the island to the Sandbanks chain ferry. At least, that's the plan of action for this one, but the weather is always influential. Once you reach Pottery Pier the race begins against the incoming tide!

Mental Miscellany

- In 1991, just a handful of local swimmers entered the race.
- In 2013, 259 swimmers took to the water.
- In 2013, the full-distance wetsuit swim was won in 1 hour, 15 minutes, 14 seconds (men) and 1 hour, 21 minutes, 45 seconds (women).
- In 2013, the full-distance non-wetsuit swim was won in 1 hour, 21 minutes, 49 seconds (men) and 1 hour, 31 minutes, 31 seconds (women).
- In 2013, the half-distance wetsuit swim was won by a woman in 1 hour, 3 minutes, 32 seconds; the first man finished in 1 hour, 12 minutes, 38 seconds.
- In 2013, the half-distance non-wetsuit swim was won in 1 hour, 28 minutes, 54 seconds (men; no women entered).
- The average swim time for the full distance is around 2 hours.
- Anyone requiring assistance or wishing to retire should raise

one arm vertically in the air while attempting to head towards the island to shallower water so they can stand and safety cover will come to assist.

* In 2013, £33,381.21 was raised for various charities.

For further information, please visit: www.rlss-poole.org.uk/ brownsea2.htm

BLOOD, SWEAT AND GEARS...

CYCLING
AN OVERVIEW

Cycle racing comes in many forms. It can be quite a complicated sport to the newcomer and has a really old school deep history of racing. Many of these are kept alive and handed down through cycling clubs. Examples are randonee or audax, criterium or road race, time trial and track racing. Track racing has numerous complicated types of events all of its own, but that's a completely separate book. It's a real divide between old school club and the new school of cycling.

Sportives are the most recent incarnation and have really taken off over the last few years. Set over various distances, 100 miles being the most popular, there are usually alternative shorter routes offered. These races usually take place over one day or over a number of days as stages, and are more about personal times than winning, and are very similar to mass marathon running events. Riders choose their start time and are set off in groups of anything up to 100 every five minutes. A transponder is attached to the bike, helmet or race number to log riders' times, which are recorded at the start, when crossing mats throughout the race and at the finish. Feed stations are provided and a sweeper wagon picks up riders who don't finish within the required cut-off times.

Traditional Time Trial races are popular individual events. Local cycling clubs organise these types of events in two versions. Club time trials, which are usually just for members of a club and used as a test of fitness levels, and open time trials, which are official individual races over set distances and open to all cycling clubs and unattached riders (those who don't belong to a club). These races have strict rules. Riders are set off in one-minute intervals by an official acting as a timer while another official will hold the seat post to allow the rider to be 'cleated' (have his feet in pedal clips) which will enable him to have the quickest possible start. Each rider has a number pinned to his back, which are handed out in sequence of riders signing up – there being tactical advantages of going earlier or later in the sequence. These races are all about the quickest time over a set distance ranging from 10 to 100 miles. There are also 12 and 24-hour versions of these types of events.

Audax or *Randonee* is the old school version of the sportive but over longer distances. Originating in Italy, Audax in the UK is the long-distance cycling association. These events are much more low key and are promoted as not being a race but more about participation and adventure, with the ultimate example being events such as the Paris-Brest-Paris race. Distances range from anything above 200km or more, going up to 1200km+ non-stop. Riders usually have a map and a card, which is stamped at checkpoints, usually in village halls with refreshments. Badges are usually awarded on finishing. These events are more about self-sufficiency between control stops and route reading. Riders can go off in groups or individually.

MARATONA DLES DOLOMITES
ITALY

Bike race over the Dolomites 55km/34 miles;
106km/66 miles; 138km/86 miles

Every year in July, the usually calm and peaceful if somewhat daunting Dolomites are besieged by thousands of avid amateur cyclists from all over the world, their colourful Lycra uniforms flashing in the sunlight as they snake their way up the winding mountain roads creating a brightly spangled spectacle that can be seen for miles.

Ever since the race first began in 1987 as part of the 10th anniversary celebrations of the Alta Badia-Raiffeisen Cycling Club, when 166 riders raced 175km/109 miles taking in seven passes, the event has grown in popularity and stature among keen cyclists everywhere, so that in 2013 more than 9,000 of them set out from the start line in the tiny village of La Ila. Certainly the organisers of that first race could never have envisioned that their celebratory club run would turn into what has become one of the most respected and important annual events in the Alta Badia valley.

The success of the race is undoubtedly due in part to the outstanding natural beauty of Italy's most famous mountain range, where the demanding routes have been ridden by great champions who have created cycling history in that most notorious of professional cycling races, the Giro D'Italia. But it is also in no small part due to the involvement of the whole community in the Alta Badia region who every year ensure the smooth running of what has become an enormous event.

The race itself is actually split into three courses with varying degrees of difficulty. These are known as the Sellaronda course, the Middle course and the Maratona course. All courses start in the village of La Ila at 0630, and finish at Corvara.

The Sellaronda course travels in a clockwise direction around the Sella mountain group and contains four passes: the Campolongo Pass at 5.8km/3.5 miles with a gradient of 6.1 per cent; the Pordoi Pass – 9.2km/5 miles and 6.9 per cent; the Sella Pass – 5.5km/3.5 miles and 7.9 per cent; and the Gardena Pass at 5.8km/3.5 miles and 4.3 per cent, giving a total distance of 55km/34 miles and a total altitude difference of 1,780m/5,840ft.

The Middle course follows the same course as the Sellaronda and the same passes, but then continues to ascend the Campolongo Pass a second time before tackling Falzarego/Valparola Pass at 11.8km/7.5 miles with a gradient of 6.7 per cent, making a total distance of 106km/66 miles and a total altitude gain of 3,090m/10,138ft.

The longest course is the Maratona course, which has a total distance of 138km/86 miles and a total altitude difference of 4,190m/13,750ft. This takes in all the same passes as the Middle course with the addition of Giau Pass at 9.9km/6 miles with a gradient of 9.3 per cent.

There are a total of seven refreshment stations around the courses offering food and drink and the whole event, including the thousands of excitable cheering Italian spectators who line the route, is broadcast live on Italian TV.

During the week prior to the race, there is an event called 'Rider's Week', which offers organised group rides, training rides and other cycling events, as well as parties!

National Geographic described the race as, 'one of the biggest, most passionate, and most chaotic bike races on Earth'.

Who would do this?

Paolo De Luca, took part in the Maratona Dles Dolomites in 2007. Here is what he had to say:

> *Because of the numerous passes and altitude gain, the Maratona Dles Dolomites is one of the toughest cyclo-sportives in Europe.*
>
> *It's classic Giro d'Italia riding, one of those burst-out-laughing events, because it's so ridiculous what they throw at you! The majority of the ride I was stood up on the pedals using 12/25 gearing – it makes the legs strong. You reach a corner and, yep, it still goes up again.*
>
> *This one remains the only race where everyone in our group got in, said nothing and collapsed at the finish for an hour. The finish was a battlefield!*

Mental Miscellany

- The inaugural event held in 1987 had 166 riders and was won by an Austrian in just over 10 hours; the only woman who entered the event came from the Netherlands and finished an hour later.
- In 1989, the race had to be abandoned because of snow.
- In 2013, 9,143 cyclists from 52 nationalities started the race; 9,004 finished.
- In 2013, entries consisted of 8,500 men and 839 women.
- In 2013, the race was won in 4 hours, 43 minutes (men) and 5 hours, 22 minutes (women).
- The minimum age for taking part in the Sellaronda or the Middle course race is 15; to take part in the Maratona, participants must be 18 years of age.
- There is a maximum age of 65 for participants wishing to take part in the Maratona.

For further information, please visit: www.maratona.it

L'ÉTAPE DU TOUR
FRANCE

Stage of the Tour de France for amateurs

The cycling race, L'Étape du Tour, meaning literally 'the stage of the tour', was created in 1993 to give an opportunity to amateur and semi-professional cyclists to experience first-hand the toughness of one of the stages of the Tour de France.

Each year a different stage, usually in the mountains, is selected from the current tour and opened up to the cyclists of L'Étape.

The event is held in July just a few days either before or after the actual Tour de France, so that the Tour's chalked markings, roadside flags and route signs are in place, giving riders a real flavour of what it would be like to be racing alongside the professionals on the same tortuous mountain roads and enjoying the atmosphere, excitement and the passion that is present throughout the Tour de France.

The timing of L'Étape also offers riders the opportunity to arrive a few days early or stay a few days after their own race and enjoy the spectacle that is the Tour de France.

Known as a 'travelling race' owing to the fact that it changes its location every year, pursuing the changes in the route of the Tour de France, the L'Étape has in previous years passed through the

Pyrénées, the Alps, the Central Massif and the Mont Ventoux.

The race itself is, of course, extremely testing and participants are advised to prepare and train specifically for the event, which is described as 'physically challenging, requiring intensive training...', although there is no qualification procedure, with riders merely needing to submit a medical certificate of fitness in order to partake.

In 2014, riders of L'Étape will cycle 148km/92 miles along the Pyrenean routes, leaving Pau

Etape

to climb the Col du Tourmalet with an ascent over 17.1km/10.6 miles and an average gradient of 7.3 per cent. They will then descend towards Luz Saint-Sauveur before facing another ascent, this time the Hautacam, covering 13.6km/8.5 miles and with a gradient of 7.8 per cent.

Each climb will be timed and points awarded according to the times taken. The cumulative number of points from all climbs will then decide the ultimate winner of the 'Grimpeur' (climber) Challenge.

Owing to the distance of the ride, the race starts early at 0700 with most riders taking over 10 hours to finish. To assist in the smooth running of the race, the faster cyclists will start at the front and the slowest at the back, causing the peloton to stretch out quite quickly over roads that are closed to traffic.

Consequently, cut-off times have been put in place to allow roads to be opened up again within a reasonable period of time, and slower cyclists may well find themselves withdrawn and eliminated from the race if they fail to meet such times.

Who would do this?

Paolo De Luca, took part in the Étape du Tour in 2011 and completed the ModaneValfrejus to Alpe D'Huez (the Col du Télégraphe 1,566m, the Col du Galibier 2,556m and the Alpe d'Huez 1,950m – a total elevation of 3,200m) stage.

After completing Ironman Austria in Klagenfurt five days before, it seemed like a good challenge to go and do the Étape a couple of days later. Let's go conquer Alpe D'Huez... why not?! It was a bonus to get the Galibier and Télégraphe thrown in on the same day. Only the Étape could throw up such a classic combination of Cols [a depression in the summit line of a chain of mountains often affording a pass from one slope to another].

We camped in Bourg-d'Oisans at the foot of the Alps. No option then but to do the customary lap up Alpe d'Huez the day before the Étape as well!

It was a classic crowds, water pouring over your back, chalk on the roads experience [the names of the Tour de France riders are chalked on the road].

Reaching the finish line

Mental Miscellany

- In 2013, there was a record number of riders in L'Étape, with 13,500 starters.
- In 2013, a record number of 10,627 riders crossed the finish line.
- L'Étape has a very strict 'green' policy, ruling that nothing should be thrown on the ground, waste should be disposed of via the selective sorting system and garbage areas, and riders should behave in an 'eco-responsible' manner at all times.

For further information, please visit: www.letapedutour.com

TOUR DIVIDE
USA

4,418km/2,745-mile single-stage mountain bike race

The Tour Divide is unarguably the longest, if not the toughest, mountain bike race/time trial in the world.

Utilising a set course within the Great Divide Mountain Bike Route (the world's longest off-pavement cycling route) in North America, the event, which can be tackled either as a race with a mass start known as the 'Grand Depart', which takes place some time within the first two weeks of June, or as an individual time trial, which can be ridden at a time to suit the individual, the challenge is to cycle along the route's endless dirt roads and jeep trails that meander through the passes of the Continental Divide. Some of the trails are unmaintained and impossible for all but the most experienced of cyclists to ride.

Travelling through the Canadian provinces of Alberta and British Columbia and the United States of Montana, Idaho, Wyoming, Colorado and New Mexico, the riders of the Tour Divide will climb nearly 60,960m/200,000ft (the equivalent of climbing Mount Everest from sea level seven times).

During the ride, which takes an average of three weeks, athletes will spend around 16 hours a day in the saddle. They will need to use navigational skills to aid them along a route which is unmarked and circuitous, travelling through remote back country where they may come face-to-face with grizzly or black bears, moose or cougars. They must organise enough food and water to carry them comfortably between services which are often more than 100 miles apart, and find shelter each night or bunk down in a bivouac alongside the trail, bearing in mind that the extreme weather and temperatures in the Rocky Mountains can turn on a sixpence, bringing high winds, rain and deep snow, while the monsoon rains of New Mexico can churn up surfaces, turning them into quagmires, and extending hoped-for time limits as riders are forced to wait for the roads to dry or carry their bikes.

The highest point on the route comes at Colorado's Indiana Pass at 3,630m/11,910ft, and during the ride cyclists will have to negotiate isolated river valleys, high desert, broad open grasslands, mountain forests and, at the end of the ride, a section of the Chihuahuan Desert.

Whether the challenge is undertaken as part of the mass start or alone, it is a self-supporting event in the strictest sense – there is absolutely no help given at any point during the race/time trial, personal support crews are not allowed, and the only places to renew supplies are the few small towns en route. In other words, it is all about the rider and his or her gear versus the route and nature. The raison d'être behind any divide race is that it is meant to be done as fast as possible; it is not a cycling tour, it is a test of speed over distance, pure and simple.

To stand even a chance of setting a winning time over such a distance means riders will need to cycle around 240km/150 miles a day, with no rest days. They will also need to maintain their own bikes.

According to the website, questions that riders must ask themselves before even considering entering the event are whether or not they have the will to suffer for days on end, whether or not they are prone to depression, whether they can be happy sleeping in the dirt while it rains all night or coping with thigh-deep snowdrifts over a 10,000ft pass – apparently entirely possible in June after a bad Rockies winter.

They should also consider whether they have enough

experience in multi-day bikepacking, whether they have ridden back-to-back off-road centuries, whether they are an expert level mountain biker, a proficient bike mechanic, a skilled navigator, competent at self-rescue. If the answer to most of these questions is 'no', they advise simply touring the route or taking more time to prepare for the Tour Divide.

In a nutshell, riders taking part in the Tour Divide are on their own. Therefore the biggest challenge they are likely to face, aside from the sheer physical effort of cycling, the varying terrain and the weather, is the mental aspect of dealing with the wretchedness of a self-inflicted plight, the endless rain, the pitch-black nights, the sense of being in the middle of nowhere, the ennui, and having nothing else to think about other than how much your legs ache.

Who would do this?

An ultra-fit bike mechanic with insomnia and a penchant for aloneness and wildlife.

Mental Miscellany

- The Tour Divide has a 60 per cent attrition rate (ie the rate at which competitors drop out of a race on average).
- In the Race Across America cyclists typically have a support crew of 8–12 people and 2–4 vehicles; the Tour Divide has none – you do it all yourself.
- Most people ride the route north to south.
- Typical times for people touring the route, as opposed to racing it, range from 6–10 weeks.
- Records on the website are inconclusive, but it appears the fastest times are in the region of 15 days (men) and 23 days (women).
- In 2013, 143 riders took on the Tour Divide.
- There are no entry fees and no prizes in the Tour Divide.
- The Tour Divide has been completed on single bicycles and tandem bicycles.

- In 2009, *National Geographic Adventure* listed riding the Great Divide Mountain Bike Route in its Top 100 best American adventures.

For further information, please visit: www.tourdivide.org

RIDE ACROSS BRITAIN
UK
1,559km/969 miles – 17,068m/55,997ft of ascent – 9 days

It didn't take long for Olympic rower James Cracknell and his two friends, Julian Mack and Charlie Beauchamp, who together founded sports marketing agency Threshold Sports on the principle of 'more is in you', to come up with an idea that epitomised the company's mission to get more people more active more of the time – a 969-mile bike ride from John O'Groats to Lands End in nine days.

The idea, which was born in 2008, became a reality in 2010, with 472 solo riders and 63 relay teams setting off from a very windy John O'Groats for the first mass participation bike ride.

The ride is broken into nine daily stages averaging around 108 miles a day and, according to its website, is one of the classic cycling challenges on the planet.

Certainly the route, which the organisers claim to be the most varied and interesting route possible, represents the unrivalled diversity of Great Britain's landscape as a whole, taking in the imposing highlands of Scotland, the lush green valleys of Wales, the barren moors of northern England, the chocolate-box villages and country lanes of middle-England and the stunning coastal roads of the south.

However, participants should be aware that the ride is not all about admiring the views: in the nine days they will be out there, come wind, rain, hail or shine – remember this is Britain – riders will face a total climb of around 15,000m/49,200ft, the equivalent of scaling Alpe d'Huez almost 13 times.

The ride in September 2014 will run from south to north, starting at Land's End, crossing the edge of Bodmin Moor and skirting around Dartmoor, ascending and descending numerous short sharp hills throughout Devon and Cornwall until 173km/108 miles later riders will rest overnight in tents pitched by the company support crew.

The second day the riders will cycle 177km/110 miles from Okehampton to Bath, facing further steep ascents and descents, crossing the Quantock Hills and climbing Cheddar Gorge.

Day three sees the cyclists heading towards the Cotswolds, crossing the Severn Bridge into the Forest of Dean and climbing steadily up from the River Wye before continuing on the undulating roads to Ludlow, completing another 159km/99 miles.

Leaving Ludlow, the riders pass through Shropshire and the Cheshire Plains, before passing over the Manchester Ship Canal via a toll bridge, and can revel in the comparatively flat ride that the day brings, even if it is 170km/106 miles from the start until they reach the night's campsite at Haydock Park.

On the fifth day, riders face a journey of 167km/104 miles, which will take them to Hutton-in-the-Forest in Penrith. Happily, en route they will be treated to some spectacular views across the Fylde coast to Blackpool Tower and inland to the Pennines. Sadly, they will also be treated to the world-famous Shap Climb from the steep side. On the plus side, should they have the capacity, they will get to enjoy some pretty potent views of the Lake District.

Day six and a nice round 100 miles will see them reach the southern edge of Glasgow and Hamilton racecourse, where they will spend the night, having first passed through Carlisle, Gretna Green, Lockerbie and the Annandale.

Just three days to go, but today is the longest stretch with a 204km/127 miles taking them from the racecourse to Fort William, having negotiated the Glasgow suburbs, the Campsie Fells, the Trossachs and Glen Ogle, and crossing Rannoch Moor and the famous Glen Coe Pass. Surprisingly, and no doubt thankfully, the final 16km/10 miles of the day are actually flat. Cheeringly, the website informs riders that the hills in Scotland are 'much less steep' – before adding, 'but tend to go on longer'.

The penultimate day and 178km/111 miles will take riders from Fort William to Kyle of Sutherland, via the Great Glen, past the memorial of the Unknown Soldier, on to Fort Augustus, along the banks of Loch Ness, to Beauly and the Cromarty Firth.

At last, the final day arrives and it's 'only' 167km/104 miles to the finish line at John O'Groats. To get there, the cyclists will face an undulating ride through the remotest part of Scotland, climbing up from Kyle of Sutherland to Cnoc Staign and Strath Vagastie before the route meanders through the picturesque and peaceful Strathnaver valley before breaking out on to the rather less placid North Atlantic coast and the final miles to the finish line.

And that's it; it's all over, done and dusted. Saddle sore and weary, the riders can now rest, relax and recuperate, having seen the best of Britain in all her greatness.

Who would do this?

This challenge seems to hold a wide appeal from bicycle-loving rugby players to novice, club and elite cyclists, as well as corporate teams and disabled riders. This is probably due to the immense support offered throughout the race by the crew, who organise the camps, setting up the pop-up tents and catering/ dining tents ready for the arrival of the cyclists. They even provide secure bike parking at night with a guard who is on duty around the clock, so cyclists can get a good night's sleep without having to keep an ear to the ground for potential bicycle burglars.

Mental Miscellany

- At the inaugural event in 2010, 472 solo riders and 63 relay teams entered the event; 94 per cent completed it.

MENTAL!

- In 2010, Ride Across Britain raised £380,000 for Paralympics GB.
- In 2010, riders and crew consumed around 200kg/440lb of porridge, 300kg/660lb of pasta, 20,000 bananas and 46,000 litres of water.
- The ride passes through 3 countries and 23 counties.
- There is a total of 17,068m of ascent.
- In 2014, 750 riders are expected to take part in the Race Across Britain.

For further information, please visit: www.rideacrossbritain.com

PARIS-BREST-PARIS
FRANCE

Cycle 1,200km/746 miles – 9,753m/32,000ft
of ascent – in 90 hours

The Paris-Brest-Paris (or 'PBP' as it is commonly known in the cycling world) is an 'audax' event – a non-competitive event in which participants attempt to cycle long distances within a pre-defined time limit, also known as a *randonneur*. Taking place during August, it's one of the oldest non-stop cycling events in the world, as well as one of the longest.

With its roots stretching as far back as 1891, the first 1,200km/745-mile ride was hailed as a gruelling test of human endurance and cycling proficiency. As such it is only held every four years.

Starting on the southern side of Paris, the route takes the riders west for 600km/372 miles to the port city of Brest on the Atlantic Ocean and returns the same way, taking in 9,753m/32,000ft of climb in total.

Back in 1891, participants had to contend with pedalling their heavy non-streamlined bicycles along dirt roads and cobblestones, whereas today's riders have the advantage of modern technology and surfaced roads. However, they still face the same perpetual hills, rough weather and exhaustive non-stop pedalling as their predecessors, and there is no doubt that the 90-

hour time limit ensures that a finisher's medal is as hard earned now as it was back then. Only the elite will manage to succeed in having their name entered into the event's *Great Book*, which has recorded every single finisher since the very first race.

Today, with the number of competitors standing at around 5,000 from all over the world, there are three staggered starts, depending on a rider's capability. The first group are given a time limit of 80 hours, the intermediate group has 84 hours and the slowest group is allowed up to 90 hours. Riders may choose which group they start in.

Starting times for the three groups are 1700 for the sub-80 hour group, 1830 for the sub-90 hour group, both on the Sunday, and 0500 on the Monday for the 84-hour group.

The route itself is split into 15 stages with each stage having its own map, elevation profile and route sheet, which is provided to the riders some months before the event. The route is well marked with large reflective arrows and is relatively easy to navigate with most of it being on quiet, country roads, although there is the occasional busy city to pass through.

The participants ride continually, stopping only at mandatory checkpoints to have their route books signed and stamped and to grab some food, or they may snatch some sleep and stop off for a sit-down meal en route. The checkpoints also provide medical and mechanical support if required.

Support crews are allowed but they can only give aid to riders at the checkpoints, which are between 65 and 90km/40 and 55 miles apart, so there are no following support cars accompanying the riders who must fend for themselves between checkpoints, in keeping with the true spirit of an audax event.

In the event of a rider having to quit, and with all of the checkpoints being relatively close to railway stations, most non-finishing participants will take the train back to Paris with their bike.

With the PBP route being so hilly, it is the weather that is likely to give the riders most cause for concern, with temperatures potentially reaching 30°C/86°F during the daytime and plummeting to a measly 10°C/50°F at night, while the sun might blast forth its damaging rays all day long or may not put in an appearance at all, being overshadowed by large black clouds dropping giant-sized dollops of rain for long periods. Race organisers recommend protection of feet and hands during the cold periods. They also recommend that riders 'always carry toilet paper as the urge may happen somewhere in the countryside, at dawn and without close restrooms'.

With some of the race taking place at night, the website recommends that riders avoid riding alone in the dark unless they are experienced and suggests that they join a group to minimise the risk of getting lost or falling asleep – saying that it is entirely possible to fall asleep on a bike!

Anyone who wishes to enter the PBP must qualify by taking part in similar events over 200km/125 miles in length, as set out in the race conditions.

Who would do this?

Cyclists come from all over the world and from all walks of life to partake in this race. Most come for the personal physical and mental challenge, knowing they will be taking part in one of the toughest physical and mental tests they will ever endure, with a constant battle between the body demanding rest and the mind denying it in an effort to complete the race within the required time limit.

Mental Miscellany

• Audax cycling is when riders attempt to cycle at least 200km/125 miles, passing through checkpoints every 10km/6 miles or so, with the aim of completing the ride within a specified time limit. All finishers receive equal recognition regardless of their order. Riders may travel alone or in groups and must be self-sufficient between checkpoints.

• Because of the non-competitive nature of the PBP, there are no official records kept of best performances or winners.

- Historically, around 20 per cent of riders will fail to finish the PBP.
- In 2011, the exact distance raced was 1,230km/764 miles.
- In 2011, there were 5,002 starters and 4,068 finishers.
- There is a shorter stage race of around 90–130km/55–80 miles for youths aged between 13 and 18 years, which has a maximum field of 30 and which allows the youths to finish with the adult riders, with the aim of 'helping, advising supervising, sometimes coddling, sometimes sermonising...' the youths so they return home with lots of memories and the desire to continue cycling in the future.
- The next PBP will take place in 2015.

For further information, please visit: www.rusa.org/pbp.html and www.paris-brest-paris.org

STRATHPUFFER
SCOTLAND

Mountain bike for 24 hours – mid-winter

The Scottish Highlands can be wild and inhospitable at the best of times, but in the worst of times, such as mid-winter with an average of 17 hours of darkness and temperatures well below freezing, it must be at its worst. The perfect time for a 24-hour mountain bike ride, then.

Recognised in 2010 by US *Bike Magazine* as one of the 10 toughest mountain bike events on the planet, and attracting competitors from all over the world, the Strathpuffer, which started life in 2005, is a 24-hour mountain bike race that takes place in the Highlands of Scotland every January. It has everything an adventurous, thrill-seeking mountain biker could want – freezing temperatures, perpetual rain, heavy snow, ice, mud, mountains and mayhem, with bikes skidding uncontrollably on black ice and cyclists tumbling off their bikes all over the place, so that by the time they finish they are covered from head to toe in dirt and are virtually unrecognisable

The ride, which takes place near the small town of Strathpuffer, is made up of laps of approximately 11km/7 miles, and takes riders along mountain tracks and forest trails, testing them with everything from sticky muddy puddles to pedal-deep snow, to death defying icy corners.

To deal with the harsh conditions, cyclists may use bikes with spiked tyres to help alleviate the icy problems and single speeds in the hope that their simplicity will mean there are fewer parts to go wrong. One of the most oft-repeated bits of advice is for cyclists to ride a bike they are used to.

Cyclists are also advised to take plenty of spare parts to replace worn or broken bits (for their bikes, not themselves) – apparently the mud is so abrasive it destroys drivetrains, and brake pads can disappear within just a few laps – as bicycle repair shops are unlikely to be open in the dead of night or early hours of the morning. Due to the changing conditions in both the weather and terrain over a 24-hour period, it is recommended that cyclists also take a selection of tyre types to suit the variable conditions.

The race starts at 10am on a Saturday and finishes at 10am on the Sunday. At this point a rider may finish the lap they are riding so long as they complete it by 11am, but may not start a new one.

Cyclists may enter the race as a solo rider, a pair or a team of four (quad).

In addition to the Strathpuffer 24-hour winter race, there is also a summer race held every July, known as the Puffer Lite. This was started in 2009 to offer riders an opportunity to enjoy the glorious scenery and trails in better summer conditions. The Puffer Lite is a 12-hour race using the same course as the Strathpuffer, although riders can expect their lap times to decrease on average by 10 minutes.

Who would do this?

According to some of the reports written about the race, it is mainly those who are fairly experienced mountain bikers although no qualification is required to enter this event – the main requisite would seem to be to have a comfortable bike that you are happy to sit on for a very long time!

Apart from those who harbour a desire to test their physical fitness and mental fortitude in an environment that would be more obviously enjoyed from inside a log cabin with a wood-burning stove, and is better suited to wild deer than to mountain bikers, the real gem of this particular challenge according to previous riders is the opportunity to push yourself beyond the limits of your normal riding and to experience the immense personal satisfaction that is guaranteed when completing a 24-hour race, particularly as such races are few and far between.

Then there is the unique experience of seeing the sun rise in such a majestic place and in such conditions: not only does it denote the move from dark to light, it also denotes the end of the race is within sight.

Those who have partaken in the event report feelings of relief once the race is over, mixed with a feeling of sadness that it has come to an end.

Mental Miscellany

- The Strathpuffer is reputed to be the only 24-hour mountain bike event held in winter conditions in the world.
- The fastest lap in 2013 in the 24-hour race was 32 minutes, 27 seconds; the slowest was 1 hour, 29 minutes, 26 seconds.
- In 2013, the 24-hour male solo race was won in 23 hours, 18 minutes, 34 seconds, with 28 laps being completed, and the female solo race was won in 24 hours, 19 minutes, 7 seconds, with 24 laps being completed.
- In 2013, the male pairs race was won in 23 hours, 56 minutes, with 37 laps; the female pairs race was won in 24 hours, 43 minutes, 12 seconds, with 15 laps; and the mixed pairs race was won in 24 hours, 18 minutes, 45 seconds, with 25 laps.
- In 2013, the male quads race was won in 24 hours, 7 minutes, 48 seconds, with 36 laps; the female quads race was won in 24 hours, 3 minutes, 34 seconds, with 24 laps; and the mixed quads race was won in 24 hours, 24 minutes, 56 seconds, with 36 laps.
- Finishers in 2013 comprised 57 solos, 46 pairs and 64 quads.
- The rules state that riders cannot accept outside mechanical assistance or parts on the course, except from other competitors.

MENTAL!

- It is mandatory for all riders to carry emergency food supplies, a whistle, a survival blanket and an emergency light.
- Waterproof shoes and gloves are recommended throughout.
- Competitors under 16 must provide written parental consent and riders under 14 must be accompanied by an adult while competing.

For further information, please visit: www.strathpuffer.co.uk

YAK ATTACK
INDIA

Highest mountain bike race on Earth

Mountain biking racing can be tough – or it can be very tough. Take the Yak Attack mountain bike race, for example. Taking place every year in March in Nepal, the Yak Attack is the world's highest mountain bike race, offering a total altitude gain of over 12,000m/39,370ft, as it follows the prodigious Himalayas for a total distance of 400km/248 miles.

Naturally, with altitude comes decreased oxygen levels, and with the course peaking at an almighty 5,416m/17,769ft such levels are decreased by a whopping 50 per cent when compared to the availability of oxygen at sea level.

And then there's the weather, which starts out at a winsomely warm 30°C/86°F for the first few days before rapidly descending down to as low as -15°C/5°F – and that's without taking wind chill into account!

Unsurprisingly, given this is the Himalayas, the terrain can be fairly hostile, not to mention changeable, too, with a vastness of variety that is breathtaking – lurching from rough, uneven ground that gives new meaning to the expression 'bone shaker', rattling riders and battering bikes alike, to the soft silken sandhills and dunes that offer a cyclist no respite but an exceedingly effective resistance-training session, to silvery streams, wobbly suspension bridges, gluey mud, threatening landslides and, more often than not, simple, yet utterly unwelcome, snow.

The race itself starts at Kathmandu, crossing the Thorong La Pass, before finishing at Khaniya Ghat. Until 2013 the Yak Attack has been divided into eight stages, but for 2014 the organisers decided to turn the tough screw a little tighter and merge four stages into two giant stages, meaning that stage two will become a mind-blowing 86km/53.5 miles with an eye-watering 2,700m/8,858ft of climb and stage four will increase its distance to 60km/37 miles with a staggering 3,200m/10,498ft of climb.

Also new in 2014 is the allocation of one porter to each rider, allowing all riders to have 20kg/44lb of gear available to them.

Race organisers describe the Yak Attack as a 'no frills' kind of race, explaining that riders will be racing through a hostile and harsh environment with only basic facilities and few, if any, refinements. They point out that things don't always go to plan, service can be irritatingly delayed, hot showers may not be available and keeping in touch with the outside world may not be possible for days at a time.

Taking these considerations into account, they suggest that only those cyclists looking for adventure and an opportunity to really test their willpower and strength against some of the toughest elements, terrain and weather known to man should apply to enter this race.

However, the website also states that for those who do fit this description, riding in the Yak Attack will be a true life experience, taking riders up to the highest high and plunging them back down to the depths of despair. They say it is a race that will leave riders physically and emotionally battered and bruised but that the memories they take away with them of a beautiful country with beautiful people will remain with them forever.

Who would do this?

Experienced mountain bikers who are used to cycling long distances over difficult terrain and in variable weather, who embrace such challenges with open arms and a firm resolve.

According to the website, those who have partaken in the Yak Attack have commented that 'the ride isn't racing, it's torture', and that it is 'the most awesome riding I've ever done'. Perhaps most telling of all is one rider's description of the event as being 'raw mountain biking'.

Mental Miscellany

- The first Yak Attack was held in 2007.
- In 2013, the race was won in 21 hours, 24 minutes, 51 seconds (men) and 26 hours, 42 minutes, 29 seconds (women).
- In 2013 there were 33 riders and 28 finishers.
- Yak Attack is run as a non-profit making event and benefits Nepali athletes and the Annapurna region (Western Nepal) communities.

For further information, please visit: www.yak-attack.co.uk

WHY DO ONE WHEN YOU CAN DO ALL THREE...?

TRIATHLON/IRONMAN
AN OVERVIEW

The triathlon consists of three disciplines – swimming, cycling and running – and is designed to test the endurance of an athlete more than if they were undertaking just one discipline at a time. In competition, the disciplines always follow the same order – swim, cycle, run. There is no rest between each discipline.

Distances of each discipline can vary from race to race, but the International Triathlon Union (ITU) distances are generally the ones used in competition, as follows:

	SWIM	BIKE	RUN
SPRINT	750m(0.5 miles)	20km(12.4 miles)	5km(3.1 miles)
OLYMPIC	1.5km(0.93 miles)	40km(24.8 miles)	10km(6.2 miles)
ITU LONG	3km(1.86 miles)	80km(49.6 miles)	20km(12.4 miles)
HALF-IRONMAN	1.9km(1.2 miles)	90km(56 miles)	21.09km(13.1 miles)
FULL IRONMAN	3.8km(2.4 miles)	180km(112 miles)	42.195km(26.2 miles)

As there is no rest between disciplines with the athletes moving or 'transitioning' directly from one to the next, they will set up their bike and running gear in the transition areas prior to the start of a race.

The first discipline, the swim, is pretty much a free-for-all, with everyone charging into the water together, jostling for position, before eventually settling down into a more orderly swim. To lose less time, athletes keep swimming until their hands hit the ground.

The first transition (known as T1) is the bike – and the most important thing to remember is where you left it! Socks, shoes and helmets should be left with the bike, and helmets should be properly secured before leaving the transition area – failure to do so may result in a penalty or disqualification.

The second transition (T2) takes athletes from the bike to the run. Cyclists will coast into the transition area, stretching out their legs while still on their bikes in order to prepare for the run. They will then park the bike, remove their helmets, put on their trainers, and head out on to the running course.

The timing of a triathlon event includes transition times between each event.

Ultra-Triathlons and Ironman

There is a general misconception that ultra-distance triathlon is anything longer than an Ironman. However, all Ironmans are ultras, but not all ultras are Ironmans. This is because 'Ironman' is a brand – a company that organises ultra-triathlons – and is the most commonly known. Many other companies and organisations also put on ultra-triathlons.

Distance-wise, an ultra-triathlon consists of a minimum swim of 3.86km/2.4 miles, a minimum bike ride of 180km/112 miles and a minimum run of 42.2km/26.2 miles.

There are also double, triple, quadruple, quintuple and deca Ironmans, the distances for which are:

	SWIM	BIKE	RUN
IRONMAN	3.86km(2.4 miles)	180km(112 miles)	42.2km(26.2 miles)
DOUBLE	7.6km(4.7 miles)	360km(220 miles)	84.4km(52.4 miles)
TRIPLE	11.4km(7.1 miles)	540km(340 miles)	126.6km(78.7 miles)
QUAD	15.2km(9.4 miles)	720km(450 miles)	168.8km(104.9 miles)
QUIN	19km(12 miles)	900km(560 miles)	211km(131 miles)
DECA	38km(24 miles)	1,800km) (1,100 miles	421km(262 miles)

In addition, there can be 10-day (deca) triathlons and double-decas, and in 2013, for the first time ever, a triple-deca Ironman (one Ironman a day for 30 days!) took place in Italy. This event was largely experimental; indeed the organisers stated the purpose of the event as: 'For understanding where a human body could go, where athletes will put their mind, how far they could resist pain, stress, mental limit.' To this end, the athletes were checked every day for changes in body composition and, prior to the event, organisers sent out a plea to local runners to run with the competitors so they would never be alone and to encourage them to keep going.

For further information, please visit: www.decaironman.com

Ironman

As stated above, an Ironman triathlon consists of a 3.86km/2.4-mile swim, a 180km/112-mile bike ride and a 42.2km/26.2-mile run. The three disciplines are raced in that order without a break and there is a strict time limit of 17 hours to complete the race.

Ironman events generally start at 7am. There is a swim cut-off time of 2 hours, 20 minutes, and the bike cut-off is at 5.30pm. All must finish by midnight.

History of the Triathlon

Triathlon originates from France when, back in the twenties, they held an event known as 'Les Troi Sports' (three sports), which consisted of a cross-Channel swim (across the River Marne), a 12km/7.5-mile bike ride and a 3km/1.75-mile run. In 1934, this changed to become a cross-Channel swim (River Marne), a 10km/6.25-mile bike ride and a 1,200m/0.75-mile run.

In the seventies, the Americans came in on the act, with the First Mission Bay Triathlon being held on 25 September 1974 in San Diego. Today, most consider this date to be the official 'birthday' of the modern triathlon, with 46 competitors swimming 440m/500 yards, cycling 8km/5 miles and running 10km/6 miles.

The Ironman came into existence in Hawaii, initially as three separate events – the Waikiki Rough Water Swim (3.8km/2.4 miles), The Oahu Bike Race (180km/112 miles) and The Honolulu Marathon (42.2km/26.2 miles). In 1978, these events combined to become the Hawaii Ironman Triathlon. The inaugural event saw 15 competitors take part with 12 finishers. By 1982 there were nearly 600 competitors and the event was broadcast by American TV channel ABC. By 2006, the number of competitors swelled to 3,000.

Since 1978, the Ironman World Championships have been held every autumn in Hawaii. The event has a reputation of being extremely gruelling, both in length and race conditions.

In 1997, disabled athletes were allowed for the first time. Cut-off times are the same as for non-disabled athletes.

For further information, please visit: www.ironman.com

Duathlon

As a precursor to participating in a full triathlon or beyond, there is the option to partake in a duathlon. These are run in the same way as a triathlon, with no rest between the different disciplines.

A duathlon incorporates running and cycling and can be of varying distances. There are also ultra-duathlons, which usually consist of a 20km/12.5-mile run followed by an 80km/50-mile bike ride, followed by a 10km/6-mile run.

The world's largest duathlon was the inaugural London duathlon (10km/6- mile run – 20km/12.5-mile bike – 5km/3-mile run), which was held in Richmond Park in 2005 with 2,500 participants. Now, on average, 4,000 people take part in this annual event.

The world's premier duathlon is the Powerman Zofingen in Switzerland. This consists of a hilly 10km/6-mile run (mostly trails), a very hilly 150km/93-mile bike ride (3 x 50km/31-mile loops featuring the Bodenburg ascent) and ends with another very hilly 30km/18-mile trail run.

With the increased popularity of extreme sports, there is also a new form of duathlon known as the 'Dirty-Du'. This is an off-road or trail run followed by a mountain bike leg, followed by another off-road or trail run.

Aquathlon

An aquathlon is a variation of a duathlon, incorporating a swim instead of a bike ride, and generally follows triathlon distances with a 1km/0.5-mile swim followed by a 5km/3-mile run or a 2.5km/1.6-mile run after which there's a 1km/0.6-mile swim and a 2.5km/1.6-mile run.

Aquabike

A more recent addition to the 'triathlon' stage is the aquabike – a swimming and cycling event. These generally take place alongside Ironman and triathlon events, on the same course alongside the main event, and follow the same format. The idea behind the aquabike is to allow people with joint problems to take part in a triathlon/duathlon-based event by simply missing out the running element.

Mental Miscellany

- Triathlon rules state that no propulsive devices may be used during the swim, no forward progress may be made without a bike during the ride, and no forward progress may be made while crawling during the run.
- In triathlon the word 'bonk' is used when an athlete has reached the point where fatigue has taken over, exhaustion has set in, and he can go no further.
- In triathlon the word 'brick' is used to describe workouts where a bike ride is immediately followed by a run.
- In triathlon/cycling terms, an 'aerobar' is not a chocolate bar filled with bubbles but an extension on the bike's handlebars that allows the cyclist to position his body more aerodynamically.
- Triathlon is one of the fastest-growing sports in popularity in recent years in the UK. Figures show that in 2011 there were over 700 triathlons, duathlons and aquathlons in the UK with more than 100,000 competitors.
- Shopping is considered the fourth discipline of triathlon!

For further information, please visit: www.britishtriathlon.org

ARCH TO ARC
UK/FRANCE

*483km/300-mile run-swim-bike Marble Arch
to Arc de Triomphe*

In 2001 an Englishman named Eddie Ette did something no man had ever done before – he ran 140km/87 miles from London's Marble Arch to Dover, then swam across the English Channel to Calais (a distance of between 33 and 56km/21 and 35 miles, dependent upon the tides and tiredness of the swimmer), and followed that by cycling 291km/181 miles from Calais to the Arc de Triomphe in Paris. He did it all in a cumulative time of 81 hours and 5 minutes (including wait/recovery periods) and set a world record.

It was the first time anyone had achieved this incredible feat as a solo performance, and for Eddie it was the catalyst that led to him setting up Enduroman, a company that today organises opportunities for others to take on extreme challenges, including the one Eddie undertook in 2001, either as a solo attempt like Eddie or as a team.

The Arch to Arc as the event is now known, is an approximately 483km/300-mile continuous triathlon challenge linking London and Paris via an English Channel swim. Anyone entering the event as a solo athlete needs to be experienced in ultra-distance events.

For those entering as a team, there can be any number of

members from a minimum of two (the usual is six), and each member will take it in turns to run, swim or cycle in 60-minute intervals. The advice on the website is that each team member should be comfortable over an Olympic-distance triathlon. Wetsuits are permissible!

The route of the challenge starts from London's Marble Arch, with the run going through Hyde Park, past Buckingham Palace and over the River Thames before progressing into the picturesque rolling hills of the Kent countryside, and finishing at Dover Harbour on the shores of the English Channel.

From here, dependent upon the weather and tides, the swimmers enter the water at either Shakespeare Beach or Samphire Hoe and, in theory at least, take the shortest 34km/21-mile route by swimming directly to Cap Gris Nez on the Calais coast. However, in practice, thanks to the force of the tides and the tiredness of the swimmers, they usually end up zigzagging across the Channel and swimming considerably further than if they were able to swim in a straight line.

Once they are on their bikes, the athletes will set out from the Calais Sailing Club following the coast road through Boulogne heading towards Paris via Abbeville, Beauvais and Persan. They will then follow the route of the Tour de France up the Champs Élysées to the undoubtedly very welcome finish line at the Arc de Triomphe.

The timing of the challenge starts the minute the athletes leave Marble Arch and doesn't stop until they reach the Arc de Triomphe. The rules state that the athletes will start the run stage no more than 48 hours (solo) or 20 hours (relay) before their allocated swim start time (these are given to the athletes in advance according to tide times). This is known as the 'Relevant Time' and allows five days to swim on the tide.

Athletes are allowed a maximum of 12 hours recovery from when the race organisers decide that the pilot boat has moored at Calais Harbour until the start of the bike stage. To ensure all routes and modes of travel are properly adhered to, the race director will be with the athletes throughout the challenge, and will also act as an official witness to their achievements.

Who would do this?

Forty-three-year old Paolo De Luca entered the Arch to Arc as one of a six-man team in a corporate challenge in 2013, to raise funds for the Honeypot children's charity.

Our corporate challenge was between three teams, each with six members. We did the run in 10km stints, the swim in one-hour stints and the ride in 30–40 mile stints. Although we didn't complete the swim leg, I can see the group-bonding potential and why it's taken on as a corporate challenge. One boat out of the nine crossing the Channel that day completed. That's why the Channel has a fierce reputation and low completion rate.

Accompanying Paolo in the challenge were fellow members of the Zoom Tri Club, Bournemouth. The following is an extract written by Paolo's teammate, Sharon Glenister, and is taken with kind permission from their blog at: www.team-hydro-velocity.blogspot.co.uk

The race started at Tower Bridge on Friday at 7.30am. Unfortunately one of our team members was stuck in New York, so didn't make the run, so Stu and Paolo 'volunteered' to do a couple of extra legs. Great run, part of it over the undulating North Downs on the Pilgrim Way.

Saturday morning, 9am, onto our boat the Optimist – heading out to Shakespeare Beach for our first swimmer to dive off the boat, swim to shore and then get the starting order to start swimming. Each of us had to do an hour in the water, non-wetsuit; luckily by now Bucky from NY had arrived.

First few hours went well until the wind picked up, sea got rougher, swimming got tougher and slower, boat started rocking more and some of the team started feeling rougher too!

Everyone did their first swim slot and then the second swim slots started. Each of us found it tough being without a nice

warm wetsuit, getting back into the water feeling seasick and not having eaten enough, but getting on with it. It had to be done.

Despite the cold and waves bashing me around, my goggles kept misting up and I had to dig deep to keep swimming. The boat was lunging from side to side and its spotlight kept going up and down; it was really hard to keep going, the last two minutes seemed to take forever as one of the team put the lights on the next swimmer.

At last he was ready and a frozen me was able to grab the ladder and get out. I have never felt so cold in my life. Discussions had to start. The pilot advised us the wind was now 20mph and we were likely to take another 6–8 hours to get to shore with no guarantee of getting to land. Everyone was exhausted and half the team felt weak with seasickness. Seven other boats had already aborted their swim and so the hardest, most disappointing decision was made – we had to abort our attempt to swim to France after 12 hours. We had done about two-thirds.

Our next challenge was a few hours away so we tried to get some sleep in the car park in our support vehicle. Not much sleep for our support crew who were still working hard to get the first bikes ready.

Sunday, 5am, bit of a panic as our first cyclist accidentally took a wrong turning and ended up on the motorway! Eventually back on track but now at back of pack, pushed on not seeing much as it was too foggy and raining. Fourth cyclist set off and ride brightened up; spirits were soaring as passed through French countryside.

Last cyclist after two cans of Red Bull, a Coke and a gel set off, adrenaline really kicking. Finally huge cheers as all the teams lined the road as we made it over the finish line around 3.30pm, in third place – a podium finish, we did it!

London to Paris – a brilliant adventure with an amazing team! Hardest challenge I've done so far but so worth it!

Arch to Arc

Mental Miscellany

- To date, only 13 people (including Eddie Ette) have successfully completed the Arch to Arc solo event – 9 men and 4 women.
- The world record for the solo Arch to Arc is 73 hours, 39 minutes and 12 seconds, set in 2012.
- The fastest time for a woman to complete the solo event is 92 hours exactly, achieved in 2012.
- The world record for the team Arch to Arc is 35 hours 53 minutes, set in 2011 by a team of six.
- Anyone wishing to take part in the Arch to Arc solo event should have completed a 6-hour sea swim in temperatures of 16 degrees or less during the year of their attempt.
- Anyone wishing to take part in the Arch to Arc team event should have completed a two-hour qualification swim in the year of their attempt.

- Athletes may use a wetsuit for the swim stage.
- All athletes are weighed before the start of the race and may be weighed at any time during the race. If when so weighed, an athlete weighs less than 90 per cent of their original recorded weight, then they will not be allowed to continue until they reach that minimum weight.
- The next Enduroman Arch to Arc challenge takes place in June 2014, although challenges may be made at other times on the spring tides.

For further information, please visit: www.enduroman.com

EMBRUNMAN
FRANCE

One of the toughest triathlons in the world

The first Embrunman event was held in 1984 but it took until 1990 before the current format and distances for the event were permanently adopted, establishing its well-deserved reputation for being one of the toughest triathlons in the world. Indeed, it is testament to that reputation that Embrun has since held stages for the World Cup triathlon on several occasions.

Such a reputation comes largely from the fact that Embrunman has stuck to the original triathlon distances – 3.8km/2.5-mile swim, 186km/116-mile cycle, marathon distance (42.2km/26.2 miles) run – which were in existence long before specific 'Ironman' (which is, as discussed earlier, merely a brand name) competitions came on the scene and long before triathlon distances were turned into the Olympic, sprint and other categorisations that we are familiar with today.

As for the name, 'Embrunman' actually comes from 'Embrun' – the area in the Hautes-Alpes in the Provence-Alpes-Côte d'Azur region in south-eastern France where the race is held – and the event forms the main part of a sporting weekend held in August, which is dedicated to the sport of triathlon, incorporating an Olympic distance event and shorter distances for youths or beginners.

The beautiful Embrun area

However, for those tackling the toughest and longest event, the race starts with a two-lap swim in the Plan d'eau D'Embrun, a lake situated 780m/2,559ft above sea level.

Following the swim, the athletes move on to what is undoubtedly the toughest part of this particular triathlon, the bike ride, which takes them up the notoriously long and impossibly steep Col d'Izoard with its 3,600m/11,811ft of elevation, and which is used in the infamous Tour de France, where it tests the toughest and finest of the world's pure-bred, specific-sport cyclists, never mind those who have already swum 3.8km/2.5 miles and have yet to run a marathon!

Indeed it is the ride up the Col d'Izoard on the north side that takes the riders close to the edge many times with climbs of six per cent and eight per cent gradient, winding up through a forest of larch to the rocky top of Col D'Izoard, while on the south side there is a long straight climb and one of the steepest parts of the ride before the road passes through a conifer forest offering some tantalising views of the valley below. However, once the riders are out of the shelter of the trees, they find themselves in an area decidedly lacking in vegetation and become exposed to the wind and the delightfully named 'Brain Deserted', an area of rocky wilderness, before finally reaching the transition area.

Hopefully reunited with their brains and adopting their running persona, the athletes will now set out to run a full marathon, consisting of a two-lap course around the perimeter of Embrun. It is a tough course, with each lap taking in a circuit of the lake, a 400m/1,312ft climb up to Embrun village and a run around the surrounding villages, which is all very scenic but offers virtually nothing in the way of shade – and remember, this is France, in August, with serious amounts of sunshine, cloudless navy skies and temperatures averaging around 26°C/78°F.

Who would do this?

Paolo De Luca took part in the Embrunman in 2011. Here is what he had to say:

> *A dark swim start, no marker lights makes it a messy free-for-all of punching and goggle grabbing.*
>
> *The bike route is OUCH! One word – Col d'Izoard – on a triathlon of Ironman proportions this is mental. Roads are still painted – Evans, Schleck, Voeckler [professional cyclists' names painted or chalked on roads by fans during the Tour de France] – from Le Tour the month before. Even on the last 10km they throw in a few more cols.*
>
> *Add to that a two-lap marathon with 800m worth of climbing. I didn't make it back in daylight! Respect to those that do and respect to any Embrun finishers...period!*

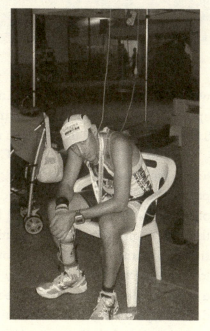

Mental Miscellany

- The website shows no results until 1990 when the event was won in 10 hours, 31 minutes (men) and 13 hours, 33 minutes (women).
- The website shows the current event records standing at 9

hours, 34 minutes, 10 seconds (men) and 10 hours, 56 minutes, 43 seconds (women).

- In 1988, the Olympic distance triathlon was added to the programme – this includes a 1.5km/1-mile swim, 43.5km/27-mile bike ride and 10km/6-mile run.
- In 1991, Embrun hosted a stage of the World Cup Triathlon for the first time; it now claims to have hosted the event more times than anywhere else in France.
- In 1993, Embrunman celebrated its 10th anniversary by hosting a stage of the World Cup for the third consecutive time, bringing record numbers to the event with 1,500 triathletes taking part in all events.
- In 2013, Embrunman celebrated its 30th anniversary, with 3,500 triathletes participating in all events, 1,500 in the long-distance event alone.

For further information, please visit: www.embrunman.com

IRONMAN LANZAROTE
CANARY ISLANDS

Full Ironman – in the heat of the Canarian sun

For most people, a trip to Lanzarote would involve basking on one of its glorious beaches, but for the 1,800 athletes who flock here every May, it's not so much about the basking as it is about their ability to endure.

For they are here to take part in what the organisers proclaim to be an unrivalled test of strength, character and mind-body excellence, all wrapped up in an Ironman competition known simply as 'Ironman Lanzarote' whose race motto is 'normal limits do not apply'.

And so it is with that portentous warning that the optimistic and self-testing amateurs, together with the glory-seeking professionals, arrive to pit themselves against the long-distance triathlon event containing the standard 3.9km/2.4-mile swim, the 180.2km/112-mile bike ride and the full marathon run of 42.2km/26.2 miles, in temperatures that will rise from around 22°C/70°F in the morning to 30°C/90°F later in the day, and strong winds, especially in the north of the island on the bike course, although these may assist later in cooling body temperatures during the run along the seafront.

The first discipline, the swim, starts at 7am on the beach at Playa

Timanfaya

Grande, Puerto del Carmen, one of the main tourist resorts on the island, and is a two-lap course in the sea – except for about 20m/66ft when, unusually, the athletes leave the water to run on the sand before re-entering the sea for the second lap. There is a cut-off time for the swim of 2 hours, 20 minutes after the race start, and wetsuits are mandatory.

Moving on to the bikes, the athletes set off on what is effectively a tour of the whole island, including 2,551m/8,369ft of climb and the strong onshore winds. On the upside, they will be treated to some stunning views and vistas as the ride passes through El Golfo, Timanfaya, Haria and Mirador del Rio, with the renowned La Graciosa island green sea view. The organisers warn, however, that the route is open to traffic, although it is controlled by the police, and riders should proceed with caution at all times. The cut-off time for the bike section of the race is 11 hours, 30 minutes after the start time.

Following their island tour, the athletes will then begin their marathon run. This consists of three laps, the first one of 21.10km/13 miles will take them to Playa Honda and the following two, each of 10km/6 miles, will take them along the seafront at Avenida de Las Playas, Puerto del Carmen, where, if they still have enough presence of mind, they can revel in the glory of their seaside surroundings, pick up a tan from the potentially searing sun, and enjoy the vociferous support of the enthusiastic spectators as

The Mirador climb

they head towards the finish. They can also refuel from any of the five aid stations that serve food and drink along the way.

There is a cut-off of 17 hours after the start time, with the race officially closing at midnight.

Who would do this?

Paolo De Luca, triathlete, 16 x Ironman, 100 Marathon Club member and ultra runner, has completed the Ironman Lanzarote three times.

The Pool Bar at La Santa proclaims this to be 'The Toughest Ironman in the World' – I'm not quite sure it merits that, but it gets a tick for tough!

Done this one three times, it's synonymous with Ironman in Europe with the standard Ironman sea swim.

Then there's the bike...wind+terrain+heat. It's all down to the elements; that's what makes Lanza so cool and lovable!

Enduroman do a double-Ironman here!

For further information, please visit: www.enduroman.com

Paolo on the course

Mental Miscellany

- The first Ironman Lanzarote took place in 1992.
- In 1992, there were 148 registered competitors and 116 finishers, of which 108 were men and 8 were women.
- In 2013, 1,767 competitors entered and 1,649 finished, of which 1,616 were men and 151 were women.
- In 2013, the event was won in 8 hours, 42 minutes, 41 seconds (men) and 9 hours, 33 minutes, 35 seconds (women), with the last finishers completing in 17 hours, 10 minutes, 55 seconds (men); 16 hours, 53 minutes, 36 seconds (women).
- Current records for the event stand at 8 hours, 30 minutes, 34 seconds (men), set in 2011, and 9 hours, 24 minutes, 39 seconds (women), set in 1995.
- For professional Ironmen, this event offers 40 qualifying slots for the World Championships held in Hawaii.
- 1,500kg/3,300lb of bananas and 35,000 litres of water will be consumed during the event!

For further information, please visit: www.ironmanlanzarote.com

NORSEMAN XTREME TRIATHLON
NORWAY

Swim ice-cold fjord – bike up mountain –
run to mountain-top finish

Rise at 0230 hours, don wetsuit and swim cap, register for race between 0300 and 0345, catch 0400 ferry, jump off ferry at 0450 and plunge into 122m/400ft of deep icy Norwegian fjord... start racing at 0500.

And this is just the start of a triathlon of Ironman proportions that will take you from sea level to 1,850m/6,070ft, via a total ascent of 5,000m/16,404ft, through some of Norway's most strikingly beautiful land, including the haunting Hardangervidda mountain plateau and the rocky peak of Gaustatoppen where the race finishes: the water will be cold, the weather may be gloriously gorgeous or dastardly dreadful, the wildlife, including reindeer, porpoises and orcas, may be abundant or invisible. Nothing is set in stone for this aptly titled 'xtreme' triathlon, but the proper preparation will give participants their best, probably only, chance of receiving one of the coveted black finishers' T-shirts at the end.

It stands to reason that entering into a swim that takes place in water with an average race-day temperature of 13–15°C/55–59°F is not something to be undertaken lightly, particularly when

306

you will be plunging into its bone-chilling depths from a ferry at 0500 hours. Reassuringly, the race organisers take the matter seriously enough to include a whole series of articles on cold-water swimming within their website, which, among other things, suggests participants should initially practise swimming in cold waters under safe circumstances, limiting exposure to short periods in shallow waters before gradually increasing duration of swims close to the shore, and being escorted by a boat, in order to become accustomed to the body's response to the cold.

This is not a matter of excessive caution either, for the Norseman Xtreme swim takes place in Eidfjord, one of Norway's major hydropower productions sites, which is surrounded by snowy mountains from which large amounts of cold mountain water are discharged into the fjord on a regular basis, ensuring there is never an opportunity for the fjord to warm up.

Of course the 3.8km/2.5-mile swim through the cold, slightly salty, magically green waters of the fjord while taking in the breathtaking mountain scenery is only the start of the day; as daybreak begins, the swimmers transform themselves into cyclists, and may or may not have heeded the warning to take the first 40km/25 miles up to Dyranut at a steady pace to allow for the 1,250m/4,101ft climb up from sea level, which will take the average cyclist around two hours.

On reaching the top of the climb, cyclists are advised to take a windproof jacket from their support crew in readiness for the chill winds they are likely to encounter on the Hardangervidda plateau. Further advice is given for cyclists to pay careful attention to the state of the uneven terrain of the road, which is full of potholes and unexpected lumps and bumps, and to keep both hands on the handlebars at all times.

Assuming the winds are favourable, the 50km/31-mile journey across the Plateau is usually the fastest part of the bike course, though riders should beware the stunning views, which can be a dangerous distraction.

Of course this is an extreme event and, therefore, there cannot be a fast-easy section without there being a slow-hard section to follow and this comes after Geilo with 45km/28 miles of steep climbs and descents and some extremely bad road surfaces. The saving grace is that this does at least lead to the final, albeit brutal, ascent, which takes the riders from 500m/1,640ft above sea level on the Uvdal Valley floor up to Imingfjell at 1,200m/3,937ft. The most important thing for riders to remember at this point is that they have still to run a marathon and should therefore not push too hard on the climb. In order to assist with this, the final section of the bike ride levels off to a large degree before descending for 30km/18 miles to the transition area in Austbygde.

Leaving the transition area next to the placid waters of Lake Tinn, the first 20km/12 miles of the run passes alongside the lake, allowing runners to view the iconic apex of Mount Gaustatoppen, where they will finish.

However, first they must ascend the pertinently if tongue-in-cheek named 'Zombie Hill' – so named by the race organisers to reflect the looks on some of the athletes' faces as they approach the top! With 17km/10.5 miles of constant so-steep-it's-impossible-to-run-it climbing still to go, most runners will be forced to walk this part of the course as fast as possible, and in deference to the mountain's challenge, there are two cut-off points at 32.5km/20 miles and 37.5km/23 miles where medical crews will check runners to ensure that it is safe for them to continue up the mountain to the top.

The final path to the finish line is described as a 'strenuous hike', including as it does loose rock and scree, all sizes and shapes of pebbles, as well as huge boulders, and will take the average athlete about 1 hour and 20 minutes to reach the finish line. Often, when the weather is at its worst and low cloud, mist and rain have closed in on the top of the mountain, the runners will be encouraged and guided in by shouts and cheers from those at the finish line, although there are red 'T' marks painted on rocks every few metres along the path as well. Of course, in fine weather, the views from the top are unforgettable, offering one of the widest vistas in northern Europe.

Cheeringly, whatever the weather, there is also a cabin and café on top offering warmth and sustenance to the weary finishers.

Who would do this?

Over half of those who participate are Norwegians, with the other half coming from more than 40 different countries around the world. However, according to the website, the race organisers suspect that, 'some may actually come from other planets, as their performances are just out of this world'.

Mental Miscellany

- The first Norseman Xtreme Triathlon took place in 2003 with a starting field of 21.
- All athletes must carry their own equipment.
- No athlete is allowed to enter the mountain alone; if a support team member is unable to accompany a runner to the top of the mountain, athletes will be held back and connected with the next athlete to arrive at the checkpoint.
- The maximum number of participants is 250 due to safety reasons.
- The maximum number allowed to finish on top of the mountain is limited to 160; anyone arriving after this must finish on the mountain plateau below the peak.
- Athletes finishing on the peak receive a black finishing T-shirt for their efforts; those finishing on the plateau receive a white T-shirt.
- The race is organised by Hardangervidda Triatlon Klubb, whose 20-odd members comprise the main crew of the race.
- As well as wearing a wetsuit and swim cap, the water is so cold that race organisers recommend also wearing neoprene socks and a neoprene cap as well.
- The swim starts to the sound of the ferry's horn.
- The website strongly recommends you read the Race Manual before deciding to enter the race.

For further information, please visit: www.nxtri.com

ESCAPE FROM ALCATRAZ TRIATHLON
SAN FRANCISCO, USA
Triathlon – San Francisco

Alcatraz, the most infamous prison in the world, situated on the inhospitable and rocky Alcatraz Island in the middle of San Francisco Bay and from which only two prisoners ever successfully escaped, would seem an unlikely place to hold a triathlon, but every year in June, up to 2,000 triathletes arrive in the city famous for its golden bridge to tackle what has become recognised as one of the most prestigious triathlons in the world.

Just before 0730, the competitors board the ferry that is normally used to take visitors to the now-closed prison on Alcatraz Island; at a point adjacent to it the ferry stops, and within six minutes all 2,000 athletes are deposited into the icy waters of the Bay.

From there they must deal with the strong currents and a 12°C/55°F-degree liquid temperature and swim the 2.4km/1.5 miles back to the San Francisco shoreline before the one-hour cut-off time.

Collecting their bikes, they will now face a hilly, 28km/18-mile ride through the Presidio district, along the Great Highway and through the Golden Gate Park. If they don't make it to the run transition area within three hours of the start time, they will be taken out of the race.

310

Assuming they do make it within the time limit, the athletes now face an 12km/8-mile run along the uneven trails of the Golden Gate National Recreation Area incorporating 91m/300ft of elevation, and 400 sand-covered steps, known as 'the sand ladder', from the beach to the top of the cliff. Due to the depth of the sand on the steps, which allows runners' feet no grip or ability to push off, athletes are advised to use the plastic-coated metal cables at the side of the steps as a type of pulley. They are also advised not to run too close to the left-hand side of the pathway at the top of the beach area because of the poison oak that grows there.

With professional as well as amateur triathletes having a go at this unusual triathlon since its inception in 1980, and despite the sub-average water conditions, the rough terrain and sandy climbs, records for the course have been set at 1 hour, 54 minutes, 41 seconds for the men, and 2 hours, 18 minutes, 08 seconds for the women, both in 2004.

Who would do this?

Anyone who's considering spending a significant amount of time in an island-based state penitentiary or prison.

Mental Miscellany

- In 2013, the race was won in 2 hours, 4 minutes, 27 seconds (men) and 2 hours, 18 minutes, 08 seconds (women).
- Teams, as well as individuals, may enter the race.
- The Alcatraz Triathlon offers corporate challenges.
- Alcatraz Island is often referred to simply as 'The Rock'.
- The federal prison on Alcatraz Island was home to criminals between 1933 and 1963.

For further information, please visit: www.escapefromalcatraz triathlon.com

ADD A KAYAK AND SOME ROPES...

ADVENTURE RACING
AN OVERVIEW

Put simply, adventure racing is a multi-event endurance based race with a minimum of two different disciplines.

The events usually comprise any combination of running/ trekking (country and/or road), cycling (mountain and/or road), paddling (kayak or canoe), swimming, climbing and related rope work, and require orienteering and navigational skills.

Less usually, events may also comprise tubing, rafting, in-line or roller skating, horse or camel riding, cross-country skiing, paragliding, hang-gliding, coasteering, caving, canyoneering, riverboarding, rappelling and zip-lining!

An adventure race may take anything from a few hours (sprint event) up to 10 days (expedition event), but whatever the time required, all races are non-stop, with the clock running continuously from the start to the finish, irrespective of the amount of time spent resting or in transition between events.

Consequently, it is up to the competitors to decide for themselves if and when and for how long to rest during an event.

Most races are held as team events, usually with a fixed

number per team and with both male and female members, although the ratio of men to women is up to each team. However, some races do have single-sex and age-based categories.

The rules of adventure racing depend upon the organisers of each race, but generally teams must travel together throughout the entire race, usually within 50m of each other; they must accept no outside assistance except at designated transition areas; and they must carry all the mandatory gear. Also, perhaps rather obviously, they should not use any form of motorised travel nor should they use GPS. Failure to abide by any of these or other rules will result in instant disqualification or, at the very least, harsh penalties.

Indeed, mandatory gear is considered so important (it may be a matter of life and death if, for instance, a competitor has dumped his emergency flares to reduce weight in his backpack) that pre-race checks may be carried out at the start of a race and again at the finish, and spot checks during the race may also take place.

Many adventure races do not reveal the course until the night before or even on the morning of the actual race. For shorter races, this is probably not a major issue, as they will usually follow a marked course. However, for longer races, competitors will be given maps marked to show checkpoints or may just be given coordinates that indicate where the checkpoints will be found.

In all races, it is mandatory to visit a series of checkpoints in a specific order and within a specified time. Failure to do so may result in disqualification, although race directors tend to take a less harsh stance in the shorter races, taking into account the fact that for many it is the first adventure race they have taken part in, and may allow them to continue racing on a reduced-length course, although they will no longer be eligible for prizes. Some races actually allow competitors to miss out checkpoints – although they will be awarded a time penalty, which will have to be made up during the race.

All races will include transition areas, the only place where teams are allowed to change to the next form of travel, ie run to bike, bike to canoe, etc. Teams may also top up their supplies, such as food and drink or fresh clothing, at transition areas.

As for equipment, aside from mandatory gear, most races will provide kayaks and canoes, with competitors bringing their own bikes, helmets and toolkits.

For many, adventure racing is a natural progression from triathlons and marathon running, blending their mix of skills and avoiding the recurrence of injuries brought about by single-event training and ageing. However, regardless of whether there is a background in other sports or not, because adventure racing is a multi-discipline event, training for a race should combine strength and endurance with the necessary skills required, although according to the various websites, expertise in all events is not necessary, although mental preparation is essential; there are training camps that specialise in preparing people for an adventure race.

At the top end of adventure racing, there are championship series events, from the UK to European to World. These races take place all over the world from Queenstown, New Zealand, to Catalonia in Spain, and offer very little in the way of prize money, but plenty in the way of sponsorship products, complimentary entry into other adventure races and, in the case of one race in Ecuador – a cruise in the Galapagos Islands!

However, whether you are a rookie or an old hand, adventure racing would appear to offer a way to refresh your training, partake in an unpredictable and exciting adventure and discover a whole load of new and extreme sports. What's not to like?

For further information, please visit: www.ukadventureracing. co.uk

ALASKA MOUNTAIN WILDERNESS CLASSIC
ALASKA, USA
Up to 400km/250 miles mountain adventure race

The Alaska Mountain Wilderness Classic began as long ago as 1982 as a 240km/150-mile foot race, since when it has pursued differing routes (this changes every three years) at different times of year (a different month is chosen each year for the race) and crossed varying mountain ranges, covering distances of up to almost 400km/250 miles and taking in some of Alaska's most beautiful and most notorious wilderness landscape.

The rules of the race are simple: competitors must make their way from the start to the finish using only their own power, with no outside support, carrying all their own food and equipment, while leaving no trace of their passing presence. Should they get into difficulties, it is up to them to get out of them. And, oh yes, by the way, there are no trails to follow, just your map and compass to guide you on your way.

Generally, those participating in this event move on foot and use a packraft (a light portable raft) for water crossings, although mountain bikes, skis and even paragliders have been adopted over the years with varying degrees of success. Since 2004, mobile phones have been mandatory for use in emergencies.

The really curious thing about this race, though, is that it is

315

a race that doesn't officially exist, given that it is not affiliated to any organisation or group. Instead it is currently run by a man called Luc Mehl, a multisport adventurer with an academic background in geophysics, who has taken part in the race himself. Arguably, he does have a slight advantage over some of the other competitors, having grown up in the sparsely populated Alaskan town of McGrath, which has undoubtedly given him an intimate and profound understanding of the unique wild rawness of the race environment.

The race itself presents unimaginable challenges, with terrain as diverse as loose boulders, scree and snowy mountains, to glaciers and quicksand, and rivers with dizzying eddies and racing rapids. As such, the race demands extreme experience and knowledge of wilderness survival, as well as bushwhacking, orienteering and paddling, not to mention the ability to swim should your packraft toss you out. It is definitely not a race for the faint-hearted.

For example, in the 2013 race report it was noted that the route from Thompson Pass to McCarthy was even harder than usual due to less snow and higher water. This caused severe difficulties during the water sections. One competitor lost his packraft on the first day after flipping in the Tasnuna River. If this wasn't bad enough, all his gear was strapped to the raft and all he was left with were the clothes he was wearing, plus a few small bits of equipment. Luckily, a couple of fellow racers found the raft and tied it to a tree, and boat and racer were later duly reunited.

It is also a race that requires superior levels of mental strength, for days may pass when racers will see not another single soul.

Who would do this?

Judging from various race reports and blogs of previous competitors, it would seem the contestants are many and varied: some work in IT, some in the police force, others are teachers or wilderness guides.

When the race organiser Luc Mehl took part in 2012, he reports that there was a lot of nervous energy at the start with nobody knowing if they had brought the right gear or what would be the best route to follow. He and another racer managed to cover 80km/50 miles on the first day but only 16km/10 miles on the second. He talks of paddling upstream in the Little Bremner to avoid the brush and travelling up eddies in the same way when possible. Because the forest was choked with fallen spruce, he found that it was quicker to climb onto the logs and 'log-walk' up the slope; the downside to this was any slips resulted in painful and bleeding shins.

For another competitor, in 2013, the race ended just 8km/5 miles from the finish when a rash he had became infected, causing his temperature to rise dangerously high, and he had to be taken to hospital. Conversely, the fellow competitor he'd partnered up with finished the race reportedly looking like nothing had happened in the past week and jogged to the ice cream shop!

Mental Miscellany

- In 2013, there were 13 starters and 5 finishers.
- The 2013 race, which followed the Thompson Pass to McCarthy via the Bremner Brush route, covered 241km/150 miles and was won in 7 days, 8 hours and 42 minutes.
- Certain areas where packrafting is required offer 'extreme caution' warnings.
- The Bremner River is classified as a Class III+ to unrunnable – and is known as 'The River of the Ten Bs' – brown water, big boulders, bugs, bears, bad rapids, bushes, bad weather, and big bucks; it also has quicksand which is stated to be a 'legitimate danger'.
- There is also a winter event called the Alaska Mountain Wilderness Ski Race that has taken place every year since 1987 and which passes through the Chugach Mountains.

For further information, please visit: www.thingstolucat.com

THE BEAST OF BALLYHOURA
IRELAND
300km/187 miles non-stop adventure race across Ireland

Every August, while visitors relax and school children play among the verdant beauty that is Ireland, a number of other people laden with rucksacks, maps, compasses, mountain bikes and tents, among other things, gather in the region of Ballyhoura and set about participating in what is a uniquely Irish, non-stop adventure race that will move from Ballyhoura and across Cork, Limmerick and Tipperary.

Split into teams of four and entirely unsupported throughout, they will run, kayak, bike and clamber up ropes over land that is both beautiful and at times threatening, especially in the depths of night, until they reach the end of the race some 40 hours later.

On their way they are likely to suffer from sleep deprivation resulting in hallucinations, not to mention blisters, aches, pains and general exhaustion as they attempt to navigate the best route to win a race that is part of the European Adventure Race Series.

In so doing, the teams of four must abide by the strict rules that state the event should be started and completed by the entire team who should stay together at all times and who should never be separated by more than 100m/328ft. In the spirit of the event they must also abide by the rule of no cheating, and should one team find another in need of medical attention, the rules state they must stop to assist. They should also strive at all times to be eco-friendly and polite.

Before setting out the teams are given all the relevant information needed about the route they must follow, but it is the responsibility of each team to copy this information on to maps using their own stationery, such as marker pens and tape. Teams are warned not to lose their maps, as they will not be replaced.

The winners are the team who accumulate the most points, having collected these at the designated mandatory checkpoints and transitions, and who complete the mandatory route of the event within 40 hours, having complied with all the rules and regulations and with time penalties being taken into consideration. In the event of two teams achieving the same score, the fastest team wins.

While a limited amount of equipment is supplied by the organisers – a set of maps, a laminated route book, bike boxes, paddles and kayak hire, and other specialist equipment hire, plus post-race food – all other food, clothing and equipment must be supplied and carried by the team members themselves.

The original idea for such an event arose out of a meeting of four men: Damien Hackett, Brendan Lawlor, Padraig Casey and Greg Clarke, who were all involved in various running, biking, and adventure racing events in some way or other. Together, they came up with the bike/run concept but it was Damien and Padraig who were particularly fascinated with the idea that with sleep deprivation comes hallucinations. In general, this would happen after 24 hours of non-stop racing and, as it is traditional for these hallucinations to be of monsters, so the idea of combining the words of Ballyhoura and monster arose, ultimately becoming the 'Beast of Ballyhoura'.

Who would do this?

A polite eco-warrior with a sense of adventure and direction.

Mental Miscellany

- The first 'Beast of Ballyhoura' was held in 2009.
- In 2013, there were 15 teams entered in the event.
- As well as running, biking and kayaking, teams must also be adept at orienteering and rope work.
- The minimum age for this event is 18.
- OSI (Ireland) maps with a 1:50000 scale are used for this event.
- There is also a short run/bike event known as the 'Ballyhoura Blitz'.

For further information, please visit: www.beastofballyhoura.com

PATAGONIAN EXPEDITION RACE
CHILE

Adventure race through mountains, glaciers and swampland

Patagonia, Chile, the closest territory to the Antarctic and South Pole, is mysterious and unique, a wild South American landscape of mountains, glaciers, forests and fjords – a land that contains the magical qualities of a Christmas wonderland but is a world away from our commercial imagery of such a world – wrapped up in the age-old secrets of its aboriginal peoples, and with a natural environment containing more than 38km(24 miles) of a coastline of active fjords that remain largely untouched by human interference thanks to an average population of just over three inhabitants per square mile.

Of course it is not only the pristine and untouched land with its immense areas of ice and granite, volcanoes and icebergs and virtually unexplored islands that mark Patagonia out as a particularly challenging region – it is also renowned for its unpredictable and erratic weather.

All of which makes it the perfect place to hold an adventure race. At least that was the opinion of Patagonian-born geologist, nature and adventure lover, Stjepan Pavicic, who having taken part in an expedition race where participants were forced to avoid cars and picnickers decided that his homeland was a much better option for such a race. He also harboured the hope that the event would promote public awareness of the importance of preserving the natural beauty and wild remoteness of his beloved home environment.

And so it was that in 2002, Stjepan, together with an international team of like-minded people, brought his idea to fruition, forming NIGSA, the company who direct and coordinate the event, and, two years' later, the Patagonian Expedition Race was born, promoting itself as 'the adventure at the end of the world', and claiming to be 'The most remote and wild race on the planet'.

For those who wish to partake, the race is an expedition in the true sense of the word, with mixed teams of four racing through hundreds of miles of Patagonia's most inhospitable areas by means of kayaking, mountain biking, climbing (using ropes) trekking and orienteering. They will receive minimal support and, apart from at the mandatory checkpoints, are unlikely to see another soul for the duration, which can be anything from 3 to 11 days.

Since the inaugural event in 2004, each edition has featured a different route, from the Torres del Paine National Park to the Beagle Channel and Cape Horn, but wherever the race takes the participants, they can be sure it will contain some of the most arduous challenges, both physically and mentally, some of the most inspiring scenery and some of the most unpredictable weather they are ever likely to encounter.

The route itself is unknown to racers until the night before the race starts, when maps and route books containing instructions are supplied. It is then up to the teams to work out the best navigational tactics.

Teams can be made up of members from different countries, but the rules state that they must comprise members of both sexes, although the ratio of male to female is a matter for each team to decide. It is also for each team to decide if and when to rest during the race.

Rules also state that teams must visit all mandatory checkpoints en route where, if there is to be a change of discipline at the next stage, such as from trekking to mountain biking, teams will change their equipment and take what is needed for the next leg with them.

Whatever the route, whatever the team composition, the race directors' stated mission is to use the race to show the world that 'there exists in an isolated corner of the planet a virgin territory of great scenic beauty and with a great diversity of native species that must be protected'.

That is their mission; their belief in the outcome of the race itself is much simpler: 'It is likely to change lives'.

Who would do this?

On 12 February 2013, 11 teams set out for Torres del Paine from the Plaza de Armas in Puerto Natales for the Patagonian Expedition Race.

The race started with an overnight bike ride and moved on to a crossing of the glitteringly icy Glacier Tyndall, which comprises a section of Campo de Hielo Sur, the third largest ice field in the world. It was the first time a glacier crossing had been attempted during the race and it proved an extremely tough initial test.

However, the race didn't get any easier and four teams retired within the first 24 hours having failed to meet cut-off times, with the Glacier Tyndall and a 25km/15-mile trek across a veritable jungle of crevasses and rivers proving just too much.

From Tyndall, the racers were faced with tortuously slow trekking through dense forests and rivers overflowing following torrential downpours, as the route looped southwards down the Peninsula Antonio Varas.

By checkpoint four, there were only seven teams left in the competition and by day six, thanks to worsening weather and intolerable weariness, this number had been whittled down to just three.

Eventually, though, the weather cleared as the remaining competitors set off in their kayaks paddling past Puerto Natales, before continuing by kayak, bike and foot through the Peninsula de Brunswick and over Monte Tarn to finish in Punta Arenas, the region's capital.

The three teams that finished the whole race had covered a total distance of 701km/435 miles and 10 discipline changes; they had faced torrential rain, howling gales and blinding snowstorms; the winners had been out there battling nature and the elements, as well as the sporting physical challenges, for an unofficial time of 9 days, 3 hours and 35 minutes, while the second and third placed teams had been out there for almost 11 days.

However, according to the website's report, despite the low number of finishers, each team had admitted that 'every hour of the journey, good or bad, made it worth braving the cold and windy nights, the seemingly endless treks across mountains and bogs, and even the misfortune of not completing the course...'

Or, as the race organisers put it: 'There are no real winners or losers in the Patagonian Expedition Race... Each team leaves transformed by the experience of racing in the Patagonian wilderness.'

Mental Miscellany

- In 2004, the inaugural race saw 10 teams from all over the world follow a 520km/323-mile southerly route, employing 8 changes of discipline, crossing windswept steppes, rivers and swamps to finish at Puerto Williams, the southernmost town in the world, approximately six days later.
- The 2004 race finished at a more southerly latitude than had ever been reached in any expedition race before.
- Teams must finish with all four members.
- During the race, racers may see colonies of penguins, seals and sea elephants, among other native wildlife.
- The website states the motivation for holding the race is to make people aware of the need to protect the Patagonian environment.
- There is a 'Race Project', which aims to raise US$20,000 to help preserve the huemul, a critically endangered member of the deer species and the symbol of Chile.

For further information, please visit: www.patagonian expedition race.com

COAST TO COAST
SCOTLAND

Run, bike, kayak – 160km/100 miles of
Scotland's mountains – in a day

If you're short on time and want to see the best that Scotland has to offer by way of historical and legendary mountain landscape, then the Scotland Coast to Coast race with its stunning views and epic course may prove to be just the ticket – providing you're used to running, cycling and kayaking long distances over rough and mountainous terrain, that is.

Covering just over 160km/100 miles of Scotland's ancient lands, the race, which can be tackled as an 'expert' (someone who is experienced in multi-sport racing over long distances) or as a 'challenger' (someone who is able to run 10km/6 miles comfortably and cycle on rough and uneven terrain), and can be entered as an individual or a team of two, includes virtually a full marathon on foot and climbs to a height of 470m/1,542ft. It will take you through various Scottish Highlands, from Inverness to Loch Ness, the Great Glen, Ben Nevis, Fort William and Glen Coe – all within a time limit of 13 hours for the 'experts' and two days for the 'challengers'.

Starting at 0630 from Fort George, Nairn Beach, with a predominantly off-road 11km/7-mile run along waymarked trails, competitors turn inland to Cawdor Castle where they make their first transition on to their bikes.

From here they will cycle 77km/48 miles to the southern shores of Loch Ness until they reach the south-west extremity of the Loch where they will then take to their kayaks for 3km/2 miles, before running a short distance to the next transition back on to their bikes.

This time they will cycle 33km/20.5 miles to Glencoe along some rough off-road sections and a further 21km/13.5 miles on the road, before reaching the next transition at Glen Nevis.

From Glen Nevis they will run a further 22.5km/14 miles, with 19km/12 miles of that on the waymarked trail along the Ben Nevis Tourist Path before crossing the Glen on to the West Highland Way Long Distance Footpath, up to the summit, then down to Sea Loch and Loch Leven.

At Loch Leven, it's back into the kayaks again for a further 1.6km/1 mile on flat water and then a short run to the finish line, completing the journey with a total of around 169km/105 miles from the North Sea coast to the sea loch inlets of the Scottish west coast's Atlantic seaboard.

Of course, being Scotland the weather can best be described as variable, especially at summer's end, and the organisers' recommended kit list, aside from the more obvious bike, cycle helmet and basic first aid kit, also includes an extra upper body thermal layer, warm headgear and gloves, a survival bag or blanket and water or windproof body cover.

For those entering the 'challenger' event, the race follows the same course over two days, allowing participants more time to admire the magnificent vistas, and includes an overnight stop on the shores of Loch Ness. Participants in this race will cover 91km/57 miles on the first day and 77km/48 miles on the second.

Who would do this?

Anyone who enjoys hopping from one sport to another and/or who has a desire to spot the Loch Ness Monster from their overnight camp on the shores of the Loch.

Mental Miscellany

- The first Scotland Coast to Coast took place in 2011.
- In 2013, the 'experts' race was won in 8 hours, 17 minutes, 57 seconds (men) and 9 hours, 35 minutes, 50 seconds (women).
- In 2013, the 'challengers' race was won in 9 hours, 23 minutes, 35 seconds (men) and 9 hours, 57 minutes, 20 seconds (women).
- All participants must be aged between 18 and 75.
- All teams must stay together throughout the race.
- There are strict cut-offs throughout the race.
- The event is self-supporting and therefore no support crews are allowed.
- Scotland Coast to Coast's official charity is Cancer Research and anyone raising funds for them will receive a £50 refund on their entry fee.

For further information, please visit: www.ratracecoasttocoast. com

COAST TO COAST
NEW ZEALAND

Run, Bike, Kayak – 243km/151 miles – West to East Coast

A s is true of many of the events in this book, the Coast to Coast race, which runs 243km from the west to the east coast of New Zealand's South Island every February, was dreamed up by a rather colourful character known as Robin Judkins.

Renowned for his brightly coloured Hawaiian-style shirts and facial whiskers, sporting event entrepreneur, Robin, has produced over 80 sporting events in his lifetime, many of which have featured on television, including the Coast to Coast race.

The two-day event came into existence in 1982, when Robin, and 11 mates, pioneered the same 243km/151-mile course used today, with the inaugural event taking place in 1983. Then in 1987, using the same course, Robin introduced the one-day event, popularly known as 'The Longest Day', as a way of keeping elite athletes motivated and inspired.

Today, Robin can be seen handing out finishers' medals and a can of Speight's (the race sponsor) beer to every finisher, although he has now handed over the race director's reigns to five-time Longest Day winner, international Ironman and former Olympic skier, Richard Ussher.

Both one and two-day races start from Kumara Beach on

the Tasman Sea and travel eastwards via the Southern Alps, including the notoriously tough Arthur's Pass – the highest and most spectacular pass in the Alps, the Waimakariri Gorge – known as the Grand Canyon of New Zealand – and its fast-flowing river, to the finish at Sumner Beach, a pretty little seaside resort situated on the Pacific Ocean.

The two-day event can be run as an individual or by teams of two or three, who will each participate in a different discipline, ie: they will either run, cycle or kayak. Teams may be made up of all male, all female or mixed gender and the race is split into age groups. The website offers competitors a chance to find teammates and/or support crews.

The one-day or 'longest day' event can only be entered as an individual and incorporates the World Multi-Sport Championships. Consequently it comes with a generous prize purse.

Both one and two-day events follow the same route, contain the same events in the same sequence, and distances within each stage are also the same.

The two-day event starts on the Friday at 0700 hours with a mass start on the beach at Kumara, with the first stage being a run of 3km/1.75 miles and a bike ride of 55km/34 miles. Stage two is the notoriously hard, mountainous 33km/20.5-mile run, which crosses the Southern Alps, following which competitors will camp overnight.

The second day sees the start of the 15km/9-mile cycle ride at 0730. This is followed by a short, approximate 600-metre run to the kayak transition area and a 67km/42-mile paddle on a Grade 2 (this indicates the degree of difficulty of rapids which runs from 1-5+, with 5+ being the hardest) river course, leading to the final stage – the 70km/43.5-mile cycle to the finish.

For the Longest Day event, this begins on the Saturday at 0600 hours in the dark and, for the top competitors, will finish some 10–11 hours later.

Rules state that kayaks may be of any type barring wave riders, surf skis or inflatables, with a cockpit (so the paddler sits inside, not on top of, the kayak) and with a 'sprayskirt' (flexible, waterproof cover used to prevent water entering the kayak). Spot checks of

compulsory mountain equipment, reflective ankle bands and bike lights and helmets are carried out throughout the competition, and failure to comply with any of these will result in disqualification. Disqualification of an entire team or an individual will also follow any failure to complete any of the stages.

Who would do this?

Elina Ussher is a 38-year-old, professional athlete from Finland (now living in New Zealand), who has won the Coast to Coast Longest Day event twice and been runner-up twice. Thanks to Elina for her account of the 2014 race, in which she finished second.

The longest day starts at 6am on the beach at Kumara, in the dark, with a 50-metre run on the sand. Then you have to climb over a bank of boulders and after that you run on a gravel road for about 500 metres before running on the main highway for around 2k.

It's quite exciting as there aren't many people about at that time and no lights at all, not even streetlights. Some people wear head torches, but I don't.

You are running for about 20 minutes and it's still dark when you get to your bike at the first transition. It's important to remember where you left your bike, like close to a tree or something! If you're lucky like I was this year and are number 3 or something like that, it's not so bad as your bike will be near the start, but if you're number 122 or something, it will be much harder to find in the dark!

A good transition is vital at this stage, as you want to be in the first bunch of cyclists, so you don't want to lose crucial minutes looking for your bike. If you are in the first group of cyclists, the boys will be at the front and will take it in turns to lead and do the work. We girls will let them and draft along behind them!

If you have a bad transition and end up in the second group of riders, it is much harder because nobody wants to take the lead and the boys will tell the girls to take a turn at the front and the girls will say, 'shut up!'

The first run and ride is tactically the hardest part of the race. If anything goes wrong you can lose a lot of time.

Next is the big run – around 34km following the rough track alongside a rocky river. The track isn't marked at all, and you have to cross the river several times during the run. Some competitors are afraid of getting lost, but you can't so long as you stay by the river. The real difficulty is in knowing which is the best track to follow. Local runners have an advantage as they will check the route before the race and work it out. You can just follow the river, but this is not the fastest way to go.

Every year the course changes a little bit depending on the depth of the water. It is slippery in places due to some plants that grow there – they are like a slimy moss and are destroying the rivers on the South Island. They grow on top of the rocks, which makes it slippery, like soap.

The run climbs up the mountain to Arthur's Pass at approximately 1,000 metres, which is the highest point of the race. From here it is 15km to the next transition area along a very narrow and rocky trail with some really steep areas and rock falls. It is so rocky and narrow you can get caught and you need to be careful and skilled to avoid catching your toes on

332

rocks, and falling. Normal people would not run there! It is a very exciting and challenging run.

After this is the 15k bike ride – it's not so hard with a couple of little steep hills on the road.

The next transition is 1k run on gravel road to the start of the paddling [kayak]. This is a 70k grade 2 paddle.

The river this year was shallow and the first hour is tricky finding your way because they have many different channels and you're supposed to follow the fastest flowing water. You need a little bit of experience and skill to read the river so you don't get stuck in shallow water.

Slowly the river gets bigger and you come to the first rapids after about 50 minutes to an hour. This bit is known as the Rock Garden and is made up of 4 rapids. It's quite bumpy and you have to find your way around the rocks. This year it was quite easy but it varies a lot from year to year depending on river and weather conditions.

For the next 30-45 minutes the water is quite flat and there's nothing too challenging before you reach the Gorge – a narrow chute in between big cliffs. It's quite exciting and quite scary – you are down on the river looking up at tall cliffs on either side.

The Gorge takes about 1.5 hours to get through. There are a few big waves in quite short sections. The main challenge here is that it's quite bendy so water moves quickly when you go around a corner and looks scary as it hits the cliff walls, with the water churning up quite badly. You think you should stay outside of that but then you can hit an eddy so you have to learn to stay in the fastest flowing water rather than go into an eddy. I'm not a good swimmer and I used to struggle with this idea but it's vital to make yourself follow the rougher looking water. Eddies may look the easiest way to go but you have to learn how to read the river and see it and avoid it. Churned up water may look worse but it's better than going through water that looks nice and flat only to find it is an eddy that spins you round and round!

The water must be respected even if it looks calm, as it can still surprise you. You need to always be aware of changes or anything flooding. But really the river is very nice and friendly – there have never been any accidents there.

It is very clean water too. This year the drinking systems on my kayak failed and the only fluid I could get was water from the river. It was very scary when I tried to take in fluid through the tubes leading to my drinking systems – there are two on my kayak – both of them were blocked.

After the Gorge, the river opens up again into a much larger area. It's now about an hour-and-a-half before you get to the next transition, depending on the river levels.

You breathe a big sigh of relief when get through the Gorge. It is not difficult but it is challenging – it feels like from there it is a long way to get to the transition.

This year at Woodstock they called out your official times – this was the first

time they have done that, they had some special underwater timing system.

Woodstock is a good place for spectators and is about an hour to the transition area. It feels like a long time and you can really struggle at this point, as you've already done 4 hours of kayaking. It's very important to remember to drink and eat and be positive, keep thinking about technique and just keep going.

I usually eat things like sports bars, bananas and boiled potatoes [in the transition area]. I refuel all the time in the kayak. It's a long section so very important to keep your energy levels up for the last 70k ride. At that point, it's all about how much energy you have left in your body. It was difficult this year because I missed the electrolytes I would have got from my drinking system.

The next transition area is Gorge Bridge, your support crew have to help you out of your kayak after 4 or 5 hours. Then there is a short run of about 500m – but uphill – it's one of the hardest runs even though it's very short, just trying to move your legs after you've been sitting in the kayak for so long is hard work.

Elina in her kayak

So you get your bike and you have 70k left. They say it's slightly downhill but it doesn't feel like it because normally there is a slight headwind coming off the beach. It is very hard. How quickly you can ride now all depends on how much energy you have left in your body.

This year, as well as the problem with my drinking system on the kayak, my second bottle on the bike which should have been a new full bottle, was the same bottle I'd used earlier so was only a fraction full.

The lack of electrolytes meant I had quite a lot of cramping on the bike. Now I wonder if I should have stopped to try and sort out the problem on the kayak, but at the time I thought I wouldn't know what to do and the support crews can only help you in transition areas and I could have wasted a lot of time. Somehow I thought I should be able to perform as well as usual, even without my usual intake of fluid and fuel!

It was annoying as I'd only been minutes behind the leader in the transition and still believed I could win but I had nothing left in my body.

I also had problems with some gels which I use all the time and never normally cause trouble. I think this was because of the lack of hydration.

335

It's hard to accept when you're such an experienced athlete that you can still make mistakes, but I did. At one point during the run, I crossed the river at the wrong point and had to go back. I was in a hurry and slipped and fell under a waterfall, I actually went under the water, the water was freezing and I got cold.

Overall, the Coast to Coast is a hard and very challenging event, but I think the harder the challenge the greater the sense of achievement when you complete it. Everyone who finishes it is very happy afterwards, and I've never heard anyone say they don't want to come back and have another go!

Mental Miscellany

- The inaugural two-day event took place in 1983, with 79 entries.
- The first one-day event was held in 1987.
- In 2014, the event celebrated its 32nd anniversary with a combined total of 600 entries for both events – 150 of which took part in the Longest Day.
- All finishers receive a can of Speight's beer.
- The first race in 1983 was rather more casual than today's professional set-up, with one bike carrying a baby seat and one kayak being made of canvas!
- The Longest Day takes top elite athletes around 10–11 hours to complete.
- The slowest ever recorded time for the event is 24.5 hours.
- Minimum age for the 2-day event is 16.
- Minimum age for the 1-day event is 18.
- There is no upper age limit for either event.
- The average age is 36, with the oldest being 79 and the youngest 15 (before the minimum age was introduced).
- Due to enforced changes in courses used each year owing to weather and river conditions, records are considered valid only for the year in which they are set.

For further information, please visit: www.coasttocoast.co.nz

OR JUST GRAB YOUR CANOE...

DEVIZES TO WESTMINSTER INTERNATIONAL CANOE RACE
UK
201km/125 miles non-stop canoe race

Easter 1948: a team of Scouts sets off from Devizes in home built canoes carrying all their food and camping equipment. They are heading for Westminster, London, 125 miles away. They will travel via the Kennet & Avon Canal before negotiating the River Thames. The challenge, the culmination of almost 30 years of similar watery wagers set over the previous 28 years by various people in a pub in Pewsey, Wiltshire, is to complete the journey within 100 hours, whereby they will secure a purse raised by the locals. The four Scouts, all aged 17 years, duly succeed in 89 hours, 50 minutes and win the purse.

Easter 2013: the 65th edition of the Devizes to Westminster Canoe Race gets underway. Paddlers from the UK and overseas, in teams of two, will race in kayaks or open canoes non-stop for the 201km/125 miles that will take them from the start to the finish. Others will join them as senior single paddlers, junior doubles, or a mixed double comprising one veteran (aged 35+) and one junior paddler, all of who will attempt to cover the distance over four days. They will be also be joined by those in the 'endeavour' race class, a class for non-competitive doubles, also to be completed over four days.

Paddlers will no longer carry their own food – this is now supplied by their support crews who line the route – and with an approximate finishing time of 16 hours for the winners of the non-stop race, camping equipment is no longer required. Those who compete over four days do not need to carry camping equipment either, as their support crews carry it on their behalf, handing it to the paddlers at designated camp sites, though the paddlers must erect all camping gear themselves and no outside help is allowed.

Despite the 'easing' of those requirements and the advances in canoe design, the race is the longest canoe race in the world and is as tough as ever, offering competitors a severe test of skill and stamina, with 77 portages (places where competitors have to carry their boat from one area of water to another), numerous locks and weirs over the first 83km/52 miles along the canal, followed by a further gruelling 88km/55 miles confronting the notorious strength and currents of the River Thames.

Not surprising then that the Devizes to Westminster race is considered one of the most testing canoe events in the world, often taking place during cold and inclement weather with the extreme distance and physical effort required causing chronic fatigue. With the majority of the course positioned out of sight of officials, spectators and support crews, the paddlers are by and large facing their challenge alone. The race organisers therefore recommend a minimum of six months' training and preparation for the race and a reminder that it is the responsibility of all paddlers to ensure that they are fully trained and competent to deal with any capsizes or mishaps that may occur.

Although not compulsory, support crews are highly recommended and play a pivotal role for all competitors, providing them with food and drink along the way, carrying spare kit, and offering advice and encouragement throughout, as well as keeping a wary eye on physical and mental wellbeing.

With the onset of health and safety requirements, the race obligingly warns of the risks of injury and death, although there has never yet been a fatality. It also warns of the risk of failure, with many teams of non-finishers appearing on the results list every year since the race began.

Despite that, or maybe because of it, the race epitomises the raison d'être for all extreme sporting challenges – that where man (or woman) has to overcome difficulties through his own physical and mental endeavours, so shall the triumph of succeeding be unrivalled, while for those who fail, they too shall yet triumph through the unique experience of lessons learned and resolve strengthened, which will serve them not only on the race course but throughout life itself.

Who would do this?

Preferably people who have taken the organisers' advice and have some experience of paddling, who also own a suitable boat or can access one, but also, judging from race reports featured on the website, those with a sense of adventure, steely determination and a taste for sheer hard work, plus, in the case of the singles event, a desire for self-reliance.

According to one competitor it was the mental side of things that proved the toughest to cope with, commenting that they would paddle for hours, reach a portage where they would get fed and watered by their support crew before setting off again only to realise at that point what little distance they'd actually covered and how much further they still had to go; adding that it was a case of just having to get on with it despite every lift, every step, every paddle stroke being a struggle.

Cramp too proved a problem for one paddler, causing him to fall into the freezing water not once, but twice.

Anyone considering taking part in the event, also needs to consider the time required to carry out appropriate training. Former participants have struggled with this aspect, either because of family and/or work commitments, getting to and from a suitable waterway or working out any tidal constraints that may arise. For some this meant using other means of upping their fitness levels, such as running, cycling or circuit training. For anyone likely to suffer from cramp, swimming might be an advisable alternative too!

Mental Miscellany

- A women's class was only introduced in 1976 because, until then, the race committee deemed the race too arduous for women. However, one woman doubled with a male partner in 1971, finishing in 48 hours, 50 minutes, only to be disqualified when her gender was discovered, and another lady entered under an assumed name in 1973, finishing in 49 hours, 57 minutes. This result was allowed to stand but the committee didn't encourage women to enter for another three years when the first all-woman crew finished in 31 hours, 6 minutes.
- Competitors are allowed to use any type of boat, so long as it is stable.
- Until 1971, the race was dominated by teams from the Forces.
- A late Easter may be warmer for competitors but will bring more vegetation in the slow section of the canal.
- In 2013, winning times were: Senior Doubles – 16:44:23; Endeavour – 18:51:14; Junior Doubles – 15:12:56; Veteran/Junior Doubles – 20:21:36; Senior Single – 16:40:18 (men) and 19:27:40 (women).

For further information, please visit: www.dwrace.org.uk

OR MAYBE
SOME OARS...

ATLANTIC CHALLENGE

*Rowing 3,000 nautical miles (c. 3,500 miles) –
across the Atlantic*

The Atlantic Challenge is a rowing race that starts in the Canary Islands and crosses the Atlantic to finish in the West Indies, covering around 3,000 nautical miles (5,556km/3,452 miles). It is held more or less every two years, starting in varying months towards the latter part of the year and can take anything from around 40 to 90 days to finish, dependent upon conditions.

Founded in 1997 by Sir Chay Blyth, who with his rowing partner, John Ridgway, became the first man ever to row across the Atlantic in 1966, the race is open to anyone who has the time, the money and the nerve to face deafening, crashing wall-like waves of up to 15m/50ft, violent, heavy-object-hurling hurricanes whirling wildly at over 65 knots/75 miles per hour, and the sheer terror, especially in the case of solo rowers, of being utterly alone at night on a boat that is less than 8m/26ft in length and 2m/7ft in width, at the mercy of a vast ocean, with its unique elements, that is capable of tossing you and your vessel into its inky depths as easily as a heavyweight shot-putter could toss a single pea into the air.

Of course if you manage to stay in or at least near your vessel, you will stand a chance of surviving the natural outcome of such a catastrophe, for the boats used for this race are all built from wood, fibreglass, carbon fibre and Kevlar (high-strength synthetic fibre) and are designed to right themselves.

The boats, which are supplied by the race organisers, come with the luxury of watermakers, which, miraculously, turn sea-water into drinking water, solar panels which power GPS (Global Positioning System) and other electrical equipment, such as tracking beacons, satellite telephones and specially designed laptops called 'tough books', which allow competitors to have contact with the outside world at all times, even when they are 1,500 miles from shore.

The boats also come with enough rations for 90 days, a first aid kit and a few small luxury items and reminders of home, but competitors are warned that the rules state that should they run out of rations and request extras, in the way of poor old Oliver Twist, they will be instantly disqualified. Indeed, the only permitted re-supplying of food or drink during the race, apart from use of the watermaker, is from the collection of rainwater and fishing. Absolutely no outside assistance is allowed throughout the race.

The rules also state that the correct number of people must be on board the boat at all times (ie, one person in solo crossings, two in pairs, four in the fours), each competitor must have rowed their boat for a minimum of 24 hours with at least 12 of those being during the hours of darkness, and each competitor must also hold a valid RYA Yachtmaster Ocean Theory certificate, First Aid at Sea certificate and RYA Basic Sea Survival Course Completion certificate, while oars must not have blades exceeding 1,530sq cm/237sq in.

Not only will competitors have to abide by the strictly enforced rules, and face whatever the ocean and elements choose to throw at them, they may also have to contend with salt rash, blisters, 'rowers claw', potentially extreme weight loss, sleep deprivation, sores from sitting, and difficulty with walking when they finally disembark.

Who would do this?

Undoubtedly the most famous people to take part in this race was the team of British Olympic rower, James Cracknell, and TV presenter, Ben Fogle, in 2005/06.

During their crossing, the two men, who kept diaries and whose entire race was filmed and later turned into a DVD, entitled, *Through Hell & High Water*, admitted to being near breaking point in every conceivable way, pushed utterly to their limits, and even breaking down in tears. Throughout the 49 days it took for them to make the crossing, they capsized once, suffered hallucinations often and even rowed naked to avoid further chafing from their clothing.

Despite all that, the two friends crossed the finish line in first place in the pairs race (third place overall behind two teams of fours), although they were later demoted to second, having been penalised for using ballast water during the race. This was at a time when they had been without water for two days but, unfortunately, in direct contravention with the rules.

Their precise finishing time was 49 days, 19 hours and 8 minutes, and in the process they raised a huge sum of money for the charity, Children in Need.

Mental Miscellany

- The first ever race took place in 1997 with 30 teams of two rowing from Tenerife to Barbados – six boats withdrew and two finished with single competitors aboard.
- Prior to the 1997 race, there had been fewer than 30 successful Atlantic crossings by rowers and to this day more people have been into space than have rowed the Atlantic.
- The race used to cross from La Gomera to Barbados, changing in 2005 from La Gomera to Antigua.
- The fours race record for the La Gomera to Barbados crossing

is 36 days and 59 hours; the record to Antigua is 39 days, 3 hours, 35 minutes and 47 seconds, precisely!

For further information, please visit: www.taliskerwhiskyatlantic challenge.com

OR JUST GO COMPLETELY MENTAL!

ZOMBIE SURVIVAL RUN
USA/UK

Run away from the Zombies over 10km obstacle course

Arriving fresh from the United States of America comes the not-so-fresh scent of the living dead, otherwise known as zombies, and a challenge that claims to test participants' speed, strength and endurance while being chased by hungry, ruthless zombies, with the first UK 10km version being held in October 2013 at Aireville Park in Skipton.

Similar in style to the now infamous 'Tough Guy' and 'Tough Mudder' type of events, the idea of the Zombie Survival Run is to navigate a supposedly horrifying 10km zombie-infected course while navigating the most hellish zombie obstacles, at the same time avoiding the ravenous, blood-thirsty, virus-spreading zombies, thus making it to the finish line intact.

With each competitor being given three lives in the form of virus-protecting life tags that must be worn on a waist belt, the aim is to cross the finish line with at least one life tag still intact. Lives are lost every time a competitor is caught by a zombie and

345

infected with the zombie virus. Naturally, the aim of the zombies is to take lives from the competitors by stealing their tags, spreading the virus and transforming the runners into zombies.

The escape route is the 10km run, with its varied terrain, mud and water, and cunningly hidden zombies attacking when least expected, forcing runners to stay alert at all times.

Then of course there are the obstacles, which are described as 'challenging but achievable', and which have been christened with potentially self-explanatory names such as Zombie Slalom, The Darkness, Tyred and Deflated, Survival Crawl, A-Mazing, Pipework, Under the Radar and High Life, to name a few, all of which are designed to hamper competitors, slowing them down and making them more vulnerable to capture by the zombie mob who are on constant patrol in the obstacle area.

The website suggests running in a group and running tactically, if necessary sacrificing another member of the group in order to save yourself – no camaraderie in this event then!

According to the organisers of the Aireville challenge, Freebird Events, who are probably better known for organising triathlon events, the deliberately theatrical fun begins the minute you arrive at the zombie evacuation zone, where you are welcomed by a zombie patrol squad who are there to guard against stray zombies and other unnamed surprises.

Who would do this?

Anton Inckle, a 37-year-old software consultant, took part in the Zombie Run in 2013.

I am a Lancashire family man who gave up local league football when the kids were born. I found running was a way of keeping relatively fit. I tend to run 10km, as that's the distance I feel most comfortable with.

I'd run the BUPA Manchester 10km for five years and wanted to combine that with a new challenge, and decided the Zombie Run would fit the bill.

While I was warming up a photographer came and asked

Anton on the Zombie Run

if I would mind wearing a head camera. I said it was fine, and then spent the rest of the time being chased by Zombies who saw me and my camera as a prime target, or being asked by other participants why I had it on – the words 'sad' and 'geek' were mentioned more than a couple of times!

At the end, the photographer admitted he'd been worried about me passing the camera to a marshal and never getting it back! Sadly, after all that, I never even got to see the film!

The run was well-organised and good fun, with the obstacles and mixed terrain keeping me on my toes throughout.

Next year, the aim is for a Tough Mudder and maybe a couple more – without the head camera though!

With thanks to Anton Inckle for this account.

Mental Miscellany

- Prizes are awarded for the most creative outfit.
- Minimum age for entry into the race is 16.
- There is a separate 5km/3 miles course for juniors aged 10 to 15.
- Competitors may enter individually or as a team.
- Anyone aged 15 or over can volunteer to be a zombie in the Zombie Survival Run – this will require a zombie makeover in the exclusive zombie makeover transformation area, including blood and make-up being used to transform them into realistic, virus-infected zombies!

For further information, please visit: www.zombiesurvivalrun. co.uk

VERTICAL RACING
WORLDWIDE
Racing up the world's tallest buildings

If you're the type of person who prefers taking the stairs to the elevator, then you should love vertical racing for, in a nutshell, that's what it is all about – racing up stairs, thousands of them, in some of the world's most iconic skyscrapers!

The concept of turning stair running into a sports discipline started in 2009 when a coordinated race circuit, known as the Vertical World Circuit (VWC), and a scientific research project came together under the auspices of the International Skyrunning Federation, which has been in existence since 2008 and which is responsible for some of the world's toughest mountain races.

The scientific research centred around the idea that stair climbing is of particular benefit to less active people, particularly those living in cities, increasing calorie consumption and thereby aiding weight loss, while also improving heart and lung function, all of which in turn help to prevent obesity, diabetes and heart disease. Using stair climbing in this way has now become generally known as 'vertical fitness'.

At the same time, the International Skyrunning Federation (whose definition 'where earth and sky meet' is not quite so literally met when it comes to running up stairs inside buildings!)

welcomed the idea of the VWC not only linking the most iconic towers across the globe and developing a new sport, but also its long-term goal for vertical racing to gain International Olympic Committee recognition.

Today, with seven races spread over the USA, Switzerland, Taiwan, China, Vietnam, Singapore and China, and more than 100,000 participants having taken part since its inception, it could be said that the VWC has been extremely successful.

As for skyrunning, this is an activity that has been in existence for centuries, since the days when running up and down mountains was a necessity of war, hunting, smuggling or just natural curiosity, with the first Ben Nevis Race taking place as far back as 1903, and the Pikes Peak Marathon in 1954, which started as a bet between smokers and non-smokers!

The idea of turning running up mountains into a sport discipline was the brainchild of Marino Giacometti, an Italian mountaineer who, together with others, pioneered records on Mont Blanc and Monte Rosa in the Italian Alps in the early nineties.

In 1993, skyrunning exploded across the world's mountain ranges with a circuit of races from the Himalayas to the Rockies, from Mount Kenya to the Mexican volcanoes, and in 1995 Giacometti founded the Federation for Sport at Altitude (FSA) to address the need for rules to govern the sport and manage the fast-growing discipline. The FSA was later taken over by the International Skyrunning Federation.

The vertical racing circuit itself begins each year in February in New York with a race up the Empire State Building. With a height of 381m/1,250ft and a climb of 320m/1,050ft, 86 floors and 1,576 steps, this race has previously been won in record times of 9 minutes, 33 seconds (men) and 11 minutes, 23 seconds (women).

After New York comes the Basel Messeturm (trade fair tower), Switzerland, in March. Standing at 105m/344ft with a climb of 100m/328ft over 31 floors and 542 steps, the record for this race is currently a spectacularly speedy 2 minutes, 36 seconds (men) and 3 minutes, 10 seconds (women).

The month of May sees the vertical racers gather at the bottom of the steps of the 448m/1,470ft-high Taipei 101 Tower in Taiwan.

This time they will face a climb of 391m/1,283ft over 91 floors with 2,046 steps. Previous best performances have been 10 minutes, 29 seconds (men) and 12 minutes, 38 seconds (women).

August, and this time it's Beijing at the China World Summit Wing Hotel, which pushes its mighty way up to 330m/1,083ft, with an equal climb over 82 floors with a total of 2,041 steps. Records here stand at 9 minutes, 55 seconds (men) and 11 minutes, 56 seconds (women).

Next comes the 350m/1,148ft-high Landmark 72 skyscraper in Hanoi, Vietnam in September. With a climb of 336m/1,102ft, 72 floors and 1,914 steps, the fastest times to the top have been 10 minutes, 6 seconds (men) and 11 minutes, 20 seconds (women).

In November, racers move on to Singapore and the Swissôtel The Stamford. Standing at 226m/741ft, with an equal climb, the race takes place over 73 floors and 1,336 steps with record times of 6 minutes, 46 seconds (men) and 7 minutes, 61 seconds (women).

Last but not least, in December, the International Commerce Centre in Hong Kong, China, plays host to the Vertical World Circuit final. Boasting 484m/1,588ft of height and offering a climb of 364m/1,194ft over 82 floors and 2,120 steps, this is the longest of all skyscraper records, with veritable marathon times of 13 minutes, 20 seconds (men) and 19 minutes, 42 seconds (women).

Who would do this?

Anyone who is interested in heavenly architecture, particularly those wishing to shed a few pounds or with an aversion to elevators.

Mental Miscellany

- Competitors wear numbered bibs just as in other sporting events.
- Racers may set off individually or start en masse, but are timed individually either way, with men and women running in separate categories.
- There is a point-scoring system employed to decide the

overall world champions, who will be crowned at the final race in Hong Kong.

- The website claims that human 'rockets' can race up to 40 flights of stairs at more than half a metre a second (3,540kph/2,200mph).
- The scientific research carried out by the International Skyrunning Federation since 2007 has shown that walking uphill consumes up to 10 times more calories than the same exercise on the flat.
- There are now some 200 skyrunning races around the world, with approximately 30,000 participants from 54 countries.
- Skyrunning has a world series of races, a European Championships and a World Championships.

For further information, please visit: www.verticalrunning.org and www.skyrunning.com

SHOVEL RACING
USA

*Race down a mountain at 112km/70 miles
per hour – in a shovel*

According to the *Oxford English Dictionary*, a shovel is 'a
spade like tool for shifting quantities of coal, earth etc,
especially having the sides curved upwards'. Nowhere does it
mention anything about grown men or women waxing its bottom,
sitting in its upwardly curving bowels and then racing down a
snowy hillside.

And yet this is what happens in various mountainous resorts
around the United States of America at various times of year,
most specifically and regularly every February in the delightfully
named alpine ski resort known as Angel Fire Resort, New Mexico.

Given this little-known competitive sport's history, however,
this particular venue is rather fitting: New Mexico is the very
place where it all began back in the seventies when ski resort
workers discovered the quickest way to get from one location
to another, particularly back down the mountain at the end of a
shift and into the local hostelries for some bone-warming brew,
was by way of their shovels, which they would deploy as a sort of
mini-sled.

Indeed, so common did this practice become that it turned

from being a mere means of rapid exit after a long day's work up the mountains into a competitive sport so popular that it actually featured in the Winter X Games of 1997.

However, perhaps rather unsurprisingly, serious injury to one of the shovel racers during a crash prompted fears that it would be banned, and thereafter the most prominent competition was held at the aforementioned Angel Fire Resort until even they lost their nerve and the event was dropped in 2005 due to liability concerns.

Fortunately, though, and maybe somewhat amazingly given today's cautious concerns over the health and safety of everyone from toothless tots to equally toothless grannies, the sport saw a return in 2009 following the banning of modifications to shovels to speed them up beyond a safe limit. Also, a rather unexpected rivalry between 'riders' to dress themselves in fancy costumes has grown year-on-year, with the sport opening up to everyone regardless of age or anything else.

To take part in a shovel race, competitors must use only a basic snow shovel (any others are deemed too dangerous and are banned), the handle of which may be taped to improve grip, and the underside of which may be waxed to increase the speed at which it travels over the snow – elite racers have been known to hit around 112km/70 miles per hour.

The rider then sits in the shovel facing forwards with legs either side of the handle and with both feet pointed forwards, and pushes himself off with his hands behind him from a starting 'pen' similar to those seen at the start of a ski race. He then leans as far back as possible, with arms held rigid and straight alongside him to achieve a streamline position, giving the appearance of a sort of strange be-handled luge (light toboggan).

The run itself takes place around a gutter-shaped course built into a ski run and top riders will take around 13 seconds to get from the top to the bottom. Novice shovel racers, however, can expect to remain seated inside their shovels for around 30 seconds – unless, of course, they crash and fall out before reaching the bottom!

Almost as remarkable as the concept itself, is the fact that the top three racers win cash prizes and gift cards, and there is also a prize for the coolest shovel race costume.

Who would do this?

Anyone with a shovel and no coal, who enjoys waxing and has a penchant for dressing up and speed!

Mental Miscellany

- There is a practise day the day before the race where experts will teach novices the proper shovel race technique.
- Each competitor will get two runs each.
- Race bibs, helmets and eye protection are mandatory.
- Competitors aged 6–9 years old compete in the 'Little Scoops' category.
- This is a genuine event!

For further information, please visit: www.angelfireresort.com/ shovelraces

WIFE CARRYING
WORLDWIDE
253.5m/832ft over track and obstacles – carrying 'wife'

Vying for the title of the most unusual challenge comes the Wife Carrying race.

Originating in Sonkajärvi, Finland, in 1992, the idea behind the event, at least according to the race organisers, is steeped in their local history. It would seem that in the late 19th century there was a brigand who only accepted men into his troops that could prove their worth by stealing a woman from his neighbouring village. Again according to the race organisers, 'Today, not even a gentle compulsion is being used, the ladies volunteer for the mission of the championships.'

And so it was that in 1992, the first ever Wife Carrying Championships were held and the rules were set by the International Wife Carrying Competition Rules Committee, as follows:

- The length of the official track is 253.5m and the surface is sand.
- Track has two dry obstacles and one water obstacle, about a metre deep.
- Wife to be carried may be your own, the neighbour's or you

may have found her further afield; she must, however, be over 17 years of age.

- Minimum weight of the wife to be carried is 49kg. If she weighs less, she will be burdened with heavy rucksack to reach the desired minimum weight.
- The winner is the couple who completes the course in the shortest time.
- If a contestant drops the wife, he has to lift her on to his back or in his arms and continue carrying.
- The only equipment allowed is a belt worn by the carrier.
- All participants must have fun.
- The contestants run the race two at a time, so each heat is a contest in itself.
- Each contestant takes care of his/her safety and, if deemed necessary, insurance.
- Wife Carrying Competition has two categories: Official Wife Carrying World Championships series and Senior series 40 years and older applicants.
- The contestants have to pay attention to the instructions given by the organisers of the competition.
- Also, the most entertaining couple, the best costume and the strongest carrier are rewarded with a special prize.

There is also a Wife Carrying Team Competition, wherein the track and rules are the same as above, but three men in the team carry the wife in turns. At the exchange point the carrier has to drink the official 'wife carrying drink' (it is not stated what this actually is) before continuing the race. The team with the best costumes will be awarded with wife-carrying products and statues.

Should you be interested in taking part in a wife-carrying contest at any point, you may wish to read the website's suggestions on how to become a master in the sport, as follows:

- Attitude – wife-carrying is composed of humour and hard sport on a 50/50 basis. You choose what attitude to take.
- Postures – there are four customary styles to carry the wife:

piggyback, wife dangling upside down on the carrier's back, thrown over on the shoulder, and crosswise on the carrier's shoulders. The style is free, you may also create a new personal style of your own.

- Outfit – it is preferable to wear clothes which won't be stripped off in full speed running and which are easy to hold on to. Some other tools known to be beneficial are a bunch of birch switches, swimming glasses and swimming slippers.
- Life – wife-carrying is an attitude towards life. The wives and the carriers are not afraid of challenges or burdens. They push their way persistently forward, holding tightly, generally with a twinkle in the eyes.
- Eroticism – you can sense the excitement in the air during the wife-carrying competition. The core of the race is made of a woman, a man and their relationship. Wife-carrying and eroticism have a lot in common. Intuitive understanding of signals sent by the partner and becoming one with the partner are essential in both of them – sometimes also whipping.
- Wife – generally the best wife is the wife of one's own, all the more if she is harmonious, gentle and able to keep her balance while riding on the shoulders of her man.
- Track – if your style is the 'wife dangling upside down', you have better to remember that in the water pool the wife's head is likely to go under the water.

Of course, wife carrying is not restricted to Finland. With its growth in popularity, competitions are now being held in several different countries, such as Estonia, Germany, USA and the UK. However, be aware that rules may vary.

In the UK for example, where wife-carrying races have been held annually since 2008, principally in Dorking, Surrey, the race entails running a distance of approximately 380m with an altitude gain of approximately 10–15m and a descent of the same, over grass, while hurdling a number of hay bales – and, of course, carrying a 'wife'. In the UK, though, the 'wife' may be male or female, married to them or not and a male can carry a female or a male, and a female can do likewise, provided they weigh a minimum of 50kg, in any one of a number of recognised holds, as follows:

Piggyback – the most popular hold, but tiring and slow.
Fireman – across the shoulders, reasonably successful.
Estonian – 'wife' hangs upside down, face out, on his/her partner's back with his/her legs over his/her shoulders – this is by far the most popular competitive hold being both fast and reasonably comfortable for both partners.
Dorking – a reversal of the Estonian hold, known as wife-carrying position no. 69, this was used for the first time in 2013 by Steven Forster, winning him and his wife a special bonus prize of £100.

On approaching the finish line, competitors are welcomed with a thorough drenching fired from water pistols and buckets.

Prizes awarded at Dorking range from tankards, beer, champagne and medals for the winners, while losers and the person carrying the heaviest 'wife' are rewarded with a pound of sausages (for strength), tins of dog food and pot noodles.

A special wife-carrying T-shirt is also available to be purchased as a race memento.

Who would do this?

Anyone from Finland, or any dog owner in the UK who likes sausages and pot noodles.

Mental Miscellany

- Contestants in the World Championships 2013 came from Australia, Germany, UK, Ireland, Estonia and USA.
- The wife-carrying world record is 55.5 seconds, held by Estonians.
- The wife-carrying Finnish record is 56.7 seconds.
- In 2013, 47 pairs competed at the World Championships in front of an estimated 8,000 spectators.

- In 2008, 3 couples entered the first UK Wife Carrying race; in 2013, 23 couples entered.
- In 2012, the UK Wife Carrying Race was named as the UK's top adventure race by *Runner's World*.
- In the UK, the first time a woman carried a man was in 2013 with TV presenter Stephanie McGovern carrying Mike Bushell – they finished last.

For further information, please visit: www.wifecarryingrace.com and www.eukonkanto.fi

AND FINALLY...

Having reached the non-end of this book, there is one question I have found myself asking throughout the research and writing of it. Why, when the world becomes less challenging, do human beings invent artificial challenges of their own and then queue up to take them on?

Well, there's the obvious answer – because they're crazy (in the nicest possible way of course) or, to answer a question with a question – is it perhaps because today's world is too soft, too easy, too comfortable and people need to test themselves, take themselves outside their comfort zone, make sure their survival instincts are still intact and capable of being activated should the need arise?

Personally, I believe the latter. I don't mean that's what those who partake in such challenges think to themselves. I mean I think it's something that is innate to man's nature, as natural as breathing, eating or drinking – all of which are necessary to stay alive.

I also believe that those who partake in such challenges are the same people who in natural or other disasters are most likely to survive. They are the people to whom those of us who don't partake in such challenges will instinctively turn, not because we've read this book (although, of course, that will help), but because they naturally exude the spirit of those who refuse to be beaten, those who will dare to think outside the box and consider alternative means to ensure they get the end result. They are those who, more often than not, triumph over adversity. They will find ways to overcome obstacles, problems and fears; they will never ever give up, never say, 'We're doomed', but more likely 'We will find a way'.

Famously, they are the James Cracknells, the Sir Ranulph Fiennes types, the Captain Cooks; less famously they may be the man next door, the guy who fixes your computer or the woman who serves your children dinner at school. They don't come in a uniform like a fireman or paramedic, but they are just as likely to be capable of saving lives – not through reading books or taking exams, but through learning from the challenges they have undertaken, building an understanding of man's basic instinct for survival, knowing the human body through pushing his or her own to its absolute limits, recognising the signs that are there for us all to see and heed but which in our cotton candy world most of us no longer recognise or respond to.

That is the danger of living too comfortably: we cut ourselves off from our innate selves, our body, mind and spirit. The very things that are capable of giving us everything we need to survive have by and large been forgotten in our quest to give ourselves greater ease on our passage through this life.

But it is those very things, perhaps only those things, that will ease us through the traumas that from time to time seep through the gaps in our cosy existence and spring up unwanted and unwelcome like weeds in a carefully tended flower bed. We can spray the strongest weedkiller, using artificial chemicals created by scientists after years of study and research – and yet the weeds will still find a way, nature will always win.

That is what we must ultimately prepare for – nature and the natural world have the final say, and we have no choice but to react and respond.

And that is what the people in this book do with the challenges featured in its pages: they pick up the gauntlet thrown at their feet, be that an ocean of wild water, a mountain or a desert, all of nature's invention; the nearest they get to taking on a man-made challenge is in the obstacle races – but even they utilise fire, water and earth – all natural elements.

In so doing, these people, these modern-day adventurers, fulfil a basic need in themselves, while keeping alive age-old skills given to every one of us that may one day save not only their own lives but also those of others.

But, of course, that's just my take on the matter; the people who really know the answer are the people who do the challenges. So I asked them...why?

Robbie Britton, ultra runner – 'Because it's nice to be good at something, because I live for competition, because I like running fast and because I want to find out just how far my body will take me. Plus, I like to sleep and this is a good way to earn it.'

Paul Ali, ultra runner – 'I enjoy the challenge of completing a long distance event, the camaraderie with other ultra runners, being out there and 'surviving' all day (and night) sometimes on your own, just relying on your own physical strength and mental determination. I enjoy the satisfaction and sense of achievement of completing an event, looking back and saying, 'Yeah, I just did that'.'

Sandra MacDougal, ultra runner – 'For me, I guess it's because I can. I never in my wildest dreams envisioned myself being in a remote area in the middle of the night with a head torch on, driven by goodness knows what inside me.'

Mark Cockbain, ultra runner – 'Simply to test myself against myself...that's it.'

Paul Navesey, ultra runner – 'The reason I run? Very simple. I love running. The reason I enter the events is also very simple: I love racing and competing. I would turn up to an event with a field of two people if it meant I could race someone!'

Ann Richardson, swimmer – 'Why? Now there's a big question. I guess there are many reasons. I love to feel fit. I love to join in rather than be an onlooker. The feeling when it goes well is pure gold; you can't buy it, you have to earn it. Self worth!!! The discipline in the training is character building. I love the people that surround me through sport, there is so much energy. I believe it is important to have a passion about something in life and for me it is open-water swimming.'

Paolo De Luca, triathlete, ultra runner, Ironman – 'Why do I do these silly challenges, why is it so addictive? The challenge obviously in part for me is about keeping fit, bettering my times, being competitive and seeing new places, but it's also about taking part in an adventure, taking on that physical challenge. It's the goal of doing something that seems so completely unachievable, unattainable, going that extra mile and pushing my own limits, stepping out of my own boundaries. It's the primal challenge, to fight and conquer against all the odds. Each adventure is different, sometimes they're so extremely difficult…your body is physically screaming to stop, you mentally question whether to continue, but it's when you get past that and conquer that challenge…that's the buzz…that's addiction. I believe that's why I'm constantly drawn to the hardest challenges…the Mental Races!'